BLINDED BY MIGHT

Can the
Religious Right
Save
America?

CAL THOMAS

ED DOBSON

ZondervanPublishingHouse
Grand Rapids, Michigan

A Division of HarperCollinsPublishers

Blinded by Might
Copyright © 1999 by Ed Dobson and Cal Thomas

Requests for information should be addressed to:

■ ZondervanPublishingHouse
Grand Rapids, Michigan 49530

Library of Congress Cataloging-in-Publication Data

Thomas, Cal.
    Blinded by might : can the religious right save America? / Cal Thomas and Ed Dobson.
        p.   cm.
    ISBN 0-310-22650-3
    1. Evangelicalism—United States.   2. Christianity and politics—United States.
3. Conservatism—Religious aspects—Christianity.   I. Dobson, Ed.   II. Title.
BR1642.U5T46 1998
320.5'5'0973—dc21   98–50196
                                                                                                CIP

This edition printed on acid-free paper and meets the American National Standards Institute Z39.48 standard.

Quotations on pages 61–62 from Charley Reese, "The World as It Is Regardless of Whether You Understand That" (*Orlando Sentinel*, 11 September 1997), are used by gracious permission of the author.

All Scripture quotations, unless otherwise indicated, are taken from the *Holy Bible: New International Version®*. NIV®. Copyright © 1973, 1978, 1984 by International Bible Society. Used by permission of Zondervan Publishing House. All rights reserved.

Interior design by Sherri L. Hoffman
Author sketches by Louise Bauer

Printed in the United States of America

99 00 01 02 03 04 05 /❖ DC/ 10 9 8 7 6 5 4 3 2 1

CONTENTS

PREFACE

A WORD TO THE SECULARIST AND MARGINALLY "RELIGIOUS"

This is not a "religious" book. It is a book about the most important social-political-religious movement of the second half and—as you will see from its earlier incarnation—the first half of the twentieth century. This movement has, and has had, many names. Some of its concerns also matter to people who do not regularly practice a faith in God. It is false to assume that only religious conservatives care about the family, values, and their country's prosperity and survival.

While both of us are followers of Jesus Christ, we believe that what we have to say in this book should interest not only conservative and evangelical Christians, but also our friends on the theological and political left and those whose interest tends more to politics and history than to religion.

In this book you will come across some Scripture verses. The reason we include them is that we have read the book in which they are contained and, unlike most of our journalist friends, we think that we understand enough of it to hold our former religious colleagues accountable. Since many conservative religious leaders affirm that the Bible is the guidebook for their lives, their profession, and their nation, we think it important to point out some things they might have missed or misinterpreted about God and his relationship to government, and in turn, about government and its relationship to God in a free society.

We don't pretend to have all the right answers, though we used to claim that we had almost all of them. And we don't pretend that some of those whose behavior and actions we critique are all wrong, though clearly their approach to politics isn't working, any more than did the approach of the liberal clergy who embraced politics.

It is also important for believers and skeptics to understand some of the dynamics behind the deep desire of conservative Christians to see our nation "revived" again. But desire does not necessarily validate behavior. It is unfair to stereotype conservative Christians as "poor, uneducated, and easy to command," as a *Washington Post* reporter once did. It is also unfair to label all those with whom such people disagree as un-American, secular humanists.

In this book we have tried to be fair. We have even interviewed a few of our former "enemies," who are now friends. We seek to hold our former associates accountable, desiring the same for ourselves. We point out where we believe they are wrong. We confess some of our own "sins" for once believing that we could make things right through the manipulation of the political system. And we propose a better way—a way that is largely ignored and untried by those who claim to be part of majorities, coalitions, and organizations that correctly proclaim the need to focus on the family (the breakdown of which has negatively affected every level of our society far more than has the matter of which party temporarily holds political office). This way is written down in the very Bible which conservative Christians proclaim as the truth, but which in regard to political and societal restoration they have mostly overlooked. Instead, they have attempted to achieve success by shortcuts through the dark and deep political jungle and have gotten lost on the journey because they are in unfamiliar territory and lack the necessary survival skills.

This largely untried way is the better way because it stands the best chance of producing the results conservatives are seeking—but can never find—through politics. If we get this way right, the political life of our nation will be vastly improved. If we don't get it right, the political life of our country will be greatly diminished.

We have come to believe that a delicate balance exists between church and state and that if each fulfills its proper role, the other is positively affected. But if one assumes the role of the other, or ignores and rejects that role, then both suffer.

If the so-called Religious Right focuses mainly on politics to deliver us, we will never get that right because politics and government cannot reach into the soul. That is something God reserves for himself.

Unlike some who have left organizations, ministries, and the personal employ of politicians and businesses, this is not a "tell-all" book. We could have written another book and appealed to the sleazy, the tawdry, and the prurient. But we chose a different, less traveled road, because we seek to influence the greater corporate body of the church and, in so doing, leave a far greater imprint on the culture.

Where examples of what we regard as wrong decisions are given, we attempt to include ourselves, where appropriate, as co-conspirators. Despite our criticism of the Religious Right, we still support much of what the movement upholds. We still believe the same doctrines about God, about salvation, about sin, about redemption in and through Jesus Christ—all part of classic Christian theology. We are not disgruntled former employees. We still respect Jerry Falwell for the good he has done as a pastor, a civic leader, a mobilizer of politically docile Christians who had withdrawn from their civic duties, and a man who has the capacity for great kindness and generosity that much of the media has ignored and, as a result, most people never see.

Politically, we still hold to what are regarded as conservative beliefs. We believe abortion is the unlawful and immoral taking of innocent human life, no matter what the Supreme Court says. We believe pornography is bad for those who consume it as well as those who produce it. We think drugs are a curse on the mind and body— human as well as corporate. We think it is better for the nation if mostly honorable people serve in high office.

But we believe that our social maladies are not the cause of our decadence. They are a reflection of it. And just as these and other horrors, such as children shooting children in our schools, were not created solely, or even mainly, by government, neither will they be resolved by government.

Our Founders believed in limited government. Those conservatives who argue that liberals used government to undermine what the Founders began should not now seek to grab the reigns of government from liberal hands in order to use government solely to fix problems that are beyond its reach and power to solve.

We are emphatically not calling for retreat or surrender by conservative Christians, or anyone else on the "right." What we are calling for is something more powerful and longer-lasting than the endeavor too many of us have devoted too much time to for too long.

Cal Thomas, Alexandria, Virginia

Dr. Edward Dobson, Grand Rapids, Michigan

January 1999

INTRODUCTION

A TWENTY-YEAR JOURNEY

A sick society must think much about politics, as a sick man must think much about his digestion: To ignore the subject may be fatal cowardice for the one as for the other. But if either comes to regard it as the natural food of the mind—if either forgets that we think of such things only in order to be able to think of something else—then what was undertaken for the sake of health has become itself a new and deadly disease.

C. S. Lewis

cal thomas The years 1979 and early 1980 were personally troubling for me. My career in journalism had stalled. I wasn't making much money, and my wife and I were struggling, like most Americans, to stay even in a weak economy. As our children grew older, we wanted to give them more but didn't have the resources. It was a common lament, especially with sky-high inflation under President Jimmy Carter.

I had voted for Carter in 1976, believing him to be a serious churchman, a moral man, and a breath of fresh air following the disastrous Watergate years of the Nixon administration. When Carter had said, "I'll never lie to you," some mocked, but I had believed him.

As the Carter administration progressed, I realized not only that the president was in over his head, but that he stood for (or did not oppose) many of the things about which I felt great concern. While I continued to regard him as personally upright, I increasingly felt there was a gap between what Scripture taught—about unborn human life, especially—and Carter's political stand. His hiring of Sarah Weddington, the attorney who argued in favor of abortion in the infamous case of *Roe v. Wade,* greatly offended most pro-lifers, including me.

One day a memo came from our youngest child's elementary school. The principal was inviting us to a meeting to discuss the growing drug problem in the school. My wife and I looked at each other and vowed to get our children out of public school no matter what the cost. I said I would work a second job if that's what it took.

About this time, I met Jerry Falwell while covering an event at which he spoke. Everything this Baptist preacher said resonated with me. His was a certain voice in an uncertain world. I did not grow up in a fundamentalist Baptist church. My background was in the Disciples of Christ denomination, and later I attended a Presbyterian church, when I chose to go. After being fired by NBC News in 1973, I made a commitment to Jesus Christ and began to seriously read and study the Bible.

Through a mutual friend, Falwell heard I was frustrated with the drift of my career and the drift of the country. He called and told me about a new organization he had founded called the Moral Majority. "I could use someone like you," he said. "How would you like to move to Lynchburg and be my vice president for communications?"

I thought, *Where is Lynchburg?* I had never heard of the town, though it was only about 175 miles south of Washington, D.C., where I was born and had lived most of my life.

My wife and I flew to Lynchburg—a short, forty-minute flight from Washington, though in many ways it seemed much farther. Falwell gave us a tour of the town, his church (Thomas Road Baptist), and the Moral Majority office, which at the time was a small office in a rented building next door to a barbecue sandwich shop.

Falwell promised full scholarships for our four children at Lynchburg Christian Academy and Liberty Baptist College (now Liberty University). He said I would help change the direction of America. I felt a rush of excitement, similar to what drug users describe as a "high." I considered Falwell's offer exceedingly generous and accepted it. I learned later that Jimmy Carter was puzzled as to why I would go to work for Falwell. I'm not sure I could have answered the question if he had asked me, except to say something noble like "I want to save America."

But add to that the fact that Jerry Falwell was the most intriguing person I had ever met. His personality was infectious. In some ways, he and President Clinton are a lot alike—using the force of their personalities to persuade people to believe in them and to follow their direction, but hiding feelings of inadequacy and fear of failure. They are superovercomers for whom defeat is taken very personally.

Jerry could be extremely generous, offering handouts from his own pocket to panhandlers (over the protestations of his wife, Macel), or full college scholarships to inner-city children as an incentive for them to complete high school. Jerry is a complex man who is difficult to know beneath the surface—again, like Clinton.

Jerry is also a practical joker, a big kid who never grew up. Sometimes he would roll firecrackers down the aisle of his private plane during takeoff and scare everyone except the pilots, who were used to it. On one flight from New York to Lynchburg, he picked up his airplane telephone, punched the intercom button, and ordered the pilots to put the plane into a steep dive just to watch the horrified expressions of his passengers.

When he was with a group of people, he liked to knock on a hotel room door at random and then run to the elevator, causing embarrassment to those with him as an irate guest opened the door in some stage of undress. Jerry often convulsed in belly laughs.

Journalism had been my career since I was eighteen. With the exception of a brief flirtation with show business (the two become ever more synonymous these days), journalism is all I ever wanted to do. So when we arrived in Lynchburg, away from the media maelstrom of Washington, I felt as if I had journeyed through a time machine to another country and another life—which in many ways I had. For the first month I entertained thoughts that this was a terrible mistake, but there was no turning back. The cord had been cut.

Jerry put me at ease. He introduced me to everyone on the staff and in the church. At virtually every meeting, even church services, he would ask me to speak or pray publicly. I was the new "star," the man who had once worked for NBC News. I was bringing credibility to the Moral Majority, and credibility was the currency one needed in order to be taken seriously.

Moral Majority was the idea of three men: Howard Phillips, president of the Conservative Caucus, and Jewish; Paul Weyrich, president of the committee for the survival of a Free Congress, a Catholic at the time (and the person credited with coining the name Moral Majority); and Falwell, a fundamentalist Baptist who even then was being criticized by "true fundamentalists" such as Bob Jones Jr. and his son, Bob Jones III, for getting too close to politics.

Reflecting on those years and my many experiences, I have realized that the political activism of believers, while a good thing, is not the best thing. In fact, it represents the most subtle of temptations.

Many people, including many church people, claim not to believe in a personal devil, or Satan. That simply proves he is doing his job, because unbelief only encourages him. The first thing the Bible says about Satan is that he is "subtle" and "crafty." His objective is to persuade people not to believe in him or, failing that, to focus attention on his agenda, diverting our attention from God's agenda and his more important objectives. Worst of all, Satan prefers us to marry God's agenda with his tactics. It is Satan's ultimate victory.

Oswald Chambers, whose devotional book *My Utmost for His Highest* has sold millions of copies, says that "the good is the enemy of the best."[1] It isn't that political activism by Christians or anyone else with a religious motivation is, in and of itself, wrong. It is just not the best. C. S. Lewis wrote in *The Screwtape Letters* that "prosperity knits a man to the world. He feels that he is 'finding his place in it,' while really it is finding its place in him."[2]

Many have written "tell-all" books about people for whom they have worked. This is not that kind of book. Others have written about how they were "saved" from fundamentalism and are now battling against it. This is not that type of book. People looking for salacious revelations about sex won't find them in this book.

Neither is this a book by disgruntled former employees who are now trying to bring down the person for whom they once worked. Since beginning my syndicated column in 1984 with the Los Angeles Times Syndicate, I have not granted interviews about my time with Moral Majority or spoken derisively about Jerry Falwell. I continue to regard Jerry as a man who has done more to awaken people to their responsibilities as "dual citizens" (of the temporal kingdom of this world and the eternal kingdom of God) than perhaps anyone else in modern times.

Ed Dobson and I still appreciate Jerry for the many good things he has done. We still believe the same things we believed when we worked for him. Our beliefs about God and the Bible have not changed. Neither has our politics.

What has changed is that we no longer believe that our individual or collective cultural problems can be altered exclusively, or even mainly, through the political process.

The religious establishment has grown so large and so rich off the contributions of others that this book may be perceived as a direct attack on their organizations, ministries, and power centers. While that is not our intent, if it is the result, and if people awaken to the greater power within themselves that does not proceed from any earthly kingdom, then our efforts will not have been in vain.

---

ed dobson It was a beautiful November afternoon in Lynchburg, Virginia, in 1980. I drove across town to pick up my son from the Lynchburg Christian Academy. As I drove, I was listening to the latest news reports of the national elections. I was shocked. It appeared that Governor Reagan was going to defeat President Carter and that the Senate was going to return to Republican control. But what shocked me the most was that much of the credit for this dramatic voting shift was going to the Religious Right, the Moral Majority, and Jerry Falwell.

Jerry was a newcomer to the political arena. For years he had preached against such involvement, but then he had a change of heart.

A little over a year before the elections, he had gathered his key staff to a meeting at a restaurant in Bedford, Virginia. There he announced his intentions to get involved in politics in order to reverse the moral decline in American culture.

Harold Wilmington, the dean of the Bible institute established by the Thomas Road Baptist Church, begged Jerry not to get involved. Wilmington argued with passion that this new endeavor was a significant step away from preaching the gospel and might in the process contaminate the gospel. Harold was the only contrary voice. Jerry listened politely, as if his mind was already made up. Then he thanked Harold for his concerns and added that he was going forward.

At the time, I had no idea that I would be involved in this new endeavor. In the weeks that followed the Bedford meeting, Jerry began to get more and more national visibility. He agreed to write a book for Doubleday and asked whether Ed Hindson (a professor at what was then Liberty Baptist College) and I would produce the material so he could edit it. We were writing the book in the weeks leading up to the elections. Part of the book was devoted to the Moral Majority. In fact, we were putting Jerry's political agenda in writing. We were so busy with the book that we had not paid much attention to the election itself.

These were exciting days. Jerry was a virtual whirlwind of activity leading up to Election Day. He was traveling all the time, giving speeches, getting Christians registered to vote, and debating moral issues on every available local and national broadcasting outlet.

When Jerry came home to preach on Sundays, our congregation loved it. He would begin with a review of where he had been that week, what he had done, and whom he had talked to. We were proud that one of "our kind" was out in the real world upholding Christian values, appearing on national television, and getting the attention of the politicians.

As I drove into the parking lot of the academy, I noticed Jerry sitting in his truck all alone. I parked my car and went over and got in the front seat next to him. He was listening to the election returns.

"Can you believe it?" he exclaimed. "I knew that we would have some impact on the national elections, but I had no idea that it would be this great."

With unrestrained excitement Jerry talked about the incredible Reagan landslide and the defeat of several liberal senators. What seemed to amaze Jerry most was that the liberal news media were giving him the credit. A new day had dawned on the political landscape. Those of us who were considered anti-intellectual, obscurantist fundamentalists were now a force to be reckoned with. We had made our mark. We influenced an entire election. Our agenda would never again be ignored. We were about to turn around the whole moral and cultural decline of our country. Our man was in the White House. The Senate was under our control. The media wanted our opinion on every issue.

Had we not been Baptists we would have danced in the streets.

In the aftermath of the election I became a part of the Moral Majority, although I was not deeply involved with it full-time. I served on the board. I traveled and debated people on moral issues. I lectured on fundamentalism. I did radio and television interviews. I served as a consultant with the Anti-Defamation League.

All the television that I did was in behalf of Jerry and the Moral Majority. When he was not available for a program, I would often stand in for him. Constant exposure to the press can be deceiving: It makes you feel that you are more important than you really are, and it can lead you to believe that you are really making a difference.

I confess that I was enjoying the thrill of traveling and debating. But my moment of truth came when I was invited to represent Jerry on Phil Donahue's TV talk show. The Boy Scouts of America had expelled an Eagle Scout who did not believe in God. He and his mother were to be on the show, along with a brief appearance by satellite of an official from the Boy Scouts. I was invited to be there in order to defend the Boy Scouts' decision.

When I was introduced as an associate of Jerry Falwell's, the crowd booed. I was thrilled! I loved hostile environments. I felt that this was a wonderful forum in which to represent truth and God. Of course, I knew nothing about the Boy Scouts. The churches I knew would never sponsor a scout troop as many churches of other denominations did—the scouts were not evangelical enough for us. But I had spent the day prior to the telecast reading all about them so that I could defend them.

The show was an hour of lively exchanges, and then it was over. I was whisked by limousine to the Newark airport, and as I walked through the terminal with my television makeup still in place, I wondered, *How many of these people recognize me?*

My wife picked me up at the airport, and all the way home I gave her a blow-by-blow account of what had happened. As we drove up to our little log cabin in the woods, Lorna spoke for the first time:

"Would you take the garbage to the dump?"

As I drove to the dump in my 1949 Studebaker pickup—my TV makeup still on—I remember thinking, *Real life is not lived in the glare of the television camera—it's taking garbage to the dump.* This was a thought that would eventually alter the whole direction of my life.

Shortly after the *Donahue* show, I was returning to Lynchburg from another television appearance. While waiting to change planes in Charlotte, North Carolina, I ran into Harold Wilmington, who was scheduled for the same plane.

"Where have you been?" he asked politely.

I went on to tell him about the television show and how great it was and what an opportunity this was to get America back on track.

He listened quietly, and when I was finished, he looked me squarely in the eye and said, "You're casting your pearls before swine. You are a preacher and a pastor and you are wasting your time and your gifts doing television shows and pursuing politics."

I knew what he meant by "casting your pearls before swine." It was a quote from Jesus, a warning about taking precious truth and throwing it out to those who would least recognize or receive it. Harold's comments made me angry, but they also made me think. Traveling all over the country seemed important, but was it really what God had called me to do? Should a pastor devote his energies to such a task? Was I making good television but not changing people's lives? Furthermore, would these people eventually turn on me?

In the months to come, I began wrestling with these questions. On one occasion I was officiating at a funeral with Jerry. We were sitting in his truck at the cemetery while waiting for the family to arrive. I asked him about the tension between being called to preach the Bible and the consuming task of political involvement. I told him that at times I felt as if I was gradually drifting away from my primary calling.

"Do you miss the days when you were just a pastor, Jerry?" I asked. He said he did.

"Then how did you work your way through the process of moving beyond the local community into a national political agenda?" I continued.

"I came to the point in my ministry when I realized that I had to do certain things for the greater good of the country. The pressing moral needs of America have forced me to prioritize my time in order to accomplish the greater good. As a result, I have had to accept the fact that I can no longer do some of the things I used to do."

Then he told me I needed to make those same kinds of choices.

"Once you move into a national arena, you can never go back."

I knew that God had called me to preach. I had been ordained to the ministry. I had pledged that I would devote the rest of my life to teaching and preaching the Bible. Yet now only a small portion of my life was devoted to those tasks.

For almost a year I went after lunch each day to the prayer chapel next to my office to pray and read the Scriptures. I longed to devote my life to teaching and preaching and nothing else. Finally, an opportunity came for me to act on what I believed. Calvary Church, a large independent church in Grand Rapids, Michigan, asked me to accept a call to be their pastor.

I will never forget the day the church in Grand Rapids voted to invite me. It was the same day that Jerry took over the PTL ministry from Jim Bakker. I had been in a long meeting with Jerry and several others to discuss how we were going to handle this new responsibility. Jerry asked if I would decline the invitation to Grand Rapids and instead go to PTL in order to help him. One of the people in the meeting held up his hands in the form of a television screen and said, "If you go to PTL, by tomorrow everyone in America will know who you are."

The fall of Jim Bakker[3] threatened the financial health of all the television evangelists. How Jerry handled PTL would have implications for everyone. I felt the pressure to help. When the church officials called to say they needed an answer, I told them I needed more time.

That night I went to my office to pray. The Scripture passage I read was compelling. It was about the temptation of Jesus: "Again, the devil took him to a very high mountain and showed him all the kingdoms of the world and their splendor. 'All this I will give you,' he said, 'if you will bow down and worship me'" (Matthew 4:8–9).

For me, the message was clear: God wanted me in Grand Rapids. The PTL was only a temptation to splendor. Jerry was not the devil, and I do not think he was wrong in taking over PTL. But for me, it was the last temptation.

I have been the pastor of Calvary Church for eleven years. When I first arrived, a friend of mine, Truman Dollar, gave me some of the best advice I've ever been given:

"There are only two things you need to do in Grand Rapids. First, preach the Bible. Second, love the people. Nothing more and nothing less."

Much to the dismay of the politically involved religious people in our community, I have avoided all political activity. No debating. No television talk shows. No marches. No voter registrations. No public comments on politics.

Perhaps I have overreacted. My beliefs have not changed. My concern for the moral decline of our country has not changed. What has changed is that I now believe that the way to transform our nation has little to do with politics and everything to do with offering people the gospel.

ONE

WHAT DID WE REALLY WIN?

When I founded the Moral Majority, my goal was to engage the religious right and, in return, to change the direction of the country on its moral and social dilemmas. Ten years later, we feel that our mission is accomplished.

Jerry Falwell, upon dissolving the Moral Majority
June 12, 1989

It was the morning after the 1980 election. Jerry Falwell and the Moral Majority were receiving credit from the networks *cal thomas* and newspapers for being instrumental in helping Ronald Reagan win the White House and in defeating five liberal Democratic senators.

A rally was held at Liberty Baptist College (now Liberty University). The auditorium was jammed, not only with students, but with the national media. It appeared that cameras and print reporters from every major publication were present. The three main television networks, the *Washington Post,* the *New York Times,* the wire services—all had sent reporters and camera crews.

I was sitting on a large stage behind a lectern with the rest of the Moral Majority leadership and several pastors. When Jerry walked in, the place exploded with cheers and victory shouts. The noise was deafening. It was as if the school's football team had just scored a winning touchdown. But instead of a traditional fight song or patriotic number, the college band struck up "Hail to the Chief," the official theme reserved only for the president of the United States. Someone might have thought that Jerry Falwell had just been elected president, not Ronald Reagan. It was an awesome and defining moment. There was no turning back now, if anyone had wanted to—and who would have in the face of this scene? The thrill of victory was ours, and nothing was going to take it away.

No one in the building (with the possible exception of the press) was not a true believer that morning. We were on our way to changing America. We had the power to right every wrong and cure every ill and end every frustration that God-fearing people had been forced to submit to by our "oppressors," whom we labeled secular humanists, abortionists, homosexuals, pornographers, and "liberals." We opposed them all with the righteous indignation we thought came directly from God. We opposed them because we knew they were the reason America was in decline. And we had been raised up by God himself to reverse that decline.

The election was proof that God was on our side and that he was well-pleased. We believed we could restore "moral sanity" by might and by power, with the Spirit of the Lord upon us. Victory and success, money and access to the White House, to Congress, and to the media—this was all the proof we needed of God's approval and blessing. Anyone who disagreed with us was a liberal, an atheist, a compromiser, or a member of the National Council of Churches (or maybe all four).

We sang the hymn "Victory in Jesus" in church, and we believed that theme in the long run. But we also believed in victory in Ronald Reagan for the short haul and we knew that he believed in us. Heaven was a long way away, and we needed something to help us make it through the political night. In Reagan we trusted.

It was said of Fred Astaire and Ginger Rogers that she gave him sex and he gave her class. We gave Ronald Reagan votes and he gave us credibility. We were no longer the backwoods yahoos who wore blue suits and white socks, drove pickup trucks with bumper stickers and a gun rack. We demanded r-e-s-p-e-c-t. And Ronald Reagan's victory was proof that we had earned it.

I visited scores of churches with Jerry Falwell and on my own during the five years I worked for the Moral Majority. On more than one occasion I saw an artist's depiction of Jesus Christ placed in close proximity to a photograph of Ronald Reagan. Sometimes the pastor was pictured shaking the hand of President Reagan; Jesus sometimes appeared to receive second billing on the pastor's wall or desk.

If any political movement should have been able to change the country by implementing its agenda, it was the Moral Majority. We had the nation's attention. We were mobilizing the nation's largest demographic unit (it has often been noted that there are more people in church on Sunday than watch NFL football games), and we had a President in the White House friendly to our objectives. For six years we also had a Republican-controlled Senate.

Our people were welcome in the White House, which some had never dreamed of visiting other than on the public tour. We were advancing. Liberalism was retreating. It was just a matter of time before our nation would be restored to what we wanted it to be. Those who doubted or questioned our power were dismissed. Those who warned of danger ahead were ignored, ridiculed, or condemned.

That was twenty years ago, and today very little that we set out to do has gotten done. In fact, the moral landscape of America has become worse. The Moral Majority folded in the late eighties, giving way to the Christian Coalition and other organizations that have taken up its agenda, using, with minor variations, the same strategies to achieve the same ends we failed to achieve.

Two decades after conservative Christians charged into the political arena, bringing new voters and millions of dollars with them in hopes of transforming the culture through political power, it must now be acknowledged that we have failed. We failed not because we were wrong about our critique of culture, or because we lacked conviction, or because there were not enough of us, or because too many were lethargic and uncommitted. We failed because we were unable to redirect a nation from the top down. Real change must come from the bottom up or, better yet, from the inside out.

Strong words?

Take abortion, an issue that has divided America longer than did either the Vietnam War or the Civil War. It is a good example of why top-down activism cannot work without the willing acquiescence of a majority of people. Abortion is not the cause of our social problems; it is a reflection of them. If the Religious Right wants to fix things at the top, it must attend to repairing things at the bottom. A stable house requires a firm foundation.

In April 1973, just three months after the Supreme Court declared a woman's right to have an abortion, a Louis Harris survey found 63 percent of those questioned agreeing with the statement "it's against God's will to destroy any human life, especially that of an unborn baby." Twenty-eight percent disagreed. The survey also found that 68 percent of respondents agreed with the statement "so long as a doctor has to be consulted, the matter of an abortion is only a question of a woman's decision with her doctor's professional advice." Twenty-three percent disagreed.[1]

The American Enterprise Institute and Roper Center examined opinion polls on abortion for the last twenty-five years. In January 1998 they concluded that despite the rhetoric and campaigns by both sides, attitudes about abortion remain pretty much unchanged.[2]

In perhaps the biggest and costliest battle waged by conservative Christians, twenty years of fighting has won nothing. And our record is no better with other moral and social issues. The gay rights agenda advances and, although Congress passed a "Defense of Marriage Act" in 1997 that allows states the right to outlaw marriages between people of the same gender, New Jersey became the first state to legalize adoption by unwed adults, heterosexual or homosexual.

Television programming is worse than ever, and language that once could have resulted in the FCC's canceling a station's license is now standard fare. In 1998, radio "shock jock" Howard Stern was given his own television show, which is syndicated on CBS, the network that once gave us wholesome comedians such as Red Skelton, Lucille Ball and Desi Arnaz, and Jackie Gleason.

The Moral Majority's campaign against pornography has had no discernible effect. Once you had to go to a "bad part of town" where, if you were seen, your reputation might be hurt. Now pornography is available in most hotels and on the Internet.

The traditional family is a distant memory for an ever-growing number of Americans. Even many declared Christians are getting divorced and engaging in adulterous affairs and premarital sex, distinguishing them not at all from unbelievers and nonchurch-goers.

If fighting crime means increasing the prison population, we have succeeded beyond anyone's wildest dreams. The United States has more people in prison than at any other time in its history.[3] Yet, a true war on crime would mean fewer criminals, wouldn't it? If criminals were a fixed number, we could order a police dragnet, get them all off the streets, and feel safe. But the culture produces new criminals faster than we can lock up existing lawbreakers. The problem resembles multiplying and spreading cancer cells, and no treatment, from President Clinton's "midnight basketball" program to conservative "tough on crime" solutions, is working.

We wanted to end, or sharply reduce, drug use among the young, but many young people turn to drugs out of frustration motivated by adult behavior, a failure to develop their character, and a sense that they are not loved. A true war on drugs would begin with a greater parental presence in the home and a deeper parental commitment to children. But a message like this doesn't help politicians win votes or political-religious leaders raise money, so the message is deliberately kept vague and nonspecific. "Traditional values" and "family values" were our preferred expressions.

For years conservatives have criticized liberals on issues such as welfare. I recall pointing out on numerous occasions that President Lyndon Johnson's "War on Poverty" was a war the poor lost. In debates on college campuses and on television I would ask my liberal opponents how much more money and how many more years it would take before the spending programs would end poverty. The answers I received were about "structural problems" and the lack of commitment and too little spending. A timetable was never offered.

But the question can be turned on conservatives. How much more money and how much more time is needed to convince a majority of the public that not only is abortion wrong (which a majority have always believed), but also that government ought to take steps to prevent as many as possible and even criminalize the procedure?

Abortion, like all other social ills, did not become a widespread practice by accident. It didn't suddenly spring on us like an unexpected storm in January 1973. If we would truly change the abortion-minded, we are more likely to be effective by changing attitudes. If we do that, laws must ultimately follow, as they did with civil rights. But if our focus is laws first, we will not succeed in our current materialistic environment.

The aphrodisiac of political power descended on Lynchburg, Virginia, with the impact of an asteroid. Politics was a better means to noble ends than the hard and often invisible efforts mandated by Scripture. Who wanted to ride into the capital on the back of an ass when one could go first class in a private jet and be picked up and driven around in a chauffeured limousine? Who wanted the role of a servant when one could have the accolades given to leaders? Who wanted the pain of Good Friday when one could have the acclaim of the masses on Palm Sunday?

It is important to understand that the greatest temptation is not to do evil. Most of us could resist the big stuff. That's why fundamentalist preachers concentrated largely on the "sins" most of their members (though not all) had a pretty easy time avoiding—liquor, movies, dancing, promiscuity. They mostly avoided the positive tough stuff—the business about feeding the hungry, clothing the naked, and visiting those in prison, along with matters of justice (see Matthew 25:31–46).

To his credit, Jerry Falwell, more than most, addressed some of these, but they were background issues because you couldn't raise money on them, and the reason you couldn't raise money is because they didn't play to people's fears and insecurities. (We will say more about this in the chapter on fund-raising.)

The impotence and near-irrelevance of the Religious Right were demonstrated on the day William Jefferson Clinton was inaugurated. Clinton's first two acts as president were to sign executive orders liberalizing rules against homosexuals in the military and repealing the few abortion restrictions applied under presidents Reagan and Bush.

With a few pen strokes, Bill Clinton erased the little that the Moral Majority had been able to achieve during its brief existence. The tragedy was not the failure to succeed, but the waste of spiritual energy that would have been better spent on strategies and methods more likely to succeed than the quest for political power.

TWO

THE VAST RIGHT-WING CONSPIRACY

Oh, we're the Moral Majority, we're holier than thou.
By God, we're here to tell you what we will and won't allow.
We're out to purge the nation of its humanistic bent.
A separate church and state we've simply given up for Lent.

Doug Mayfield, Minneapolis schoolteacher
Recorded song, "The Moral Majority"
July 29, 1981

With the founding of the Moral Majority in 1979, evangelicals and fundamentalists ventured into the political *ed dobson* process. They were not welcomed with open arms by either the political or religious establishments. Rather, they kicked down the door and marched in with such fury that they sent panic through most sectors of American society.

The media were shocked. Where did all these fundamentalists come from? Who were they, and what did they want? Since the general public had assumed that fundamentalists disappeared after the infamous Scopes "Monkey Trial" in 1925, it was at a loss to explain their sudden public resurgence. A kind of paranoia set in, and some began to assert that hoards of bigoted "Bible-bangers" had formed a conspiracy to take over America. In September 1980, *Newsweek* magazine stated, "What is clear on both the philosophical level—and in the rough-and-tumble arena of politics—is that the Falwells of the nation and their increasingly militant flock are a phenomenon that can no longer be dismissed or ignored."

Twenty years have passed since conservative Christians burst on the political scene. They are now part of the political landscape, but there is still a great mistrust of them and their agenda in the secular corridors of power and influence. Some still believe that there is a right-wing conspiracy to take over America and turn it into a theocracy. In the aftermath of the Monica Lewinsky accusations against President Clinton, the president's wife went on NBC's *Today* show to defend her husband and deny the allegations. She stated that the real problem was that there was a vast right-wing conspiracy to get her husband and that this conspiracy was led by people like Jerry Falwell.[1]

Now, Jerry Falwell has never been a fan of President Clinton. Jerry told me one time that he did not see how a real Christian could vote for Bill Clinton. On another occasion he sent me a harsh note about some of the things I had said about the president. I had attended a breakfast meeting at the White House with fifteen other clergy to discuss the issue of HIV/AIDS, and I was seated next to the president. During the course of the dialogue, someone began criticizing the Religious Right and their rhetoric on the issue of homosexuality. Several people agreed that something had to be done about the nastiness of these conservative bigots. Then it was my turn to speak.

"In regard to the Religious Right," I said, "you need to know that I worked for Jerry Falwell for fifteen years, and that I was a member of the board of the Moral Majority."

At that point the room became silent. The president looked at me as if to say, "How in the world did you get in?"

I continued, "I think your assessment of the Religious Right is unfair. When my friends find out that I met with the president and, furthermore, that I sat on his 'left' side, I'm doomed."

Everyone laughed. The president threw his arm around me, leaned over close, and said, "Take a picture and send it to Rush Limbaugh!"

Shortly after the meeting, I was quoted in *Christianity Today*— some comments I made that were favorable toward my meeting with the president. Then I heard from Jerry Falwell. He faxed me a copy of the article in *CT* and underlined my comments. In the margin, he wrote, "Unforgivable compromise. Don't ever call me again."

I think he was a little ticked.

Several months later, Jerry and I were together at a funeral. As we walked away from the graveside, he took me aside and said, "Remember what I wrote about your comments in *CT?* Well, everything is OK."

In fact, Jerry's initial response to the Monica Lewinsky accusations have been rather remarkable: he called for prayer on behalf of the president. Mrs. Clinton was dead wrong in accusing Falwell of being behind the Lewinsky accusations. She was also dead wrong in her belief that there is a vast right-wing conspiracy operating for the destruction of her husband.

There are, however, millions of conservative people in this country who share many common beliefs and moral standards. Jerry Falwell is one of them. But he does not speak for everyone, nor does any other Christian leader. That is what the press and many critics of conservative Christians fail to understand. And that is also why the Religious Right is doomed to fail unless it changes its behavior. What started as a legitimate and rational response to the threat of theological liberalism evolved into a political agenda motivated more by fear than conviction.

The fundamentalist movement took its name from the publication of a series of booklets in 1909 named *The Fundamentals: A Testimony of Truth,* written by scholars from around the world. The authors represented Presbyterian, Methodist, and Episcopal denominations and people of varying theological positions. These articles were designed to identify the essential (fundamental) doctrines of the Christian faith, which were under attack from the then-current tides of scientific inquiry. Five fundamental doctrines were identified as the basic tenets of the Christian faith:[2]

1. *The inspiration and infallibility of the Bible.* The fundamentalist concept of inspiration and inerrancy is that in the original autographs all Scripture is equally inspired, and that inspiration extends to the very words themselves. The logical consequence of inspiration was a document free from any error in all its statements and affirmations. This meant that the Bible

error not only in theology but also in matters of science, history, geography, and the cosmos.

2. *The deity of Christ.* This was the most crucial doctrine of all. The argument as written by Princeton theologian B. B. Warfield was twofold. First, Christ claimed to be God. Second, the deity of Christ was evidenced by the personal experience of every believer. The Virgin Birth was considered intrinsic to the deity of Christ, the means by which the Son of God became the Son of Man. To deny the Virgin Birth, as many liberal theologians did, was to deny the essential personhood of Jesus.

3. *The substitutionary atonement of Christ.* The liberal theologians had begun propagating the idea that the death of Christ was merely that of a martyr and provided nothing more than a moral influence on society. That is, his death was a good moral example from which all people could benefit. To the fundamentalists this was a denial of the heart of Christianity and the soul of the gospel. Christ died a substitutionary death, and in so doing, he provided atonement for the sins of mankind.

4. *The resurrection of Christ.* Liberal theologians advocated a spiritual rather than a literal resurrection. They claimed that Jesus did not come out of the grave physically and bodily, but only in spirit and influence. They believed that the Resurrection was only in people's hearts. The fundamentalists, by contrast, loudly proclaimed the literal resurrection of Jesus. They believed that their salvation was sealed by the death and resurrection of Christ. The Scriptures clearly taught a bodily resurrection from the dead and recounted many post-resurrection appearances of Christ to his disciples. To deny the Resurrection was to deny the clear teaching of the Bible and the core truths of salvation.

5. *The second coming of Christ.* The fundamentalists believed not only in a literal, bodily resurrection, but also in a literal, bodily return of Christ to the earth. Their hope was that the coming of Jesus would be the culmination of all history. By contrast, liberal theologians and church leaders, who questioned the meaning of the death of Jesus and denied his resurrection, were in no position to advocate the return of someone whom they believed was dead.

The birth of fundamentalism at the beginning of this century was not the birth of a fanatical, militant, and irrational minority. It was the reemergence of the traditional and conservative Christian orthodoxy that had existed throughout church history. Threatened by liberalism and its accommodation to unbelief, fundamentalists rose to defend minimal doctrinal essentials—without which the Christian faith would cease to be valid.

By 1918 the liberals and the fundamentalists had clearly articulated their positions and were ready for a head-on collision. Conservative Christians held their first major national conference in Philadelphia that year, with more than five thousand people attending. The next year they met at the Moody Bible Institute of Chicago and decided to go on the offensive against liberalism by establishing their own organization, which would later be known as the World's Christian Fundamentals Association. They also began advocating the establishment of new Bible institutes and conferences to combat the influence of liberalism. This was a major change of direction. Instead of staying in the major denominations and fighting against the liberals for control, the early fundamentalists withdrew and began their own organizations.

Just as conservatives were building a head of steam, a local courtroom drama was played out in the national press that would have a profound impact on how they would be perceived by others as well as by themselves. John Thomas Scopes was a public school teacher in Tennessee, where it was illegal to teach any hypothesis contrary to biblical creationism in the public school system. Scopes was encouraged to teach evolution and thereby challenge the law. He did so and was brought to trial in Dayton, Tennessee, on July 10, 1925, in the sweltering summer heat.

The main characters of the trial were the two attorneys. William Jennings Bryan defended the cause of creationism while Clarence Darrow defended Scopes and evolution. Bryan was a prominent politician, with an exceptional gift for oratory, who was an unsuccessful Democratic nominee for president three times. He served as the secretary of state under Woodrow Wilson. Toward the end of his life, Bryan devoted more and more time to religious causes. He seemed to be the most logical choice to defend biblical creationism. By contrast, Darrow was a brilliant defense attorney who was accustomed to defending unpopular causes and was at ease in the heat of a courtroom trial.

All America followed the trial. Thousands attended. The press covered the unfolding drama in detail. Indeed, it was more than a trial; it was a reflection of the larger issue of the confrontation between biblical supernaturalism and secular empiricism. During the years leading up to the trial, conservative Christians in all the major Protestant denominations were struggling with several major intellectual issues. First, they were dealing with the issue of Darwinian evolution. Charles Darwin (1809–1882), an English naturalist who had studied for the ministry for a while at Cambridge, shocked the nineteenth-century world with his theory of evolution based on natural selection. Darwin postulated that life did not exist as a result of the direct act of creation by a supernatural God. Rather, he theorized, life evolved from simple singular cells to complex mammals, including humans.

The issue of evolution became the hottest intellectual issue of the nineteenth century. In time it affected theology as well as education, sociology, and law. Most people concluded that if humans were mere animals, then God was unnecessary. By advocating the scientific process of critical analysis, Darwin unleashed a barrage of critical thinking on almost every area of academic pursuit. Some Christians, who eventually came to be called "liberals," advocated broadening their thinking to include the idea of evolution. The fundamentalists rejected evolution as a rejection of the biblical account of creation.

Second, conservative Christians were dealing with the issue of higher criticism. In both England and Germany, liberal theologians, influenced by the scientific approach, began to question the authenticity of various books of the Bible. In time nearly every book of the Bible fell under the critic's knife. Conservatives rejected these new "scientific" approaches to the Bible as a rejection of the inspiration and authority of the Bible.

Third, conservative Christians struggled with the issue of anti-supernaturalism, the notion put forth by scholars that what could not be documented through rigorous scientific inquiry would not be accepted as real or true. The stupendous miracles of the Old Testament, like the crossing of the Red Sea, were rejected as scientifically impossible. Eventually the miracles of the prophets and the apostles, the miracles of Jesus, the Virgin Birth, and the Resurrection were all rejected.

The Scopes trial was really the final confrontation between science and the Bible for that era, and the Bible lost. The turning point of the trial came when Darrow called Bryan to the witness stand. Darrow's cross-examination resulted in the humiliation of Bryan in the eyes of the press, due in part to Bryan's inconsistent and ill-informed testimony. The next day, the judge ordered Bryan's embarrassing testimony stricken from the record. Darrow asked that the jury return a guilty verdict so the case could be appealed to a higher court. The jury pronounced Scopes guilty. Technically, Bryan (who died just five days later) won the trial, but in the court of public opinion he suffered a great loss—a loss not only for him, but also for conservative, Bible-believing Christians, who had become the laughing stock of the media and the nation. In the aftermath of the trial, fundamentalists withdrew from the public square and focused on building their own subculture of churches, denominations, schools, organizations, radio stations (and eventually, television), and associations.

When conservative Christians reemerged on the political scene in 1980, the media were shocked. Where did all these millions of people come from? The assumption was that religion in America was either dead or dying. But it was not. Conservative Christians had been winning people to Christ throughout the half-century following the Scopes trial. Churches that had started in storefronts had become the largest and most influential in nearly every town. Generations of young people had been trained in hundreds of Bible colleges and Christian liberal arts colleges. Entire denominations and fellowships had been formed. Dozens of parachurch organizations had been created. Christians controlled a vast empire of radio and television stations as well as publishing houses and magazines. People like Jerry Falwell and Pat Robertson were taking in more money than the Republican and Democratic parties. But until these Christians entered the political arena, they were ignored by the media.

There are two popular but false notions about the founding of the Moral Majority and the reentry of conservative Christians into public life. First, many think that the founding of the Moral Majority and other such groups is part of a vast right-wing conspiracy. They think that people like James Dobson, James Kennedy, Donald Wildmon, Jerry Falwell, and dozens of others get together on a regular basis at some remote location as part of a secret society to take over America. Nothing could be further from the truth. The Moral Majority was not the result of some high-level consultation between the power brokers of the Religious Right. It was the idea of one man: Jerry Falwell.

With the encouragement of several pastors and politically connected people, Falwell founded a political organization to deal with the crucial issues of the day. The purpose of this "nonpartisan" organization was to promote morality in public life and to combat legislation that favored the legalization of immorality. The Moral Majority took its name from Richard Nixon's earlier use of the term "silent majority." Falwell had always been a Nixon supporter. The first time I went into Jerry's office at Thomas Road Baptist Church, I was impressed with the huge photograph he had on the wall. It was a picture of President Nixon standing beside the presidential helicopter and waving.

The second false notion is that the purpose of the Moral Majority was to take over America. Again, nothing could be further from the truth. The Moral Majority was founded as a reaction against a secular society that was increasingly hostile to conservative Christians. Christians believed that they were an oppressed minority and that if they did not stand up, they would be buried by the secularists and the humanists. The Moral Majority was seen as an organization to stop the rising tide of secularism. It was a fortress to protect, not a battleship to attack. We were not interested in taking over America. We were only interested in making sure we did not get overtaken. Falwell himself wrote,

> As a pastor, I kept waiting for someone to come to the forefront of the American religious scene to lead the way out of the wilderness. Like thousands of other preachers, I kept waiting,

but no real leader appeared. Finally I realized that we had to act ourselves. Something had to be done now. The government was encroaching upon the sovereignty of both the church and the family. The Supreme Court had legalized abortion on demand. The Equal Rights Amendment, with its vague language, threatened damage to the traditional family, as did the rising sentiment toward so-called homosexual rights. Most Americans were shocked, but kept hoping someone would do something about this moral chaos.[3]

Then Jerry Falwell did something.

Shortly after the founding of the Moral Majority, I signed a contract with Ed Hindson and Jerry Falwell to write a book for Doubleday about the rise and influence of fundamentalism. Toward the end of the book we discussed the rise of the Moral Majority. We also included the original agenda. The platform had ten points:[4]

1. We believe in the separation of church and state. Moral Majority, Inc., is a political organization providing a platform for religious and nonreligious Americans who share moral values to address their concerns in these areas. Members of the Moral Majority, Inc., have no common theological premise. We are Americans who are proud to be conservative in our approach to moral, social and political concerns.

2. We are pro-life. We believe that life begins at fertilization. We strongly oppose the massive "biological holocaust" that is resulting in the abortion of one and a half million babies each year in America. We believe that unborn babies have the right to life as much as babies that have been born. We are providing a voice and a defense for the human and civil rights of millions of unborn babies.

3. We are pro-traditional family. We believe that the only acceptable family form begins with a legal marriage of a man and a woman. We feel that homosexual marriages and common law marriages should not be accepted as traditional families. We

oppose legislation that favors these kinds of "diverse family forms," thereby penalizing the traditional family. We do not oppose civil rights for homosexuals. We do oppose "special rights" for homosexuals who have chosen a perverted life-style rather than a traditional life-style.

4. We oppose the illegal drug traffic in America. The youth in America are presently in the midst of a drug epidemic. Through education, legislation, and other means we want to do our part to save our young people from death on the installment plan through illegal drug addiction.

5. We oppose pornography. While we do not advocate censorship, we do believe that education and legislation can help stem the tide of pornography and obscenity that is poisoning the American spirit today. Economic boycotts are a proper way in America's free-enterprise system to help persuade the media to move back to a sensible and reasonable moral stand. We most certainly believe in the First Amendment for everyone. We are not willing to sit back, however, while many television programs create cesspools of obscenity and vulgarity in our nation's living rooms.

6. We support the state of Israel and Jewish people everywhere. It is impossible to separate the state of Israel from the Jewish family internationally. Many Moral Majority members, because of their theological convictions, are committed to the Jewish people. Others stand upon the human and civil rights of all persons as a premise for support of the state of Israel. Support of Israel is one of the essential commitments of Moral Majority. No anti-Semitic influence is allowed in Moral Majority, Inc.

7. We believe that a strong national defense is the best deterrent to war. We believe that liberty is the basic moral issue of all moral issues. The only way America can remain free is to remain strong. Therefore, we support the efforts of our present administration to regain our position of military preparedness—with a sincere hope that we will never need to use any of our weapons against any people anywhere.

8. We support equal rights for women. We agree with President Reagan's commitment to help every governor and every state legislature

to move quickly to ensure that during the 1980s every American woman will earn as much money and enjoy the same opportunities for advancement as her male counterpart in the same vocation.

9. We believe the Equal Rights Amendment is the wrong vehicle to obtain equal rights for women. We feel that the ambiguous and simplistic language of the amendment could lead to court interpretations that might put women in combat.

10. We encourage our Moral Majority state organizations to be autonomous and indigenous. Moral Majority state organizations may, from time to time, hold positions that are not held by the Moral Majority, Inc., national organization.

For fear of being misunderstood, we also articulated what we were not.

1. We are not a political party.
2. We do not endorse political candidates.
3. We are not attempting to elect "born again" candidates.
4. Moral Majority, Inc., is not a religious organization attempting to control the government.
5. We are not a censorship organization.
6. Moral Majority, Inc., is not an organization committed to depriving homosexuals of their civil rights as Americans.
7. We do not believe that individuals or organizations that disagree with Moral Majority, Inc., belong to an immoral minority.

Then we launched into a series of concerns under the following major categories: moral issues, social issues, ethical issues, political issues, and religious issues. The moral issues included the sanctity of human life, humanism in the public schools, sex education in the public schools, pornography, and homosexuality. The social issues included the dignity of the family, racial injustice, and world hunger. The ethical issues included artificial insemination, selective breeding, genetic engineering, and euthanasia. The political issues included a strong national defense, the communist threat, and the state of Israel. The religious issues included national revival, church planting, and Christian education.

In retrospect, we were not passionate about all the issues we listed, and some of them therefore suffered from neglect. I am not sure that we did much about racial injustice or world hunger or speaking in favor of the civil rights of homosexuals. We should have done so. On the other hand, we worked hard to defeat gay rights issues and pressed for action on the issue of abortion. We probably chose too many issues. In practical terms, we attempted to do too much aimed in too many directions. I think the list of issues represented our general concerns, and we wanted to do something about all of them. I remember the feelings of euphoria during those days. We knew we were in the middle of something big and significant. We knew we were a force to be reckoned with. We knew we were no longer an alienated minority. We possessed political power, and we intended to use it for good.

The Reagan-Bush landslide in 1980 was the greatest moment of opportunity for conservative Christians in this century. We had been disgraced in 1925 at the Scopes trial. But now we were vindicated. We had helped elect our man to the White House, and he openly praised the efforts of Falwell and the Moral Majority. The Republican landslide brought in new senators, and for the first time in twenty-six years the Republicans had a Senate majority. Along with the Moral Majority, groups like the Christian Voice, the Religious Roundtable, the National Christian Action Coalition, and several pro-life organizations published target lists and moral report cards. The new right was successful in defeating senators George McGovern of South Dakota, Frank Church of Idaho, John Culver of Iowa, Birch Bayh of Indiana, and Gaylord Nelson of Wisconsin. Of the targeted senators, only Alan Cranston of California survived.

Between the presidential campaigns of 1980 and 1984, the Religious Right continued to lobby Congress and register new voters. According to various reports, by 1981 new right groups had enlisted 70,000 clergy and had registered four to five million new voters. The Reagan presidency took a conservative posture toward issues such as abortion, the Equal Rights Amendment, homosexuality, and school prayer. The Religious Right lined up behind this Republican platform. Jerry Falwell and other religious leaders visited the White House on a regular basis. President Reagan became the hero of the conservative Christians in America.

Every Wednesday night we had a church service at Thomas Road Baptist Church. I almost always sat on the platform next to Jerry Falwell. At some point in the service, Jerry would tell where he had traveled that week and where he would be the rest of the week. His schedule was a blur of activities—several different cities each day. He was continually being interviewed by the press, speaking on college campuses, visiting political leaders in Washington, or preaching in churches all over the country.

We always looked forward to the report Jerry would give afterward. It was exciting to know that the American public was finally hearing from conservative people of faith, and we were proud of Jerry as our representative. After the report, we would have a time of prayer. We would divide into small groups and pray together. I would kneel next to Jerry and pray with him. He always prayed for the president and his advisers. He prayed for their protection. He prayed that the president would seek godly advice and do what was right. He poured out his heart to God on behalf of the president. Then he would ask forgiveness for the terrible sin of abortion and pray that this would be changed. They were powerful prayers that I will never forget.

By the time of the 1984 election, the Religious Right had been galvanized behind the Republican party. However, as is typical of second-term victories, there was no landslide effect in the House or the Senate. This time there were no report cards or target lists. The civilizing of the Religious Right was already taking place. Conservative Christians were no longer an outside group. We had been invited to the table, and now we were required to practice table manners.

After the reelection of Reagan, a mood of apathy set in among the Moral Majority. The two most influential vice presidents, Ron Godwin and Cal Thomas, resigned in 1985 to pursue careers elsewhere. Jerry Falwell announced that he was getting out of politics in 1986 and going back to the basics of his ministry. He began shutting down the Moral Majority. Then in 1986, Pat Robertson, who had managed to stay out of earlier campaigns, announced he might run for the Republican nomination in 1988. He stated that he would run if he got the support of one million people by the fall of 1987. He got the support and became a Republican candidate for the presidency. He also gave up his ordination papers so that he would not be running as a minister but rather as a broadcaster and lawyer.

The Religious Right had come a long way in their thinking in seven years. In 1980, through the influence of Jerry Falwell and others, conservative people of faith were convinced that it was acceptable for Christians to be involved in politics. We were also convinced that it was legitimate for pastors to be engaged in the process. Although we had criticized black pastors for their involvement in the civil rights struggle, we had now changed our minds and had jumped in ourselves. With the candidacy of Pat Robertson, we were now declaring that it was also desirable for a minister to become president. This change in thinking and action is miraculous, given the short period of time in which it took place. Or was it deception?

Did the Moral Majority really make a difference? During the height of the Moral Majority, we were taking in millions of dollars a year. We published a magazine, organized state chapters, lobbied Congress, aired a radio program, and more. Did it work? Is the moral condition of America better because of our efforts? Even a casual observation of the current moral climate suggests that despite all the time, money, and energy—despite the political power—we failed. Things have not gotten better; they have gotten worse.

In 1992, when the vast majority of Americans believed that the alleged sexual immorality of the president had no bearing on his job performance and was exclusively a private matter, then we knew that Christian values had long since been forgotten. That 70 percent still approved of his "job performance" on the day of his impeachment is another indication of the Moral Majority's impotence. Crime is still rampant, judging from the overcrowding of our prisons. Drugs are even more readily available to our children than they were twenty years ago. Pornography has moved from the back shelf to the television sets in our living rooms. The number of abortions performed each year has declined only slightly. Homosexuality is shrugged off as an acceptable, alternative lifestyle. And even within our churches, divorce rates continue to climb, mirroring those of people who do not attend church.

On practically every plank of our platform, we have failed, at least from a legislative and judicial perspective.

So, were the efforts of the Moral Majority a complete waste of time and money? Absolutely not. The Moral Majority had a profound impact on American life. First, the Moral Majority forced public discussion on moral issues. Abortion became a front-burner issue. Jerry would often say, "Now you can't run for dog catcher in any town in America without having a stand on abortion," and he was right.

Second, the Moral Majority forced discussion of the role of religion and religious people in the political process. Liberal churches and liberal clergy had shared a monopoly on religion and politics. The Moral Majority forced new and heated discussion in this arena. Although we have not resolved the appropriate role between religion and politics, the resurgence of conservative Christians into the public square made ongoing dialogue on this issue necessary.

Third, the Moral Majority awakened millions of Christians to their civic responsibility. New voters were registered. These voters became informed on the moral issues and voted their conscience on these issues. For decades these Christians had ignored the political process, but now the sleeping giant had been awakened. The liberals hoped the giant would go back to sleep, but it did not and it will not—thanks in large part to the Moral Majority.

But there were blind spots in the Moral Majority's vision. In 1988, I wrote a book with Ed Hindson entitled *The Seduction of Power: Preachers, Politics and the Media.* In the book we argued that the Moral Majority lacked a long-term vision for its political involvement. We suggested that the organization was better at confronting and opposing issues rather than offering positive steps to change the things they opposed. We offered some advice on how to go about making a difference over the long term. We called for a philosophy of Christian political involvement. This philosophy would include several key factors that bear repeating:[5]

1. We need a theological and philosophical basis for our involvement. If we are going to affect American political and social life, we must understand what it is we are trying to accomplish. We are not merely advocating the election of certain officials as an end in itself. Francis Schaeffer clearly understood this when he argued that Christ must be Lord in all of life. Schaeffer wrote, "He is Lord not just in religious things and not just in cultural things ... but in our intellectual lives, and in business, and in our relation to society, and in our attitude toward the moral breakdown of our culture." Acknowledging his lordship involves placing ourselves under the authority of his kingdom and acting as citizens of his kingdom as well as citizens of earth.

It is in this regard that the Christian understands the wrongs of society are not merely social ills. As such, these wrongs require spiritual help, not merely political adjustment. Ultimately, there are no permanent solutions to the problems of society in a fallen world. But that does not mean that we should retreat to a monastery and allow social anarchy for the rest of the world.

Because the Christian is a citizen of two kingdoms—one earthly, the other heavenly—he has an obligation to both. He cannot divorce himself from either. He is under divine mandate to both. Nevertheless, he realizes that the one is temporary and the other is eternal. Yet that in no way prohibits his involvement in the temporal; in fact, it enhances it. The Christian cannot merely sit by and passively watch society self-destruct. Something within him—namely, the Spirit of God—cries out for truth and justice. Wherever the cry has been articulated into action, truth and justice have prevailed.

2. We need a long-range strategy. There are no instant solutions to complex problems. The New Right has often been criticized for offering simple answers to complex questions, but this doesn't have to be the case. We do have valuable answers to the really important issues of the day, and those answers need to be articulated clearly and thoughtfully. This is not the time for arrogance or overstatement of our case; neither is this the time for capitulation. No one ever said this process would be easy. Those who naively thought Ronald Reagan

THE VAST RIGHT-WING CONSPIRACY 45

would solve all the ills of American society by himself have been severely disappointed. On the other hand, conditions have improved so that religious conservatives have been able to make their voices heard in a way that was not possible prior to 1980.

One of our greatest needs today is for a long-range strategy to enact moral goals and objectives. We cannot rest on past strategies, successes, or failures, or the future will catch us unprepared. Serious questions need to be addressed now. Where do we go after Reagan? What if the next president is more hostile to our agenda? Do we give up or do we dig in deeper?

3. We need to make careful use of power and influence. People expect politicians to talk about politics, but when preachers start talking about politics, they begin using the power of their position to legitimize political issues. Preachers are perceived as spiritual leaders and religious authorities by the general public. When they defend political or social issues, they are perceived as somehow speaking for God. It is difficult for the average layperson to distinguish between whether the preacher is speaking for himself or God, whether the preacher is a Catholic bishop or a Pentecostal evangelist.

The particular power of preachers who use television is that they are the only preachers some people listen to. Many viewers lack spiritual discernment to evaluate properly what they are hearing. So we must be cautious in the statements we make regarding religion and politics. We must also exercise caution with regard to those with whom we disagree. When preachers start talking about politics, it becomes tempting to label our opponents as the "devil" and their views as "anti-Christian." (Unfortunately, this has been the case throughout most of church history.) In some cases, our political opponents will even be fellow believers who need to be respected as such, even though we may seriously disagree on political matters. This is perhaps the most difficult issue of all for Christians in politics. We are all so quick to believe that "God is on our side" that we tend to see our political opponents as God-hating, Christ-denying hypocrites. Unfortunately, this kind of prejudice has been used on the New Right as well as by the New Right.

4. We need financial integrity and accountability. Certainly the misuse of funds uncovered during the PTL scandal serves as a

reminder to every ministry that integrity in fund-raising and account-ability in financial expenditures is essential. We must not become deceived by the tyranny of the urgent and lose sight of our ultimate objectives. Some preachers have found politics to be a great potential fund-raiser and have lost sight of why they are raising funds in the first place. Sociopolitical issues are not important because they raise money; they are important because they touch on matters of eternal truth. It is also true that some issues raise more money than others. Preachers need to be especially careful that they do not focus only on those issues that are financially profitable, but on all issues of truth, whether or not they are popular or produce funds. Defending the rights of the unborn, for example, may not be lucrative, but it is certainly one of the great issues of our time.

5. We need to remember the priority of justice. According to Scripture, the ultimate authority of law comes from God and is a reflection of his nature and character. In this sense, even majority rule is not always right. Paul Marshall of the Institute of Christian Studies in Toronto, Canada, has correctly recognized that "at times even constitutional limits are not sufficient, and great injustice can still be done even while following constitutional rules." He cites the case of Hitler, who was supported by a large majority of Germans and was able to function within legal parameters while slaughtering millions of innocent people.

At times, the greater issues of human justice transcend political boundaries. The real issue today is not whether one is a Democrat or a Republican, but whether one is committed to justice for all. This means we must defend the rights of those with whom we disagree. Suppressing their freedoms in the name of religion is just as wrong as for them to suppress ours. We are only asking for the opportunity to be heard in the debate on public policy.

The Moral Majority served an important role in mobilizing many previously uninvolved and decent American citizens to return to the public square and reclaim some of the ground they had lost. As a pastor and one who was involved in the movement, I will always urge people to exercise their rights as citizens through the political process. But we who are Christians are deluded if we think we will change our culture solely through political power. One of the major reasons the Religious Right failed is that they were seduced by one of the oldest temptations known to man.

THREE

SEDUCED BY POWER

My theory is, there is something about politics and religion together that makes most Americans fight. They didn't like it when Jimmy Carter talked about salvation, and they liked it even less when Pat Robertson began talking about foreign affairs.

Darrell Laurant, columnist
June 23, 1989

A woman approached me after Sunday services and asked with frustration in her voice, "How can we persuade some Republicans not to withdraw from the party because they don't agree all the time with other Republicans?" She was, of course, referring to conservative Republicans who were threatening to bolt from the party because it would not take a strong stand against abortion.

Taking advantage of this unique church-state moment, I replied, "You can't apply the principles of a kingdom not of this world to a kingdom of this world. The purists want to apply the principles of a kingdom that knows no compromise to a kingdom that is all about compromise." What this woman and many like her do not realize is that where politics is about power, the Christian faith is about truth. Whenever you try to mix the two, power usually wins, at least for the short haul.

Please don't misunderstand us. We are not calling people of faith to settle for a lesser or weaker power. Rather, we are challenging them to utilize a superior and more effective power. To those who suggest that any compromise with political purity is a call for retreat from the public square, we say it is nothing of the kind. It is, in fact, a call for enlistment in another army that has better weapons, a superior battle plan, and a far better Commander-in-Chief than any candidate for high political office. One of my favorite hymns, "Lead on, O King Eternal," expresses it best: "For not with swords' loud clashing, or roll of stirring drums; with deeds of love and mercy the heavenly kingdom comes." The Religious Right certainly knows about that kind of power, but has chosen instead to use a far weaker arsenal.

From the beginning, men and women have sought power. In the Garden of Eden, Adam and Eve wanted the power to be like God. China's Mao Zedong said power comes from the barrel of a gun.[1] Lord Acton's often-quoted remark about power is that it is corrupting and when it becomes absolute, it corrupts absolutely.[2]

Power is defined as "possession of control, authority, or influence over others."[3] Such power can be had through persuasion and example that one's ideas are correct and beneficial. This kind of power leads others to willfully accept a belief or idea. Power can also be imposed from the top, as in a dictatorship, which may cause many to bow down to authority, but persuades few. When this dictatorial power is overthrown or dissipates through internal rot, little remains.

The late Senate Chaplain, Richard C. Halverson, often spoke of power. He worked among men and women who pass laws that have the power to deprive people of liberty by putting them in prison or taking their lives, property, or money if they break the law. Yet Halverson never saw this as real power. He spoke to me about the "powerlessness" of political power in that it lacks the ability to change hearts.

Political power is about numbers. If one group defeats another by amassing greater numbers at the polls, that doesn't mean the group is right. It just means it won a battle in a never-ending war for political supremacy. The defeated party then tries harder the next time to amass enough numbers to beat the victor in the previous election. And so it goes, forever, with neither side scoring a victory in the battle for truth.

Power is the ultimate aphrodisiac. People may have wealth, position, and fame, but unless they have power, many of them believe their lives are incomplete. Power cannot only seduce, but also affect judgment. It can be more addictive than any drug, because it deceives the one who "takes" it. Power can be used to rationalize the most outrageous behavior because the power abuser sincerely believes his ends are justified and so any means of achieving them are legitimate.

When a preacher or any other person who claims to speak for God, and who already holds sway over sometimes large numbers of people, is seduced by power, he can become destructive, not only to himself and to those he is charged to lead, but to the cause and objectives of the One he is supposed to be serving. A prime example on the political and religious left is the Rev. Jesse Jackson, who once made strong pro-life statements on behalf of the unborn, but caught the pragmatism virus when he decided the opposite view was more favorable to his political ambitions.

During President Clinton's personal and political difficulties with the Independent Counsel and various women, Jackson signed on as a "spiritual adviser" to the president and his family. On a trip to Africa with the Clintons in March 1998, Jackson told *New York Times* columnist Maureen Dowd that he, Jackson, understands the extremes of politics—the adulation of a big speech and then the loneliness of a hotel room. In responding to charges of extramarital affairs against the president, Jackson told Dowd, "Obviously, there was a lot of torment there. Some can turn pain into despair. He can turn pain into energy." Added Jackson in a mixed metaphor, "Sex is not the one string on the guitar. There are nine more commandments."[4]

Here is a clear example of how a religious leader's knowledge of the truth succumbed to the seduction of power. Had he told the truth and urged the president to repent, he might have lost his coveted position as confidant to the most powerful man on earth.

Compromising spiritual integrity for access to power is not limited to liberal clergy. In the same month that Jackson traveled to Africa, evangelist Billy Graham appeared on NBC's *Today* show and seemed to grant absolution to President Clinton for sins real and alleged. Graham offered forgiveness to Clinton (although the President had consistently denied any wrongdoing, leaving in question whether anyone can forgive an innocent man). Then Graham offered up an excuse for Clinton's alleged wanderings. After saying, "I think that a president should attempt, with God's help, to have a higher moral standard than perhaps the average public has," he added, "but we're living in a whole different world today, and the pressure on anybody today is difficult." Then he said of the president, "He has such a tremendous personality that I think the ladies just go wild over him."

In my syndicated column I suggested that not only should Graham devote his remaining years to preaching, but that it was long past time for all preachers to declare a moratorium on personal friendships with presidents of either party. It can only corrupt the preacher and the purpose of the church. Although Dr. Graham has generally been a model of integrity when it comes to his friendships with nine presidents, the marriage of religion and politics almost always compromises the gospel.

The late Roman Catholic priest Henri J. M. Nouwen wrote about power in a little book called *In the Name of Jesus: Reflections on Christian Leadership*. His remarks are so worthy of consideration that I will quote them at length.

Nouwen writes that men and women who are dedicated to spiritual leadership are easily subject to very raw carnality. "The reason for this," he says,

> is that they do not know how to live the truth of the Incarnation. They separate themselves from their own concrete community, try to deal with their needs by ignoring them or satisfying them in distant or anonymous places, and then experience an increasing split between their own most private inner world and the Good News they announce. When spirituality becomes spiritualization, life in the body becomes carnality. When ministers and priests live their ministry mostly in their heads and relate to the gospel as a set of valuable ideas to be announced, the body quickly takes revenge by screaming loudly for affection and intimacy. Christian leaders are called to live the Incarnation, that is, to live in the body—not only in their own bodies but also in the corporate body of the community, and to discover there the presence of the Holy Spirit.[5]

Nouwen says that confession and forgiveness are the disciplines by which spiritualization and carnality can be avoided. But think quickly about preachers who use television. How many can you name who are associated with confession and forgiveness? More often their messages are full of condemnation and judgment. When we consider that all of us have failed to live up to such a standard, a dose of humility might be in order, but as former U.S. Senator Alan Simpson once observed, if one travels the high road of humility (in Washington) he will not encounter heavy traffic.[6]

The third temptation of Jesus was the most subtle and the most dangerous, and it speaks clearly to those of us who want to use politics to usher in his kingdom. Those familiar with the story recall that Satan, who has had a lot of practice at this sort of thing (and gets new people to practice on with every generation), led Jesus into the wilderness. The record says, "And he led Him up and showed Him all the kingdoms of the world in a moment of time. And the devil said to Him, 'I will give You all this domain and its glory; for it has been handed over to me, and I give it to whomever I wish. Therefore if You worship before me, it shall all be Yours'" (Luke 4:5–7 NASB). The temptation, of course, was rejected, but today some are giving into it. In the early days of the Moral Majority we were taken up to the mountain, and we saw how we could finally win the battle for Jesus' sake. Unfortunately, the voice we were listening to was not that of Jesus.

Many who claim to speak for Jesus and seek earthly power to help him usher in his kingdom forget that he emptied himself and took on the form of a servant (Philippians 2:6–8). Nouwen writes, "The temptation to consider power an apt instrument for the proclamation of the gospel is the greatest temptation of all."[7]

And finally comes perhaps Nouwen's most profound insight: "What makes the temptation of power so seemingly irresistible? Maybe it is that power offers an easy substitute for the hard task of love. It seems easier to be God than to love God, easier to control people than to love people, easier to own life than to love life."[8]

Registering people to vote and persuading them to vote a certain way on issues and for certain candidates is one way power can be used to manipulate. The other way is fund-raising. The Moral Majority, like all other organizations in the Religious Right, was dependent on the contributions people made to it. Over the years we raised millions and millions of dollars. Most of the money came in as a response to our fund-raising letters.

If you were to do a content analysis of the fund-raising letters of the Religious Right, you would discover that they are all basically the same, regardless of the organization. First, they identify an enemy: homosexuals, abortionists, Democrats, or "liberals" in general. Second, the enemies are accused of being out to "get us" or impose their morality on the rest of us or destroy the country. Third, the letter assures the reader that something will be done: We will oppose these enemies and ensure that they do not take over America. Fourth, to get this job done, please send money (and the letter often suggests a specific amount).

Fund-raising letters almost always focus on the negative, not the positive. I remember asking, "Why don't we ever send out a positive letter on what we've accomplished with people's money?" Jerry Huntsinger, who was a partner in a Virginia firm that specialized in fund-raising for religious and other nonprofit organizations and who was a consultant with the Moral Majority, quickly replied, "You can't raise money on a positive." Fund-raising letters too often focus on people's fears; they identify the enemy.

One of the fund-raising letters we sent out during the days of the Moral Majority was titled "Who is the #1 enemy of the American family in our generation?" I wanted the letter to ask "what," not "who," and my answer would have been "divorce." Instead, the letter identified America's worst enemy as Norman Lear, founder of the liberal political group People for the American Way, which was created by the television producer specifically to fight the Moral Majority and the "intolerant" Religious Right.[9]

A reporter for the Associated Press in Richmond called me and asked whether I thought Norman Lear was the foremost enemy of the American family in our generation. "No," I said. "I think that's a bunch of crap." I added that "the Lear thing was a Frankenstein of the direct-mail folks, and it went out before I saw it." Norman Lear was becoming a friend of mine, and I felt it more important to develop a relationship with him than to call him names.

Sometimes fund-raising letters made incredible claims. Pat Robertson once sent out a letter that claimed an associate reported to him that God had told the associate he wanted Pat to help usher in the Second Coming. In order to do that, the recipient of the letter was asked to send in money to keep Robertson's Middle East radio station on the air so that Jews would come to believe in Christ and prophecy could be fulfilled, hastening the Messiah's return.

A year after leaving Moral Majority, I mentioned this letter on an ABC News special hosted by Ted Koppel. Robertson was upset. He wrote me and said I had told "a deliberate falsehood. I never said in a fund-raising letter what you said I said." When I produced a copy, he said it wasn't meant to be taken literally: "I did not claim in that letter ... that I personally was going to bring about the coming of Jesus." Then, on his 700 Club television program, he took an on-the-air phone call from a viewer, who sounded to me as if she knew enough details to be a staff member. The caller wanted to know what Robertson thought about my remarks on the Koppel program. He launched into an attack on me, saying I had once applied for a job with his organization and had been let go. It was the old "disgruntled employee" routine: To avoid dealing with one's own culpability, attack the critic. It works in politics and in religion.

The fact is that Robertson had begun a nightly network news program and had asked me to do a brief commentary once or twice a week. The show was canceled after a few months. I was already writing my column and doing a number of other things, and there seems to be little longevity in television anyway, so being "let go" from a canceled television show is hardly unique. It has happened to me (and others) many times. But one must constantly have enemies, conspiracies, and opponents as well as play the role of righteous victim in order to get people to send in money. So I became another of Roberton's "enemies."

Sometimes the mail sent out by the Moral Majority produced funny results. We accidentally sent U.S. Senator Ted Kennedy a "Moral Majority membership card." It was especially amusing because Kennedy, a Democrat from Massachusetts, was often mentioned in our appeals for money (as Falwell was in letters Kennedy and his liberal friends sent out). The *Washington Post* called me and inquired whether we would ask for the card back. "No," I said, "we don't believe any man is beyond redemption. In fact, we'd like to invite the senator to visit Lynchburg and see Jerry Falwell's school." The quote was printed in the newspaper.

Two weeks later, a top Kennedy aide, Larry Horowitz, called and said, "The senator has decided to accept your invitation."

"What invitation?" I asked.

"The one for the senator to visit Lynchburg."

Ted Kennedy came, and it turned out to be a great evening. The day before Kennedy's visit, I spoke to a gathering of the entire student body and faculty at Liberty. I told them that if Ted Kennedy was going to see Jesus, he would have to see him in them, so whatever their feelings about his politics, I said I hoped they would treat him with respect.

They couldn't have been nicer. The senator first came to dinner at Falwell's house and gave Jerry a copy of two books—one about his mother, Rose, the matriarch of the Kennedy family, the other a collection of his brother Jack's presidential papers. Then the senator delivered a speech on tolerance and diversity that was warmly received. The press loved it. Every network, the major newspapers, still photographers, the national news magazines—all were there.

I wrote a column on the occasion for the *Washington Post* called "The Man Who Came to Dinner."[10] An accompanying cartoon depicted Satan and two demons standing just inside the gates of hell in a snowstorm. Satan is reading the *Hades Gazette* newspaper. The headline is "Senator Kennedy Dines With Rev. Falwell, Then Addresses Liberty Baptist College Students."

Hell may not have frozen over that night, but that was the beginning of a treasured friendship between Kennedy and me. Falwell met with Kennedy on several subsequent occasions. More of eternal value was accomplished that night and in the subsequent relationship than years of political bashing and one-upmanship had produced.

At the height of Moral Majority's "power" in 1982, Americans gave $54 billion to charitable organizations. Religious groups received 46 percent, or $25 billion of that total, according to Russ Chandler of the *Los Angeles Times*. In a story for Religious News Service on January 21, 1983, Chandler quoted John Groman, religious consultant for Epsilon Data,

Inc., of Burlington, Massachusetts, which at the time served seven of the nation's top ten revenue-raising television preachers, including Falwell.

"What's the difference between Robert Schuller and HBO?" asked Groman. "They both need subscribers to keep on the air." The "difference," of course, is that a preacher of the gospel is supposed to be constrained by the ethical and moral boundaries spelled out in Scripture, which is not a code embraced by the entertainment industry.

The pressure for increasing amounts of money from a shrinking pie occasionally produced scandals that made instant headlines. The ones involving PTL's Jim Bakker and evangelist Jimmy Swaggart stunned the nation. It was the unholy trinity of money, sex, and power (along with a staff and a public that refused to hold these men accountable) that helped lead to their downfalls.

My mailbox is cluttered every week with fund-raising letters from a variety of religion-based organizations. I read them with a high degree of skepticism, and over the years I have developed a series of compelling questions about the need for money. First, how much of the money I give goes to the cause identified in the letter and how much goes to overhead and expenses? Any organization that raises money for a specific cause and then gives only a small percentage to that cause while using the rest for overhead (salaries, postage, advertising, radio and television air time) does not deserve my money. Ask every organization that seeks your support what percentage of the money you give actually goes directly to the cause.

Second, does the tone of the letter reflect the admonition of Jesus to love our enemies? Speaking the truth can be done in sound bites; loving our enemies cannot. We are called upon by Jesus to love our enemies, whether they be homosexuals, abortionists, Democrats, or liberals.

Third, if I give to this cause, will I really make a difference? After all the millions that have been given to organizations in the Religious Right, it is fair to ask the question, "What has actually changed?" Unfortunately, the answer appears to be, "Not much." Maybe the time has come for people to withhold their monies from national organizations and invest it in their own communities to deal with the real issues around them.

The subordination of conviction to the pragmatic was also evident in politics—which is one of the great dangers of too close an
association by the church in affairs of state. Politics is all about compromise. The church is supposed to be about unchanging standards.
Historically, when the church joins the political game, it only sometimes enhances the state's understanding of and commitment to principles. More often, this marriage of church with state results in the
church's getting its theological pocket picked.

The temptations occurred early for Moral Majority. Not only were
we forced to say nothing about Ronald Reagan's selection of the previously pro-choice George Bush as his running mate, but only one month
into the Reagan presidency, we were faced with the ultimate litmus test.
Associate Justice Potter Stewart announced his intention to retire from
the Supreme Court. Conservative groups had long believed that the
Court had acted as an unelected legislature. We thought that Reagan's
presidency offered a possible once-in-a-lifetime opportunity to reshape
the Court in a conservative, or "strict constructionist," image.

Reagan nominated a relatively unknown Arizona Appeals Court
judge and former state senator, Sandra Day O'Connor, to replace Stewart.

Judge O'Connor was supported by Paul Laxalt, a Nevada senator
and close Reagan friend, as well as other prominent Republicans,
including Barry Goldwater and Justice William Rehnquist, one of the
two dissenters in *Roe vs. Wade*. But because of Judge O'Connor's ques-
tionable record on abortion, many conservative groups immediately
opposed her. They felt the conservative movement had not come this
far only to be compromised at the moment of victory. Besides, we rea-
soned, with Reagan in the White House and a Republican-controlled
Senate, any nominations to the Supreme Court should be a "slam
dunk."

In an interview with Gerald and Deborah Strober for their book,
Reagan: The Man and His Presidency, Jerry Falwell revealed how politicians—even Ronald Reagan, who supposedly was above compromise—can use the prospect of future access to cause one to
compromise a principle.

Said Falwell, "I was at Myrtle Beach (South Carolina). The president called me and said, 'Jerry, I am going to put forth a lady on the (Supreme) Court. You don't know anything about her. Nobody does, but I want you to trust my judgment on this one.'

"I said, 'I'll do that.' The next day he announced the nomination of Sandra Day O'Connor. About two weeks later he called me again and said, 'Jerry, I've had a chance to talk to her, and my people have, and I can tell you that her views will not disappoint you, and I hope you can help me bring the troops in.' so I began calling conservatives, asking them to back off.

"I think she has done well; she broke the (all-male) tradition in a dignified way. The president knew that I would be concerned, and that the Religious Right would be upset, but I believed in and trusted him. And I haven't been sorry I did."[11]

But Justice O'Connor has been the swing vote that, in virtually every case, has beaten back any and all challenges to the "right" of a woman to abort her child at any stage of pregnancy. It is difficult to see how Jerry Falwell could not be disappointed in such a Justice or how he could speak of "the Religious Right" in a detached way when, in 1981, he *was* the Religious Right, or at least its primary spokesman.

That O'Connor broke the all-male tradition is irrelevant. Her gender wasn't as important as her ideas and legal reasoning. What is the difference between a male pro-choice judge and a female pro-choice judge?

Justice O'Connor has consistently held with the Court majority to keep abortion "safe and legal," and conservatives lost a golden opportunity to put someone on the bench at that time like the subsequent appointees Justice Antonin Scalia and Justice Clarence Thomas, about whom there is no doubt when it comes to the issue of abortion. But Falwell didn't want to upset Reagan, and he believed at the time it was more important to maintain access to the president.

When I went on *Nightline* with Ted Koppel and George Will to oppose O'Connor's nomination, I was later berated by Moral Majority's executive vice president, Dr. Ronald Godwin, who also made the case for access and not principle.

Whenever the church cozies up to political power, it loses sight of its all-important mission to change the world from the inside-out.

Along the way it gets caught up in an escalating demand for more and more. Every year, budgets must grow and more souls must be saved than last year. University enrollment must go up. No one talks about discipleship or maturation in one's faith. "The deeper life" was often mocked by fundamental evangelists who wanted scalps. The more the better. It was like birthing newborns and then leaving them to take care of themselves or giving them only basic nourishment.

Jesus said to go and make disciples, not converts (Matthew 28:19–20). It is the disciples who are then employed in making converts, and the way they do this is with the quality of their lives as well as their message. The faith about which Jesus spoke was to shine like a light before men and women. It was to be demonstrated before it was spoken. Today we too often reverse the process.

Worse, the church now resembles a corporation. People have been robbed of their privilege (or have relinquished it) of visiting those in prison, clothing the naked, and feeding the hungry (Matthew 25:31–46). This privilege was an individual, not a corporate calling. We now have institutions that do these things for us. A prison ministry will take care of visiting prisoners for $20 per month. A ministry to the homeless will visit the homeless if you contribute. A hunger ministry will feed the hungry for a gift. Church staffs have grown to the point where there is a pastor to do everything. If we drop enough money in the plate to meet the ever-growing budgets, we can sail through life and never once have to do anything Jesus asked us to do because we have hired people to do it for us.

Jesus emptied himself of power that was rightfully his. We try to fill ourselves with power that belongs to the world and seek to usher in a kingdom not of this world by using tools that are of this world.

In the 1994 congressional elections, religious conservatives celebrated the Republican takeover of Congress. The euphoria was so intense that one might have thought they heard the trumpet preceding the Second Coming. It was only a matter of time, they felt, before all the dreams and plans that began with Ronald Reagan would be fulfilled: a ban on abortion, bringing the gay rights movement to a halt, the "clean-up" of television, and a reversal of the explosion in pornography and drug use. This was possible, many believed, because even though they realized these were primarily moral and spiritual problems, their faith was strong that legislative and judicial solutions would also work. Somehow we forgot how quickly Mr. Reagan's promises to us were broken, because it didn't take long before frustration set in and many of the newly empowered Republicans began behaving like "normal" politicians.

When the Republican majority started planning to spend a lot of the budget "surplus" on a massive highway bill, resembling the Democrats they once criticized, the *Wall Street Journal* editorialized about their copy-cat tactics:

> Both fiscally and philosophically, all of this must be demoralizing for those who thought a GOP Congress might be different. It was at first. But as they've grown to enjoy incumbency, Republicans have begun to accumulate power and money for themselves rather than return them to voters. We hope they enjoy their road revels, because voters may decide that if Republicans are going to spend like Democrats, they might as well vote for the real thing.[12]

Writing in the *Orlando Sentinel,* columnist Charley Reese noted that the reason the culture is sterile and depraved is not because of bad politics, but because of an anemic faith.

> As much as agnostics and atheists would like to deny it, all cultures, good or evil, are derived from religion.
>
> That's because religious beliefs produce political and social consequences. America's culture has always been based on Christianity. Europe, from which we came, was known as Christendom. But early in the 19th century, American Christianity developed a split. This split caused, and still causes, political conflicts.
>
> The liberal has an unshakable religious faith that given sufficient money, the right program, the right education system and sufficient power to coerce, then human ills can be eliminated and a paradise on earth can be created. By placing man first and God second, the liberal view inevitably evolved into eliminating God altogether—hence, a secular and egalitarian culture developed.
>
> But we conservatives are in danger of doing the same thing. We don't want to eliminate God, of course. But we do want to

bring him down to earth and appropriate him for our narrow political agendas.[13]

Reese concludes, "If you're looking to politics for solutions, you're looking in the wrong place."

In Romans 8, the apostle Paul writes that God has built "futility" and frustration into his creation "in hope" that the creation will turn to him. Instead, we ask God to bless our tactics, our techniques, and our zeal for him. He will have none of it, because to succeed in our strength would mean we don't need God. We would be as guilty of self-enhancement as those people who built the ancient tower of Babel, which God destroyed on the grounds that if they accomplished this, they would have no need of him (Genesis 11:1–9).

The Bible, which conservative believers love to wave (rhetorically and sometimes visually), contains many admonitions that those who claim to believe the Book frequently ignore. One admonition that is often overlooked and is a rebuke to those who are trying to "return this nation to moral sanity" through the ballot box and political process comes from the apostle Paul:

> For though we live in the world, we do not wage war as the world does. The weapons we fight with are not the weapons of the world. On the contrary, they have divine power to demolish strongholds. We demolish arguments and every pretension that sets itself up against the knowledge of God, and we take captive every thought to make it obedient to Christ. And we will be ready to punish every act of disobedience, once your obedience is complete (2 Corinthians 10:3–6).

The strongholds and pretensions can only be demolished under two conditions: one, that we don't fight with the world's weapons, but with divine ones; and two, that our obedience is complete. We have been trying to use the world's weapons of political power, and we have not been sufficiently obedient to the call of Jesus to care as he cares and do as he did. No wonder conservative Christians continue to run into brick walls.

The weapons of this fallen world are fashioned out of human pride and arrogance. How can—and why should—a holy God whose attributes are the antithesis of these things honor such attitudes and strategies? If he did, we would have no need of him.

In God's economy, everything is reversed. Weakness is strength. The last shall be first. The foolish things of the world God uses to confound the wise. The meek inherit the earth. Those who wait upon the Lord shall renew their strength, rise up with wings as eagles, run and not be weary, walk and not faint. The mustard seed. The last place at the table. The washing of feet.[14]

How many times do the words and actions need to be said and done before we see the picture, understand the message, and obey the commands? And when will we learn from previous failed efforts of the church to change society exclusively through political power?

FOUR

PROHIBITING EVIL

We have a message of redeeming grace through a crucified and risen
Lord. Nowhere are we told to reform the externals. We are not told to
wage a war against bootleggers, liquor stores, gamblers, murderers,
prostitutes, racketeers, prejudiced persons or institutions, or any other
existing evil as such. The gospel does not clean up the outside but
rather regenerates the inside.

Jerry Falwell, during the civil rights movement of the 1960s
As quoted in Jerome L. Himmelstein, *To the Right* (University of
California Press at Berkeley, 1990), 118

 One of the dangers of mixing politics and religion is that
you begin to think the only way to transform culture is by
ed dobson passing another law. Most of what we did in the Moral
Majority was aimed at getting the right people elected so that we
would have enough votes to pass the right laws. While we believe
Christians need to support effective legislation, history has shown us
that we can't rely totally on laws. Perhaps the most instructive example of how the well-intentioned efforts of Christians to correct a horrible problem failed to bring about the desired results is the attempt
to ban alcohol at the beginning of the twentieth century.

The temperance movement began in the early nineteenth century
in reaction to the tremendous volume of alcohol consumption and the
social "evils" connected with it. Strong drink was an accepted part of
life where men were concerned. It is estimated that during the 1830s,
the amount of alcohol consumed per year averaged out to between six
and seven gallons for every American.[1] There was growing concern

over the consequences of alcohol abuse: decreased worker productivity, increased poverty, and drunk husbands who abused their wives and ceased to provide stable homes and incomes, not to mention crime and political corruption.

Many temperance groups arose during the 1820s, and by 1835 they claimed about one million members. Prominent among these was an army of evangelical Protestant churches, including both laypeople and clergy. The church saw intemperance in part as a spiritual problem—a hindrance to its mission of saving souls—in the belief that alcohol impaired reason, dulled the conscience, and diminished the fear of God. And it also viewed alcohol as a social problem, fostering ungodliness, immorality, disease, and death. Therefore the church sought to change society through the power and force of law. According to this view, the Christian's duty was "to use the secular power of the state to transform culture so that the community of the faithful might be kept pure and the work of saving the unregenerate might be made easier."[2] The church championed the temperance movement in varying degrees over the course of a hundred years.

There were other forces besides the church giving impetus to the temperance cause. Temperance was very much a women's movement because it addressed important problems in their daily lives. The American saloon was almost exclusively a man's domain. Women and children were the victims of alcohol abuse, but they had no legal power to protect themselves from it. Moreover, women tended to be viewed as the spiritual and physical guardians of both the home and the community. In fact, they banded together under the motto "For God and Home and Native Land." They wanted communities where they could "walk the streets unmolested, where their sons' worldly prospects would not evaporate in an alcoholic fog, and where their daughters would marry men who cared for them more than for the bottle."[3]

In 1873 these temperance crusaders launched the largest mass movement of women to that point in American history. In 1874 the national Women's Christian Temperance Union (WCTU) was created, and by 1892 it had nearly 150,000 members—mostly church-going Protestants motivated by their religious convictions.[4] They approached liquor dealers with hymns, prayers, and requests to desist from their ruinous business. Praying in saloons became a common tactic.[5] They circulated total-abstinence pledges and persuaded boards of education to include temperance literature, songs, and "scientific" education in school curriculums.[6] Eventually women saw the need to exert their influence through politics and began the battle for the right to vote. For twenty-five years the WCTU led the crusade against alcohol until the growth of the Anti-Saloon League in the early twentieth century.

The Anti-Saloon League was formed during the 1890s to bring organization to more than a hundred temperance societies operating along denominational, fraternal, and partisan lines.[7] The League called for renewed unity and action against the saloon and turned to the church to influence and organize the masses for social change. Their goal was national Prohibition—the regulation and prohibition of alcoholic beverages as national policy. Their motto became "The Church in Action Against the Saloon." Clergymen made up three-fifths of Anti-Saloon League leaders, and pastors were encouraged to enroll their congregations in the league.[8] The WCTU assisted the League in forming public opinion and lobbying before the state and national legislatures. The League consolidated the temperance forces in places where they had the greatest strength, and they succeeded in driving the liquor business from various cities and towns.[9]

The temperance movement finally got what it was working for when the Eighteenth Amendment was ratified in 1919, prohibiting the production, transportation, and sale of alcoholic beverages. Several factors contributed to this long-sought achievement. The generation of voters and politicians who passed the Eighteenth Amendment were raised on the educational platform designed by the WCTU that had been incorporated into school curriculums across the country.[10] Another factor was the First World War, which aroused a spirit of sacrifice and idealism among the people and at the same time weakened the power of the liquor interests.[11] On January 16, 1920, the Eighteenth Amendment went into effect, Prohibition began, and America became a dry nation by law.

But not for long.

Initially, making alcohol illegal seemed to work. Prohibition brought the lowest level of alcohol consumption per capita in America's history in 1921. But consumption rose as bootleggers and rumrunners became better organized; by 1927, consumption was back to the level of the late nineteenth century.[12] Law enforcement agencies could not control the liquor consumption because too many people opposed the laws on principle, too many people were making money from the illegal traffic, and too many officials were corrupt or at least not dedicated to upholding Prohibition.[13] A report by a commission to investigate criminal justice found that since the passage of the Eighteenth Amendment, drinking had increased, bootlegging and official corruption were widespread, and judicial and penal systems were overburdened by prosecutions; states were slackening their efforts at enforcement, and respect for the law was being eroded by Prohibition.[14] There was a growing, widespread feeling that national Prohibition did not and could not "work" and that law and order were breaking down.[15] It was feared that this failure to enforce Prohibition would ultimately undermine respect for all laws.[16] Prohibition was not living up to its promises of making America a more productive, safer, moral, and prosperous country.

As you might expect, it wasn't long before this law faced opposition and the threat of repeal. When you attempt to change a social problem exclusively through the legislature, it's only a matter of time until opponents line up enough votes to undo your agenda. The campaign to repeal the Eighteenth Amendment started with the wealthy, who had never given up drinking but simply paid more for it on the black market. Their businesses also paid higher income taxes to make up for the lost revenues from the liquor business. The Association Against the Prohibition Amendment was founded and grew in power and influence at the same time that the Anti-Saloon League was losing strength because of weak leadership and a scandal involving a national leader of the organization. The tide of public sentiment had turned.[17]

By the 1932 presidential election, neither the Republican nor Democratic party embraced Prohibition. The Republican party wanted continued federal action on liquor control, while the Democratic party wanted a full repeal. The fate of national Prohibition was sealed when the Democrats won the White House. The Twenty-first Amendment, repealing the Eighteenth Amendment and putting an end to national Prohibition, was approved by Congress early in 1933 and ratified by the states later that year.

What began as a noble attempt to correct a tragic alcohol problem in American society ended in a defeat that made religious people look like a band of moralizing killjoys. Ironically, at the same time that the tide of public sentiment was turning against Prohibition, fundamentalists lost another public relations war through the Scopes trial and various efforts to make the teaching of evolution illegal. In many ways, conservative Christians have never shed the image of these two landmark events.

As a pastor, I am familiar with the damage that alcohol has inflicted on American society. I work every week with recovering alcoholics. Most of them lost their jobs, their families, and their human dignity before they began the long and difficult journey on the road to recovery. Alcohol abuse has ruined lives, has torn families apart, has led to physical and emotional abuse of women and children, has caused the death of thousands at the hands of drunk drivers. But I don't think we can solve this problem by passing more laws. Prohibition was a noble ideal, but it did little to change alcohol consumption in America.

I have thought a lot about Prohibition because it is so tempting to try to save America through the political process. The crusade for Prohibition involved thousands of good people who sincerely wanted to eradicate the source of much pain in society. What can we learn from their well-intentioned but unsuccessful campaign?

1. The leaders of the temperance movement expected the government to do the work of the church. As we saw earlier, they felt it was a Christian duty to use the secular power of the state to transform culture. They failed to understand that mere laws do not change people or culture. You can pass a law to restrict the making and selling of alcohol, but no law can force a person not to drink. A change in people's behavior comes from a change of heart, and only the gospel can bring about that change. The leaders of the temperance movement had hoped to lower alcohol consumption and diminish the consequences of alcohol abuse on women. They hoped to transform the culture by making alcohol illegal. They succeeded in making alcohol

difficult to obtain, but they failed in changing people, families, and the culture. Things did not get better—they got worse. Government cannot change people or culture.

2. The leaders of the temperance movement failed in "trickle-down morality." They believed that there was a shortcut to moral transformation. That shortcut was using the power of the state to dictate moral behavior among its citizens. But morality is never activated from the top down. It is achieved from the bottom up—one person at a time, one family at a time, one street at a time, one community at a time—until the entire culture is changed—not by laws, but heart by heart. This work of individual transformation is slow and takes a long time. The net effect cannot be easily measured or observed. It is easier to pass a law. But laws do not change people. Trickle-down morality does not work.

3. Respect for the law is based on a moral consensus. Even though Prohibition passed, it was not acceptable to the masses of people. In fact, people ignored the law altogether. They made and sold and consumed alcohol illegally. It was feared that the disrespect and disregard of this law would eventually lead to the disrespect and disregard of all other laws. Some believed that America was on the road to anarchy and corruption.

Legislation must reflect the consensus of the people governed, or they will just disregard the law. Before morality can be shaped by legislation, there is the difficult work of shaping a moral consensus among the people. For example, we who are conservative Christians believe in the need for a law to protect human life—especially the unborn. If we were to succeed today in passing a law that would "ban" nearly all abortions, it is unlikely that it would be effective. Why? Because it does not reflect the moral consensus on the issue. America is still deeply divided.

While we work toward legislation, we must also do the more difficult task of changing people's minds and beliefs on the matter. The most effective laws *follow* moral consensus—they do not bring about moral consensus. Our task as believers and followers of Jesus is to continue the tedious work of moral transformation in our culture. As we move toward that goal, legislation will be the natural consequence of that moral transformation; it will never be the cause of moral transformation.

4. Let the church be the church. The mission of the church is to declare the good news of the gospel of Jesus Christ. This gospel has the power to transform and change people's lives forever. The temperance movement would have served its cause better by bringing about change in individual lives rather than marshaling its forces to pass a law. Christians in the temperance movement had the ultimate answer, but surrendered it for a lesser answer that turned out to be no answer at all. They exchanged the gospel for political solutions and in the end lost on both accounts.

Recently I baptized Bob. Bob is a successful businessman in his early fifties—successful in business, but a complete failure in every other aspect of life. He was an alcoholic. Over the years he lost every relationship that he cherished. Finally he checked into an alcohol rehabilitation center. As part of the spiritual component of his recovery program, he was encouraged to attend the nontraditional Saturday night service at Calvary Church and then attend the AA (Alcoholics Anonymous) meetings that we sponsor in the church.

After a few weeks, Bob committed his life to Jesus Christ. The night I baptized him, he had been free of alcohol for one hundred days. Before he was baptized, he apologized to his family and friends for the incredible hurt he had caused them over the years. He pledged to make restitution wherever possible. His life has been transformed, and he continues to grow and rebuild his life without the aid of alcohol.

Bob's story reflects the lives of hundreds of people in our congregation who have discovered that Jesus can and is transforming their lives. On the surface it does not appear that we are making a huge dent in the problems of alcohol and drug abuse. But below the surface we are seeing God change people—one heart, one life at a time. We do not have a national organization. We do not get our name in the media. We do not print magazines about it. We are just the church being the church in a local community.

Every time I receive another piece of mail from a Christian organization that is trying to change society through the political process, I worry about people like Bob. They don't need more laws.

They need the church to be the church.

FIVE

CROSSING THE LINE

But I tell you: Love your enemies and pray for those who persecute
you, that you may be sons of your Father in heaven.

Jesus Christ (Matthew 5:44–45)

But I tell you who hear me: Love your enemies, do good to those who
hate you, bless those who curse you, pray for those who mistreat you.

Jesus Christ (Luke 6:27–28)

Grovenor High School is one of the premier high schools
in all of Northern Ireland. It is steeped in real British tradition. Getting into the school is not that easy. Every elementary student takes an exam at age eleven. A small percentage of
those who take the exam pass, and they are sent to various high
schools to prepare for college. Those who do not pass the exam are
sent to secondary schools, where they are taught a trade.

I remember the Saturday when the results of the eleven-plus exam
arrived at our house. If the envelope was thick, it meant that you
passed. If it was thin, it carried only a terse notice that you had failed.
My heart was in my throat as the mailman approached our door, for
I knew that my future was in the envelope he carried. As the mail fell
to the floor, I saw a large envelope.

Grovenor required a dress code, as did all the high schools. Every
morning I would put on the same short pants, shirt, tie, blazer, socks,
sweater, and cap. Then I would get my bicycle out of the shed and
ride to school. After putting my bike in the school's bike shed, I would
join my classmates for homeroom. Attendance would be taken, and
then we would all gather with the rest of the school in the gym for

opening exercises. We would line up by form (grade). We would sing a hymn out of the official hymnbook. Then someone would read the Scriptures and pray. We would also sing the British national anthem, "God Save the Queen." Having done our religious and patriotic duties, we were then off to class to learn and become the next generation of Northern Irish leaders.

Although this was a public school, it was also a British and Protestant school. There were no Catholics. The Catholics had their own schools and their own religious and national obligations. I had never attended school with a Catholic student.

One of the first things I had to do when I was admitted to Grovenor was to choose among the Protestant religion classes. Every student was required to take religion classes taught by various ministers in the community. This created a problem for me in that we were Brethren and considered a nonconformist Protestant group. We believed that if you were really Christian, you would not belong to the Orange Order, the main Protestant political and cultural group. My grandfather, who lived in the village of Castledawson, played the "big drum" in the local Orange Order band until he became converted. After his conversion, he quit the band and the Orange Order. He felt that aligning with a group that mixed politics and religion was incompatible with his new relationship with God.

Now I was faced with a similar dilemma. My father had taught me not to hate Catholics and not to be caught up in the passions of the Orange Order. Most of the main religious denominations had close ties to the Orange Order, and many of their ministers were leaders in the Order. My dad solved the problem by telling me to sign up for the Presbyterian class, which I did.

Still, no one at Grovenor was immune from the political divisions between Catholics and Protestants. Every week we would take a double-decker bus to the "baths" (the local swimming pool), and along the way we would sing good old Protestant songs. The Irish are known for their enjoyment of music, and we could tell our history through our songs. These songs spoke of the terrible Catholic killings of Protestant children. They celebrated the various defeats of the Catholics, including the most famous of all: the Battle of the Boyne, fought in 1690, when William, Prince of Orange, defeated the Catholic forces of King James II of England and established Protestant ascendancy.

One of our favorite songs spoke of the helplessness of the Pope and how he got help from King Billy:

Oh, the Pope he had a pimple on his bum
And it nipped, nipped, nipped so sore.
So he called for King Billy
To wipe it with a lilly
And it nipped, nipped, nipped no more!

We were taught that Catholics were never to be trusted—that they were lazy, had too many children, were living off the good welfare of the British government, that they hated us Protestants and wanted to reunite Ireland. And above all, they would do anything the Pope asked them to do. They were, in fact, so it was said, the chief cause of all the problems in Northern Ireland.

Of course, none of us boys had ever been in a Catholic home or lived in a Catholic neighborhood. We had never been in a Catholic church or attended a Catholic school. But we knew all about the Catholics and had a history to prove we were right. It never dawned on us that the Catholics actually held some fundamental biblical beliefs that were the same as our own. All we needed to know was that they were Catholic and nationalists and we were Protestants and British. Our political beliefs and our religious beliefs were almost one and the same.

At Grovenor High School, we studied Irish history with a Northern Irish bent. The battle cry of the Protestant majority in the north is "Kick the Pope and no surrender." We were taught that the Southern Irish government was totally dominated by the Catholic church and the Pope in Rome. To prove our point, we pointed to the Irish constitution of 1937. It recognized "the special position of the Holy Apostolic and Roman Church as the guardian of the faith professed by the great majority of the Citizens."[1] The law banned divorce, contraception, and abortion. For us Protestants this was too much. This was the imposition of Catholic doctrine into the public square. And we knew what happened to Protestants when the Catholic church was in political control—it meant persecution for Protestants. Remember the Inquisition—not to mention our own history in Northern Ireland. Union with the south of Ireland was out of the question. It would mean the end of religious liberty and the end of life as we knew it. On this issue there was "no surrender."

The 1950s and 1960s were relatively peaceful in my home country. There was some improvement in the conditions of the Catholic minority. But underneath the surface the deep divisions remained. In 1964 there was a riot in Belfast when Liam McMillan, the Republican candidate for West Belfast, flew the Southern Irish flag over his campaign headquarters. It was this incident that propelled the Rev. Ian Paisley to the forefront of Northern Irish politics. Paisley lived around the corner from us in Belfast. He is a large man with a booming voice, and he expressed the feelings of the typical working-class Protestant in the North. And in this instance he demanded the removal of the flag.

I remember the night Paisley spoke at our church. The place was packed. There were no empty seats, and I was sitting on the steps of the platform to make room for adults. Paisley preached a powerful sermon without political overtones. When the sermon was over and the congregation dismissed, Paisley turned to pick up his overcoat and with a smile on his face said, "To hell with the Pope." Several people around him laughed, but I was somewhat surprised. I had heard this phrase many times from people at school, but never from the mouth of a minister in a church. "How could a minister wish that anyone could go to hell?" I thought. "Not even God wants that."

Later that same year, our family emigrated to the United States. We were spared the terrible troubles that were to come. In 1969 the British sent the army to Derry and Belfast to protect the Catholics and restore order to a quickly deteriorating situation. At first the Catholic minority welcomed the British soldiers, but soon they were perceived as the symbol of hated British control. By January 1970, the Provisional IRA (Irish Republican Army) was formed, and the stage was set for the horrible killing and bombings of the '70s and '80s. In response to the IRA, the Protestants formed their own paramilitary groups, who killed suspected IRA terrorists and Catholics. Between

1969 and 1981 there were 2,161 deaths from "the Troubles," as the strife has traditionally been called. Violence bred violence and hatred begat hatred in an endless and unbroken cycle.

For most of my life in Ireland, I lived in Belfast. My grandfather lived in a little village called Castledawson, where he owned a grocery store on Bridge Street. I loved to visit Castledawson. On one occasion my dad sent me to my grandfather's house for several months while my mother recovered from a serious illness. I attended the one-room schoolhouse in the village, and I made many friends there. My grandfather allowed me to help in the store, which was part of the family house where my grandparents had reared a large family. But Castledawson was not immune from the troubles. My grandfather's store was bombed. One of the saddest moments of my life was walking through the charred ruins of the store and house when I was on vacation sometime afterward. Although the store was still in operation, it was not at all as I remembered it.

In Belfast I had two relatives who worked for their father in the family business. They were not connected to any of the paramilitary groups. One day their father left them in charge while he went to lunch. While he was gone, IRA triggermen came into the store and shot them in cold blood as a reprisal for Protestant killings of Catholics.

Several years ago I was preaching in a large Baptist church for the weekend. After the evening service, we went to a restaurant. When we arrived, the pastor asked if Colleen was working and if we could sit at one of her tables. The pastor and his wife were frequent customers at this particular restaurant and had become fond of one of the waitresses.

After we were seated, Colleen passed out the menus and began taking orders. She was short, thin, in her early fifties, and had blond hair. As I began looking through the menu, the pastor's wife interrupted. "By the way, Ed, Colleen is from Ireland." I thought, *Here we go again.*

Since coming to America, I had met many people who had relatives or friends who came from Ireland and when they found out I was from Ireland they assumed I might know them or at least know where they were from. Nearly all of them were from the South, which meant they were Catholic. Most Americans don't realize that Ireland is really two countries; whenever I try to explain that, it tends to just confuse them. So I would let people assume I was from the South, even though it betrayed my Protestant roots.

"What county are you from?" I asked Colleen.

"County Antrim," she replied in an accent that was clearly northern. Since County Antrim is one of the six counties in Northern Ireland, I was at least excited to be talking with someone who would understand the real situation in Ireland.

"You know, I was born in Magherafelt in a one-room thatched cottage," I responded.

"I was born a few miles from Magherafelt," Colleen said. "Can you believe it? We were born a few miles from each other in Northern Ireland, and here we are in the same restaurant on a Sunday night in the United States of America!"

She came around the table and hugged me, and I immediately broke into my Irish accent, and we laughed and talked about the old country.

"If you don't hurry up and order, I'll give you a dig in the bake," she said.

"Watch you gub," I responded.

"How about some flies graveyards for desert?" she replied. And on and on we went, using Northern Irish sayings that no one else at the table understood.

After Colleen went to the kitchen, I explained to the pastor and his wife that "bake" refers to your face. "Gub" is your mouth. "Flies graveyards" is a dessert made of currants. The currants look like dead flies. I guess you had to be there to really get the picture.

Every time Colleen came back, we talked more about Ireland, and I knew sooner or later one of us would have to ask the relevant question. If you are Irish, you cannot separate the political from the religious, but somehow that seemed irrelevant as we laughed and joked together in the restaurant. But eventually I asked her about her faith.

"I'm Catholic," she said.

If we were having this conversation in Ireland, neither of us would speak to each other anymore. But we continued, carefully approaching the subject of the conflicts our people were facing back in Northern Ireland. After a few minutes, she paused and became very serious.

"Nine years ago my husband went out one evening to take the dog for a walk. As he walked down the street, he was gunned down by Protestant extremists. You are the first person I have told in a long time about his death."

I didn't know what to say, since by now she knew I was a Protestant.

"The way they killed him was brutal. It was like—it was cold-blooded. It was 6:30 in the evening. You know, there's a little garden and then a stone wall. He went through the garden and had just gone out the gate when they shot him. Seven times—through the heart twice. I mean, there were so many bullets in him. There was no way he could have survived—no way. He crawled back into the house, leaving a trail of blood from the gate all the way back to the house."

By now I was crying. I was looking at the wife of a man who conceivably could have planned the bombing of my grandfather's store in Castledawson. But I was also looking at a widow whose husband had been brutally murdered by Protestants, some of whom I would undoubtedly know. I cannot describe the feelings deep inside. Of course, Colleen was crying, too.

"I can't see how anyone, Catholic or Protestant, can pull a trigger and snuff out a human life," I said.

"It is brutal, really brutal, terrible!" Colleen said. "You see, to mix religion with politics is very, very bad. People are people. Many of my friends were Protestant. They were beautiful people."

I stood to my feet. Colleen came around the table, and we hugged. We walked slowly to the exit with our arms around each other. It was as if we didn't want to say good-bye. For a brief moment it didn't matter that she was Catholic and I was Protestant. At that moment we had more in common than what divided us. We wanted to hang on to this moment forever, because we knew we would never be able to do something like this in Castledawson, Northern Ireland.

Northern Ireland is a long way from the United States, where Catholics and Protestants live in relative harmony. But there are important lessons about the blending of politics and religion to be learned form the troubles in Ireland:

1. *When religion and politics are one and the same, the situation tends toward intolerance.* In Northern Ireland the intolerance is both political and religious. Protestants believe that the Catholic church is the church of the Antichrist and that the Pope is the forerunner of the false prophet who will establish the one-world church at the end of the world. This church will be the instrument of Satan and the Antichrist. They believe that the Catholic church is "the great whore" of the book of Revelation (chap. 17). Catholics view Protestants with the same disdain. Neither side believes that the others are real Christians. These views are inseparable from their politics, and it is not difficult for otherwise decent people on either side to rationalize the taking up of arms.

2. *When pastors become entangled too deeply with politics, they harm the gospel of Jesus.* Jesus becomes synonymous with a political party or platform. Ian Paisley is one of the leading ministers and politicians in Northern Ireland, a member of the British and European parliaments. He has the reputation of being a good politician and representing his district well; even Catholics will testify to that.

But even though Paisley has been a leading politician in Ireland since the late sixties, what has this done for the gospel? And if, for the sake of argument, we assumed that Catholics were *not* real Christians, is it our Christian duty to kill them? Has the Rev. Paisley succeeded in sharing the gospel with the Catholic community? The obvious answer is that he has failed. For Paisley, the gospel has been wrapped in the flag of the Orange Order and the Protestant political platform. The message of Jesus has been drowned out by the rhetoric of politics.

In my opinion, the Christian Coalition and other Christian political groups in America are making the same mistake as Paisley. They are selling their religious priorities for a mess of political pottage. In the process, they are harming the gospel. They are implying that there is a proper Christian position on nearly every political issue. They are implying that disagreement with their political positions is, in fact, disagreement with Jesus. They are alienating others from themselves and the gospel they believe. They have forgotten the words of Jesus, who said, "My kingdom is not of this world. If it were, my servants would fight to prevent my arrest by the Jews. But now my kingdom is from another place" (John 18:36). They have forgotten the words of the apostle Paul who likened our Christian responsibility to that of a soldier in the army of God: "Endure hardship with us like a good soldier of Christ Jesus. No one serving as a soldier gets involved in civilian affairs—he wants to please his commanding officer" (2 Timothy 2:3–4).

We have politicized the gospel with our agendas. To be part of the Christian right is to be part of the Republican party. For some, this means that to be a *real* Christian, you must be a Republican. That is heresy and is only a short distance from the extremism of my Irish counterparts.

3. *The harsher the rhetoric, the more it is likely that it will lead to violence.* The saddest part of the situation in Northern Ireland is the ongoing violence that accompanies the political and religious differences. Several thousand citizens have been killed, and millions of dollars of damage has been done to properties. Fortunately, despite the harsh political rhetoric of the Religious Right, we have been spared from violence. But that kind of rhetoric gives permission to an already unstable person to take the next deadly step. While I believe it is unfair to attribute the recent abortion-clinic bombings to the pro-life movement, we need to recognize that words do matter. In Northern Ireland, fiery language almost always leads to violence. In the current American religious and political scene, the rhetoric has become more confrontational and threatening.

One of the reasons my parents came to America was to escape the volatile mixture of politics and religion. They saw what happened when religious leaders used their God-ordained power to whip people into a hateful frenzy. They wanted none of it, and neither do I. As Christians we have a responsibility to be salt and light in society (Matthew 5:13–14). We are not called to change the political beliefs of our opponents, but to announce the Good News.

That is our only hope of transforming culture.

SIX

THE USE AND ABUSE OF GOD

I say beware of people who claim to have a monopoly on the word of God because they're usually bigots.

Dr. Sol Gordon

All politicians, Democrats and Republicans alike, love God. Or more accurately, they love to use God to baptize their political agendas. In the Congressional Directory, which lists biographical and staff information about members of the House and Senate, no one is an atheist. Even those who have not been to a church or synagogue in years (or have never gone) and probably claim nothing more than a generic Protestant, Catholic, or Jewish "faith" list themselves as something under the category "Religion." You never know when it might help you to be religious.

Until the Clinton administration (with the brief exception of Jimmy Carter, our first self-professed born-again president), Republicans pretty much had a corner on God and believed him to be on their side, or at least not on the side of Democrats. One of my lecture-circuit laugh lines is that Democrats appear in the Bible (pause). Yes, the Bible says that Jesus dined with (re)publicans and sinners. Those sinners were Democrats! Yes, my Democrat friends counter, but he rode into Jerusalem on a donkey. To which I reply, "I think the biblical record refers to the animal as an ass."

In the 1980 and 1984 presidential campaigns, when some Republicans and conservative ministers brought religious ideas into the public square to support certain policies, many Democrats cried foul and said such language was a threat to the First Amendment and to pluralism.

They said religion should be kept out of politics so that it might remain pure and unsullied by exposure to the temporal world.

But just as Bill Clinton has been accused of stealing Republican ideas on welfare and the economy, so, too, did he and other Democrats begin using religious language in support of their agendas. The problem for them has been that some are new to the church-state linguistic game, and thus they often misquote Scripture or misstate its intent (a sin that is not unknown among some on the religious and political right). Since the closest most journalists get to a Bible is the one in the drawer of a motel room, the big media never picked up on the misquotations or misrepresentations of Scripture by Democratic (and a few Republican) politicians. In fact, Jerry Falwell used to joke that as much of a pain as the press is, their ignorance about religious matters sometimes worked in our favor. Unfamiliar with the beliefs and terminology of the Christian faith—and apparently unwilling to learn—they never knew the right questions to ask or the proper biblical quotations to cite, leaving them powerless to challenge the positions of some pastors.

In his acceptance speech at the 1992 Democratic National Convention in New York City, Bill Clinton quoted the Bible as saying, "Our eyes have not seen, nor our ears heard, nor our minds imagined, what we can build." The only verse that comes close to what Clinton said is 1 Corinthians 2:9: "But as it is written, Eye hath not seen, nor ear heard, neither have entered into the heart of man, the things which God hath prepared for them that love him" (KJV). Different words and decidedly different meanings.

During the 1996 budget showdown between Congress and President Clinton (the one that closed the government for a number of days), fifteen leaders of the National Council of Churches met for forty-five minutes with President Clinton in the Oval Office. At the end of the meeting they "laid hands" on him. They prayed that he would be "strong for the task." What task did they have in mind? Perhaps it was an NCC resolution, passed a few days before the meeting, calling on the president and Congress to protect the most vulnerable of society as they worked out their differences over the budget. Translated, this meant that it was God's will that Republicans not cut any social programs.

Diane Knippers, president of the Institute on Religion and Democracy, called the "laying on of hands" ceremony in the Oval Office "a disturbing misuse of prayer for blatantly partisan purposes."

Al Gore's acceptance speech at the 1992 Democratic Convention was an even better example of attempts to appropriate and manipulate biblical language for political purposes. Gore said, "In the words of the Bible, 'Do not lose heart. This nation will be renewed.'" No such verse appears in the Bible. The press faulted Dan Quayle for misspelling a word; it gave Clinton and Gore a free pass for misquoting the Bible.

The Rev. Jesse Jackson, who campaigned for the Democratic Party's nomination for president and who fancies himself a spiritual advisor to President Clinton, has referred to the Virgin Mary as homeless. It's a good story that directs a lot of attention to a serious social problem, but it's wrong. Mary and Joseph were tax-paying citizens who presumably owned a home and were trying to find a place to spend the night while on a trip.

In 1988, Democratic candidate Michael Dukakis said he sought religious benefits from his association with the Greek Orthodox Church. Some leaders of that denomination criticized him for his position on social issues, including abortion, and there was no evidence that Dukakis was a regular attender at Sunday services.

During one of the 1984 presidential debates, journalist Fred Barnes asked former vice president and Democratic presidential nominee Walter Mondale whether he was "born again." Mondale responded that he didn't know exactly what that meant, but said he had sung in more church choirs than any other presidential candidate, which he thought might qualify him for heaven.

George Bush, whose background is Episcopalian, a denomination normally not associated with evangelicalism, played with "God words" in an attempt to shore up his political base among conservative Christians. Commenting on the Democrats' 1992 party platform, Bush said the party "left out three simple letters, g-o-d."

Bush was also quoted as saying, while president, that when he was shot down during World War II, "I thought about mother and dad and the strength I got from them—and God and faith . . ." and he quickly added, lest any lawyer from the American Civil Liberties Union be offended, "and the separation of church and state."

Why should this misuse of the Bible matter to anyone but theologians and the devout? Because as a politician thinks in his heart, so is he (a liberal interpretation of Proverbs 23:7). If political leaders claim to believe in God and to order their lives according to Scripture, but misinterpret, misunderstand, or misapply biblical instructions, disaster can result. The Bible is full of instances wherein leaders (and followers) did precisely that. If Democrats are going to join Republicans in invoking religious imagery and biblical truth, they had both better get it right or they run the risk of receiving the verdict Isaiah 28:15 pronounced on those who misquote and misrepresent God and his intentions: "For we have made falsehood our refuge and we have concealed ourselves with deception" (NASB).

Another way politicians use God for their own ends is in selling their programs to the public. In August 1994, President Clinton addressed a black church congregation in Maryland. He said it was "the will of God" that Congress pass his crime bill. He didn't say whether God would accept any amendments, so one was left to believe that God wanted the entire package.

During an anti-impeachment rally in Washington the week before Christmas 1998, John Boyd of the National Black Farmers Association took the use of religious figures and imagery to new depths. According to an account of the event by Tucker Carlson of *The Weekly Standard* magazine, "Jesus himself has come to Washington to judge the impeachment proceedings: 'He's looking at the wrongdoing of the Republican Party,' Boyd told the crowd, and His verdict is clear: Republicans had better rethink their position on Clinton. Otherwise, Boyd warned, 'on judgment day they might not get through.'"[1]

When Republicans and Christians claim divine approval for public policy initiatives, Democrats and groups like People for the American Way denounce them for their hubris. No liberal group criticized the president for his remarks, but then, conservative religious leaders hardly ever criticized Reagan and Bush when they said or did something with which conservatives disagreed.

You would think our astute religious leaders would see through this abuse of religion for political gain. Most of them do, but they refuse to hold politicians accountable for their blatant misuse of personal faith. Why? In the end it's about access. If you want to maintain your access to powerful political leaders, you must frequently compromise your supposedly cherished and deeply held convictions. That's the primary danger that accompanies a too-close association between church and state. Faith knows no compromise—but compromise is the essence of politics. That is why politics and government are greater dangers to the church than the church is to politics and government.

One news magazine thought it was complimenting the Christian Coalition when it said the organization had finally "won a place at the table" in Washington. Is this what the kingdom of God should be about—winning a place at the political table alongside labor unions, political action committees, civil rights advocates, and other petitioners for power, all of whom compete for the government's attention and, in some cases, tax dollars and tax breaks? There is great danger in Christian political activism because the inexperienced and unsophisticated can easily be burned. Participants are often not content with doing the grunt work that brings change by increments, so they sometimes overreach, alienating those who don't always share their agenda. They usually win little or nothing and, worse, offend and turn off those they might be winning to their cause if they employed other means.

That is what happened to the Moral Majority. We had the attention of the public because of heavy publicity, but we won few converts outside of a small band of true believers. Again, the ignorance of the press about religious things worked to our advantage. The press didn't know that most of our "state chapters" were little more than a separate telephone line in a pastor's office.

Democrats are trying hard to become as adept at misusing and abusing God as Republicans, but they have a long way to go because they haven't been at it as long as Republicans have and they lack the core of true believers, who are mostly in the GOP. Both parties now shamelessly invoke God to bless public policies with which they agree—and frequently invoke him wrongly—but ignore his instructions when he speaks clearly about matters with which they don't agree. In other words, they use only enough of the Bible or their Christian convictions that will accomplish their political objectives—so much so, that I'm convinced both parties would have applied focus groups or the line item veto to one or more of the Ten Commandments. Politicians want God on their side whenever possible because they see him giving legitimacy to their ideas and a personal feeling of moral satisfaction.

Does this mean that politicians should never mention their personal faith or allude to their beliefs? Absolutely not. But they need to be sincere, and they need to be very careful about using God-talk to manipulate voters. Frankly, it would be refreshing to see more politicians demonstrate a vibrant faith, but to do so would open them up to the kind of criticism Justice Antonin Scalia faced when he spoke at a 1996 prayer breakfast in Jackson, Mississippi. Justice Scalia spoke not only of his personal faith, but of the reaction by the press and the rest of the secular establishment to people who believe in an authority higher than government. He even spoke of his faith in miracles, which led some commentators to place him in the same category as people who call psychic hotlines. *Washington Post* cartoonist Herblock drew Scalia reading a Bible while his fellow justices read the Constitution. I wonder how Herblock would have drawn Abraham Lincoln, who said of the Bible, "But for this book, we would not know right from wrong"?

Justice Scalia urged the 650 people present to ignore the scorn of the "worldly wise" and merely stand up for their beliefs. That's pretty good advice in an age when some call for the "Christian equivalent of the ACLU" to force secularists to treat believers fairly. Some believe that to be persecuted for their beliefs is wrong. To the contrary, Jesus said that if we are persecuted for righteousness' sake (an important prerequisite), we should be glad because we stand with a long line of prophets (Matthew 5:11–12).

Prophets, however, were never popular, and they certainly could not get elected to public office in America today. Conservative Christians would do well to remember that the next time we hear a candidate quote the Bible.

SEVEN

BETTER WEAPONS

Last November's victory was singularly your victory. Fellow citizens, fellow conservatives—our time is now, our moment has arrived.

Ronald Reagan, speaking to Conservative Political Action Conference, March 1981 As quoted in Jerome L. Himmelstein, *To the Right* (University of California Press at Berkeley, 1990), 13

Two things amaze me about conservative Christians: our hand-wringing over all that is bad in the world, and our reluctance to use what we have been given to influence the world. We should know better.

In the book of Matthew in the Bible, Jesus taught his disciples an important lesson on how they should view the world and the evil things that occur in it. He used three parables, or stories, to make his point. The first one was about a landowner who planted wheat, but when it sprouted, his servants noticed weeds were also growing. The servants offered to pull them out. The landowner said to wait until the harvest and then they would pull the weeds and burn them.

The second parable was about a tiny mustard seed that, once planted, grows into a large tree. And the final parable was about a woman who mixed a small amount of yeast into a large amount of flour.

If you are confused, you are in good company. The twelve disciples to whom Jesus told these stories were also confused and asked him to explain what he meant.

Jesus answered their question this way:

The one who sowed the good seed is the Son of Man. The field is the world, and the good seed stands for the sons of the kingdom. The weeds are the sons of the evil one, and the enemy who sows them is the devil. The harvest is the end of the age, and the harvesters are angels.

As the weeds are pulled up and burned in the fire, so it will be at the end of the age. The Son of Man will send out his angels, and they will weed out of his kingdom everything that causes sin and all who do evil. They will throw them into the fiery furnace, where there will be weeping and gnashing of teeth. Then the righteous will shine like the sun in the kingdom of their father. He who has ears, let him hear (Matthew 13:37–43).

These parables say something important to those who are putting at least partial faith in government and politics to turn the nation around. It is that they should not focus their primary attention on eliminating weeds, but on nurturing the wheat. And these parables suggest that while this might seem like a small, even ineffective (as we measure effectiveness), thing to do, the mustard seed is a reminder that big trees can grow from little seeds. Furthermore, the yeast can only do its work when it penetrates the dough and becomes invisible. It is only this penetration and invisibility that makes the dough rise.

Penetration and invisibility were principles embraced by Communism that allowed it to infiltrate governments and organizations so effectively for most of the twentieth century. The substance of Communism was wrong, and eventually it collapsed when pushed, but some of Communism's tactics were straight out of the Bible.

It is the same with the salt analogy used elsewhere by Jesus (Matthew 5:13). Politically conservative Christians like to use the salt metaphor as the rationalization for their political involvement. They say that political activism is part of the "salting," or preserving process. But this is not entirely true, perhaps not even mainly true.

Salt does its primary work when it is invisible, not when it's seen. Salt preserves, not while in a shaker or in a box on a store shelf, but only when it penetrates the meat or other substance that would spoil without its application. Salt only slows down the spoilage process; it does not preserve forever. If religious conservatives really want to change Hollywood, for example, so that it produces movies more to their liking, more of them who have the required talent should penetrate Hollywood. If they are tired of one-sided journalism, people who don't like what journalism has become and who have the necessary skills should penetrate journalism. The example works in every field: education, politics, media, the arts, even churches.

Bashing these institutions from the outside has little, if any, effect. It is like taking a battering ram to a fortress that is sufficiently protected to guard against external assaults.

So why are religious conservatives devoting so much time, effort, and money to reforming the "field" (the world) by trying to stop evil (the weeds, which are sown by the devil), instead of sowing more good seed (by bringing more sons and daughters into the greater kingdom)? It is the ultimate temptation.

Too many Christians today apparently feel a need for government to reflect their values in order for them to feel significant. Ed Dobson and I have found in our travels to many parts of the world that this is a distinctly American concept.

In China, where house churches are trying to survive against an officially atheistic government that has persecuted the church since 1949, the focus of believers is not on the toppling of the government leadership and their replacement with Christian leaders or others more favorably inclined toward religious freedom (though many might say they would like to see that day come). The focus is on living a holy life and spreading the news about a higher and better kingdom. To the extent that they interact with government, it is usually when government seeks to suppress, not just their political activities, but the application of their faith, which Beijing sees as the ultimate threat to Communism's hold on political power.

Why do so many American Christians need to feel wanted and appreciated and see their politicians reflecting the way they pray and behave? Why do they seek validation in visibility? Is it because of some deep sense of inferiority? Is their faith so fragile that it is only in seeing it manifested in the corridors of political power in Washington that they feel justified?

When I was working as a reporter for a Houston television station in the 1970s, I interviewed Madalyn Murray O'Hair, the atheist "credited" with the lawsuit that led the Supreme Court to declare organized prayer and Bible reading in public schools unconstitutional. I asked Mrs. O'Hair why so many people were afraid of her. I will never forget her reply: "I'll tell you, Mr. Thomas, why some Christians are afraid of me. They're not sure that what they believe is really true. If they were sure, I wouldn't be a threat to them at all."

That may have been the only time in my life I found myself agreeing with Madalyn Murray O'Hair about anything.

Too many religious conservatives, especially conservative Christians, have an inferiority complex about their faith. If they aren't in the majority and seeing their faith reflected in every organ of government and culture, they feel personally diminished and corporately powerless. They want respect, and they think respect is necessary in order for their faith and its principles to advance. In fact, the opposite has been true throughout history. The early church flourished without government approval. A sound argument can be made that the church does poorly when it seeks or receives the blessing of government and does better and exhibits real power when it is out of favor with government or is being persecuted.

One of the more outrageous examples of the inferiority complex exhibited by many conservative Christians occurred in the mid-1970s. The National Religious Broadcasters convention invited *Hustler* magazine publisher Larry Flynt and former Black Panther leader Eldridge Cleaver to speak at their convention in Washington, D.C.[1] (For years the NRB has met in Washington in what has to be the ultimate flirtation between church and state.) Flynt had supposedly been converted by Jimmy Carter's evangelist sister, Ruth Carter Stapleton. Neither Flynt nor Cleaver lived up to his advance billing, but the scene was instructive. Delegates needed to feel accepted by the world. They hungered for significance, and they wanted validation by the same people who grant "significance" to celebrities. If the NRB could produce high-profile "converts" like Larry Flynt and Eldridge Cleaver, then that would prove to the cynical, unbelieving world that their faith was legitimate.

Sadly, but not unpredictably, parading these two "converts" around the convention turned out to be another embarrassing fiasco. It was the last time Flynt would ever appear in public at a religious gathering. He quickly returned to publishing his dirty magazine. As for Cleaver, after a stint as the Black Panther the white churches loved to invite to speak, he flirted with the Mormons and the Unification Church. Cleaver died in 1998. The religious celebrity circuit didn't have time to make sure the conversions of these men were real, much less instruct them in the essentials of biblical principles, because they needed them in order to feel relevant and important. So they pushed them on the stage before they were examined and certainly before they were ready.

I have watched preachers at these celebrity gatherings move through lobbies with security details and public relations flacks carrying walkie-talkies. There is never time for these important leaders to mingle with the masses. They are constantly hurrying to news conferences and to meetings. It looks more like a presidential detail than a preacher greeting his flock. You couldn't get a meeting with these guys unless you had an appointment, and you often could not get an appointment unless you were important or wanted to give lots of money.

These religious sideshows take on the trappings of a political convention. The president is always invited, but clearly the delegates prefer a Republican. One year, George Bush was a speaker at the NRB convention and said that his favorite Bible verse was "John 16:3." Unless he had dyslexia, he meant to say John 3:16, but the moment taught a lesson. Someone must have said, "Here, give them a Bible verse, mention God, and they'll vote for you next time."

In the 1980s, people were led to believe that changing government leadership would keep their teenage daughter from getting pregnant, would clean up television, would reduce drug use, and would restore "morality" to America. They believed it because we in the Moral Majority knew they wanted to believe it, so we convinced them it could happen. Many books were sold with quotations from the past, suggesting that the time of the Founders was more moral than the time of Carter and Clinton. (Somehow Republican presidents got a free pass even when they failed to do what we wanted.) But those of us who criticized liberal attempts to use government to impose what we regarded as an unrighteous standard were trying just as hard to use government to impose a righteous standard. We criticized big government, but what we were really criticizing was the other guys who had control of it when we wanted control. So it wasn't big government per se that was evil. Our primary objection was that we weren't running it.

What a tragic irony it would be if conservative Christians would turn to the government gods that failed and repeat the error of the political and theological left. One reason the National Council and World Council of Churches no longer have the moral power and authority they once enjoyed is that they married government to God. In the process, their moral power evaporated and they became, as the Religious Right has become, just another special-interest group to be appeased by politicians.

In fact, that is precisely what was said of former Christian Coalition executive director Ralph Reed in a *Time* magazine cover story. Reed and Christians in general had "finally arrived," said *Time*.[2] So the kingdom that is not of this world is of this world after all? And Christians are now to receive the same attention as, but no more than, other competitors for political power and influence.

The temptation is always to do good, never evil. That's what makes it so subtle, and that's why so many fall for the deception. Even the noblest political causes (and there is great nobility in saving the innocent unborn) can be a form of corruption when they divert our attention and effort from the work of Jesus in the world. For believers, this vision of worldly power is not a calling, but a distraction— another case of the good being the enemy of the best. It is a temptation Jesus rejected—not because it was dangerous, but because it was trivial compared with his greater mission.

Listen to the advice of the devil Screwtape, in C. S. Lewis's *Screwtape Letters*, on how to corrupt a Christian:

> Let him begin by treating patriotism ... as a part of his religion. Then let him, under the influence of partisan spirit, come to regard it as the most important part. Then quietly and gradually

nurse him on to the stage at which the religion becomes merely a part of the "cause," in which Christianity is valued chiefly because of the excellent arguments it can produce.... once you have made the world an end, and faith a means, you have almost won your man, and it makes very little difference what kind of worldly end he is pursuing.[3]

Faith in Jesus (and it ought to be in Jesus, not Jesus plus or minus anything else, including agendas and politics) is not, or should not be, a means to any end. It is the end itself. But this presents a paradox. It is precisely when we concentrate on God's agenda that we are most useful to the world around us. It is only when our goal is heaven that we are of any earthly good.

America is coming slowly and surely to a recognition. Our society's most dangerous diseases have developed an immunity to politics. They are rooted in the decay of sexual standards—leaving so many of our children diseased and dying. They are rooted in the decline of civility—turning our republic into a civil war. Our language of right and wrong, honor and duty, has become a dead language, like Latin—quaint, curious, and forgotten.

We suffer, not from failures of political organization, but from failures of love. Our most pressing problem is not the federal debt, but a deficit of time and attention that parents give their children. In increasingly violent streets and schools and in broken homes, the cry of anguished souls is not for more laws, but for more conscience and character.

We must fulfill our political duties as citizens. But a crisis of moral authority will not be solved by an appeal to political power. Our public interest depends directly on the private virtues of our people. If we cannot change this, the reform of our society will be impossible. If we manage to change this, the reform of our society will be inevitable.

Lasting, fundamental social change cannot, has not, and should not come from government alone. It is a byproduct, not a goal—the byproduct of believers' living as Jesus calls them to live. This should not be confused with living as we think he wants us to live or as what makes us feel good. The calling of Jesus is not to victory, and it is not to power or comfort. We have tried to marry him to another suitor, and the relationship has gone sour.

The urgent question that comes to us is not "how can believers have more political influence?" It is the scriptural question, "When the foundations are being destroyed, what can the righteous do?" (Psalm 11:3). The answer should be this: Rebuild the foundation; restore the moral infrastructure that sustains our laws and our culture. Our constitutional order rests on the underpinning of the Ten Commandments and the inspiration of the Beatitudes. Our goal must be to change minds and hearts, not just change our government.

If people who claim to follow Jesus and his kingdom get too cozy with government, it won't be the government that gets injured. It will be the church that is compromised. "Religious leaders" who seek favor with the king especially run the risk of refusing to speak truth to power out of fear that they won't be invited back. Politicians know how to manipulate people and tell them what they want to hear without doing anything about their concerns. Religious people are more vulnerable to this seduction than anyone else because they have been taught to respect government leaders (at least Republican ones) and they lack sophistication in the ways of the political world.

We live, as President Vaclav Havel of the Czech Republic has said, "In a world of appearances trying to pass for reality." It sometimes appears that when a voice is not amplified by the megaphone of politics and the media, it is irrelevant. It sometimes appears that nothing important can be done without a place at the political table and a piece of the political action.

The reality is quite different—because we have a different definition of power, or should have. It is different from cynical political insiders; different from grassroots activists; different even from Rush Limbaugh and a host of conservative opinion leaders who dominate talk radio and increasingly penetrate the newspapers with opinion columns.

It is a power that comes from making disciples, helping the poor, visiting the sick, rearing a child, and comforting the dying. It can change a jaded society, because it can transform a hardened heart. But that change comes from within, not without.

The message of Christian leaders must be clear: It is not enough to support a welfare reform bill; they must also mentor the children of poverty who live without fathers and without hope. It is not enough to fight the gay rights lobby; they must comfort AIDS patients preparing for a lonely and painful death. It is not enough to support a constitutional amendment against abortion; they must provide young women in trouble with a home and a sympathetic ear.

What we must not do is demonize those with whom we disagree.

One prominent pastor visited a large church and concluded his politically charged sermon with these words: "Thank God, we don't have any liberals or feminists here today."[4] Those liberals and feminists would have been friends of Jesus. He would have been less likely to invite the religious plutocrats to dinner.

Jerry Falwell has urged Christians to pray for President Clinton, but he also distributed a highly critical videotape called *The Clinton Chronicles,* produced by some of the Clintons' more notorious adversaries.[5] How sad! Even if every accusation against the Clintons were true, there is a criminal justice system and a legal process that deals with these things, and even as we write, that system is working. It is the worst possible witness to unbelievers to have a minister running down the president of the United States. To his credit, Falwell acknowledged in an interview that as a pastor he should not have distributed this video. But he did not refund people's money that had been donated.

The church cannot and must not become an appendage to the power games of the world. Theologian Richard John Neuhaus has put it bluntly: "The church as a tool is a church of fools."

The church that belongs to Jesus is not part of anyone's agenda. In fact, people who belong to him provide the only agenda that ultimately counts. It is the agenda of the kingdom of God breaking into human history—the central feature in the history of the world. It is the only force that can make an enemy into a friend, a criminal into a saint, a biological father into a real parent. And it makes the most ambitious political agenda we can possibly imagine look trivial by comparison.

And that's the main point. The good is the enemy of the best. We settle for less than could be had and, by settling for less, ensure that we will not even get that. It is easy to "amen" in assent, but the application is sometimes hard. Let's apply this principle to abortion, which Falwell has correctly called "America's shame."

We vigorously support a constitutional amendment to restore government's recognition that the endowed right to life ought to be protected from the moment of conception. We believe our political leaders have an obligation to defend human life without apology and without equivocation. And we believe that if the Republican party abandons the pro-life movement, then pro-life Americans should abandon the Republican party (as many have abandoned the Democratic party for the same reason).

But we also believe that the pro-life movement has much to learn from history.

Most Americans do not realize that in the middle of the nineteenth century the abortion rate per capita in America—in a smaller population—was almost what it is today. In 1860, based on per capita statistics, abortion was as large a moral crisis as it is more than a century later. Ads for abortions ran in reputable newspapers. Intellectual leaders, even some of the clergy, defended abortion as a right. The *New York Times*—clearly under different management from today— ran a headline in 1871 calling abortion "the evil of the age."

A committed, effective pro-life movement sprang up across America. By 1910, the abortion rate had been cut in half—remaining low until the 1960s. How did the movement accomplish this? How did they save millions of unborn lives and prevent millions of women from making a mistake that many today say they now seriously regret?

It was not primarily laws that restricted abortion, though laws were eventually passed.

The nineteenth-century pro-life movement provided women in trouble with positive alternatives to abortion—practical help in times of crisis. The Salvation Army, the YWCA, and Florence Crittenton Homes concentrated their efforts on prostitutes and young, urban women abandoned by their child's father. Between 1833 and 1933, Crittenton Homes helped 500,000 unmarried women. Evangelists like Dwight L. Moody always carried in their pockets the names and addresses of families who would provide a room in their homes to unmarried women who found themselves pregnant and without resources.

In addition, the early pro-life movement tackled the issue of sexual ethics. Groups such as the White Cross Society urged men to abandon a sexual double standard, which persists today, and "treat the law of purity as equally binding on men and women." The society realistically warned young women to be skeptical about any promise from men that was not guaranteed by a marriage license. The power of the pro-life movement was that it appeared to be sticking up for young women against irresponsible men.

This earlier pro-life movement hoped to pass legislation, but that was not its primary focus. It stood for compassionate alternatives and moral standards. It recognized that society had to be transformed before laws could be reformed and enforced. Professor Marvin Olasky concludes his careful historical study of the pro-life movement:

> In short, the practice of compassion a century ago and today, means giving a woman undergoing a crisis pregnancy a physical home and a spiritual rock. It means the adoption of hard-to-place children. It means counseling and standing by desperate women. Particularly in a politics-obsessed age, the one-to-one practice of compassion may be less thrilling and may seem less important than dramatic protests or power politicking, but it is the major way in which lives have been saved. . . . yes, protective laws and enforcement help, but the most effective pro-life efforts have always concentrated on one life at a time.[6]

We are not political quietists or separatists. To be such, we would have to invalidate and recant everything we said and did with the Moral Majority. Believers must be energetically engaged in politics, without either weariness or wishful thinking. In a constitutional republic, this is both an opportunity and a duty—a way to show love for our neighbors and to shape a future fit for our children.

But if our goal is "Reclaiming America for Christ"—a slogan currently being used by Dr. D. James Kennedy, pastor of Coral Ridge Presbyterian Church in Fort Lauderdale, Florida—we must always ask ourselves, "Where do we place our faith? What is the source of our hope?" Will it be God, or government? It cannot be both that will restore us. One can guard what has been restored, at least for a time, until the people become restless and decide to play God themselves. But government does not have the power to force virtue on a people who do not wish to be virtuous.

EIGHT

RELIGION AND POLITICS: WHAT DOES THE BIBLE REALLY SAY?

Most Americans believe churches and the clergy should speak out on the social issues, but they are strongly against churches and clergy becoming involved in politics.

Associated Press—NC News Poll

August 18, 1981

When I traveled for the Moral Majority, I often used a line about politics and God that always brought a laugh from *ed dobson* even the most hostile audiences. "God is neither a Republican or Democrat—and he is sure not a Democrat!" But beneath the humor is the obvious question about whose side God is on. Is God the God of the religious and political left with its emphasis on the environment and the poor, or is he the God of the religious and political right with its emphasis on the unborn and the family? Both groups claim to speak for God. Both groups claim to operate with a divine mandate.

When Joshua led the Hebrew people into the Promised Land, he learned that it was more important to be on God's side than for God to be on his side. Before the people attacked the city of Jericho, Joshua was confronted by a man with a drawn sword. Joshua asked the logical question, "Are you for us or for our enemies?"

"Neither," the man replied. "But as commander of the army of the LORD I have now come."

Joshua was standing before an incarnate appearance of God. God was not interested in sides; he was interested in submission. Joshua fell facedown to the ground and asked, "What message does my Lord have for his servant?" (Joshua 5:13–15).

Many in the Religious Right have fallen for the temptation of taking sides and declaring that God is on their side. The most blatant attempt to co-opt God is the Christian Coalition. The very name places the divine stamp of approval on their agenda. Unlike Joshua, the Christian Coalition does not even ask whether God is on their side or on the side of their enemies. They assume he is on their side. Maybe God is on neither side, as in the day of Joshua. In that case, what we need is to fall on our knees like Joshua and ask, "What message does my Lord have for his servant?"

For those of us who believe the Bible (and that includes most people in the Religious Right), God has already given us a message. This message includes an understanding of our relationship to political powers as well as the role of the church in the culture. I am afraid that in the current tide of political engagement, as at other times in history, we have conveniently ignored the Bible and have become "practical atheists." We believe in God and the Bible, but we don't pay much attention to either. What does the Bible say about these issues?

1. *All political power comes from God.*

When God told Joshua that he was neither on the side of Joshua nor on the side of his enemies, he was declaring the truth that God transcends all nations and political parties. He is God. In fact, all political authority is derived from God. When Jesus was on trial, Pilate faced a dilemma. He wanted to set Jesus free because he believed Jesus had committed no crime worthy of the death penalty. But the Jews were insisting that Pilate order his crucifixion. So Pilate questioned Jesus—yet Jesus refused to answer.

Pilate was frustrated and asked, "Don't you realize I have power either to free you or to crucify you?" (John 19:10).

Jesus answered, "You would have no power over me if it were not given to you from above" (v. 11).

Pilate was the representative of the Roman government. He had the authority to administer capital punishment or to set a prisoner free. Pilate's political authority was absolute in human terms—but Jesus reminded him that he had no real authority apart from God. Ultimately, Pilate's authority was derived not from Rome, but from God.

The idea that all human authority, including political authority, comes from God is a truth taught consistently throughout the Bible. In the Old Testament, God had a special covenant relationship with the Hebrew people. God chose Abram and entered into a covenant relationship with him and his descendants:

> I will make you into a great nation
>   and I will bless you;
> I will make your name great,
>   and you will be a blessing.
> I will bless those who bless you,
>   and whoever curses you I will curse;
> and all peoples on earth
>   will be blessed through you (Genesis 12:2–3).

It would appear from these promises that God is for the Jewish people and against everyone else. Had I been Abram, this would have been my assumption based on what God had said. But Abram was soon to learn that God was the God of all nations. Abram traveled to the Promised Land with his nephew Lot. Eventually they separated, and Lot settled in the city of Sodom. A coalition of armies attacked Sodom and took Lot captive. Abram led a private army and rescued Lot from captivity.

As Abram returned home, he was met by Melchizedek, the king of Salem who was a priest of God Most High (Genesis 14:18). Melchizedek blessed Abram, who in turn gave him a tithe, or tenth, of all his possessions. Abram might well have thought that he himself was the only one connected to the true and living God. After all, God had chosen him. Then he met this king from a pagan city and discovered that the king was a priest of the same God. Abram discovered that God was at work beyond his limited perspective. He learned that God has many people, and they do not all wear the same label.

God's sovereign choice for the Hebrews as a special people did not exclude his interest and involvement with the rest of the peoples and nations of the world. In fact, God's intention for the Hebrews was to bless all the nations and people of the world through them.

Moreover, not only was God the God of all the nations, but also he used pagan nations to do his will. He used these pagan nations to bring judgment against the Hebrews. God gave the Hebrew prophet Jeremiah the following message:

> This is what the LORD Almighty, the God of Israel, says: "Tell this to your masters: With my great power and outstretched arm I made the earth and its people and the animals that are on it, and I will give it to anyone I please. Now I will hand all your countries over to my servant Nebuchadnezzar, king of Babylon." . . .
>
> I gave the same message to Zedekiah king of Judah. I said, "Bow your neck under the yoke of the king of Babylon; serve him and his people, and you will live" (Jeremiah 27:4–6, 12).

These words contain some compelling truth about the working of God in the affairs of human history. First, God is the Almighty One and is in control. Second, he delegates his authority to people and nations as he pleases. Third, he uses pagan kings to do his will and calls them his servants. Nebuchadnezzar was the king of Babylon—present-day Iraq. Saddam Hussein, the current ruler of Iraq, sees himself as the modern equivalent of this ancient king. If the message of Jeremiah were delivered by e-mail today, it might well read as follows: "Now I will hand over your countries to my servant Saddam Hussein."

The Bible makes it clear that God has not abandoned this world. In the Wisdom literature of the Old Testament we read, "The king's heart is in the hand of the LORD; he directs it like a watercourse wherever he pleases" (Proverbs 21:1). In the New Testament, the apostle Paul writes, "Everyone must submit himself to the governing authorities, for there is no authority except that which God has established. The authorities that exist have been established by God. Consequently, he who rebels against the authority is rebelling against what God has instituted, and those who do so will bring judgment on themselves" (Romans 13:1–2). In language similar to the prophet Jeremiah's, Paul declares that those in political power are the servants of God (Romans 13:4).

The truth that all authority comes from God and that God is equally involved in all the nations of the world raises several important questions.

First, does the United States have favored-nation status with God? An analysis of the contents of the letters, broadcasts, and speeches of the leaders of the Religious Right shows that all of them perceive that America has a special relationship with God. It is a "nation under God." It has been chosen by God as a light to the rest of the world and therefore we must devote our efforts to protecting and defending her against the threats of secularism, humanism, and liberalism that are on the verge of destroying her. According to many, America is a Christian nation and is drifting from her Christian roots in a dramatic way.

Much of the rationale for Christian political involvement is connected to this idea that America has been chosen by God. Jerry Falwell writes, "When will America sit down and cry? When will this country finally return to the Judeo-Christian values upon which it was founded? . . . With this in mind, I have determined to address the nation—live, via satellite—in a prime-time telecast that will be a moral and spiritual State of the Union Address. . . . I believe this special, live prime-time telecast can be the vehicle which helps turn this ship of state."

But this thinking is flawed. It is not the thinking of biblically informed people. While it is true that God was sovereignly involved in founding this nation, he is no less sovereignly involved in the affairs of Iran or Iraq or any other nation. That is not to say that America has not been blessed by God. It has benefited from what Francis Schaeffer called the "Christian consensus" of its Founding Fathers. That consensus was crucial to the kind of nation the United States became. Schaeffer observed, "This does not mean that it was a golden age, nor that the founders were personally Christian, nor that those who were Christians were always consistent in their political thinking." But, he said, their belief in a Creator to whom they were responsible in their commitment to biblical standards of morality made all the difference between the American Revolution and the French Revolution, or later the Russian Revolution.

America has enjoyed unparalleled prosperity because of its adherence to the biblical principles of freedom, justice, equality, integrity, honesty, and hard work. This is not to say that we should or even can go back to "the good old days." The same people who founded our nation participated in the reprehensible slave trade. My African-American friends do not want to go back, because going back for them means going back to slavery.

The second question is, is God responsible for the wickedness of the nations that reject his principles? The apostle Paul explains the workings of God in the nations when he writes, "We are bringing you good news, telling you to turn from these worthless things to the living God, who made heaven and earth and sea and everything in them. In the past, he let all nations go their own way" (Acts 14:15–16). God is sovereign in the affairs of nations but does not violate the freedom of those nations to "go their own way."

God allows nations to make choices, just as he allows individuals to make choices. But he also holds both nations and individuals responsible for the choices they make. If a nation chooses to disregard God, it will pay the consequences of that choice. By contrast, if a nation chooses to honor God and his principles, it will reap the benefits of that choice. The writer of the book of Proverbs states, "Righteousness exalts a nation, but sin is a disgrace to any people" (Proverbs 14:34). To put it another way, living by God's principles promotes a nation to greatness while disregarding those principles brings disgrace.

At this point the argument appears contradictory. How can God be in control of all the nations and at the same time permit them to go their own way? If God is in control, then the nations can only go his way; if the nations can go their own way, then God is not really in control. However, this apparent contradiction can be resolved with another important question. If God is in control, why does he *allow* the nations to go their own way? The answer is that even when nations go their own way, God is still working to accomplish a greater purpose than may be evident at the moment.

There is one further question, which we will explore later in this chapter: "If God allows nations to pursue wicked agendas, what is the responsibility of Christians to resist that wicked government?"

2. Government has a God-ordained role to play in society.

According to the leaders of the Religious Right, government should reflect their values. It should hold to a Judeo-Christian worldview and should promote and defend the principles inherent in it. But is this the role of the government of the United States or any other nation? More precisely, what should we expect out of government? The writings of the apostles Paul and Peter both identify the specific role of government in society.

> For rulers hold no terror for those who do right, but for those who do wrong. Do you want to be free from fear of the one in authority? Then do what is right and he will commend you. For he is God's servant to do you good. But if you do wrong, be afraid, for he does not bear the sword for nothing. He is God's servant, an agent of wrath to bring punishment on the wrongdoer (Romans 13:3–4).

> Submit yourselves for the Lord's sake to every authority instituted among men: whether to the king, as the supreme authority or to governors, who are sent by him to punish those who do wrong and to commend those who do right (1 Peter 2:13–14).

Both Peter and Paul argue that the primary purpose of government is to maintain an ordered and structured society where good is promoted and evil is restrained. For this reason, government has been given the sword—the authority to inflict punishment. This is a God-given role, and when the government exercises this role properly, it is acting as a servant of God.

We should not expect the government to promote the gospel or prayer or religion. This is not its role. We should not expect the government to promote compassion for the poor. That is not its role.

What should Christians expect from the government of the United States? We should expect the government to maintain an ordered society so that we can live out our faith and pay attention to the greater purposes of God in calling people to faith in Jesus Christ. Paul writes,

> I urge, then, first of all, that requests, prayers, intercession and thanksgiving be made for everyone—for kings and all those

in authority, that we may live peaceful and quiet lives in all godliness and holiness. This is good, and pleases God our Savior,
who wants all men to be saved and to come to a knowledge of the
truth (1 Timothy 2:1–4).

We are to pray and give thanks for everyone in authority whether
we agree with them or not. The objective of our prayers is to promote
an environment in which we are left alone by the government to live
peaceful and quiet lives. But life is not to be a retreat from the society. On the contrary, God wants everyone, including those in politics,
to be saved, and we are to devote our energies to the task of sharing
the gospel with everyone.

The main purpose of government is to promote an ordered society. The main purpose of a Christian is to live a godly life so that
people will be attracted to the gospel. For Christians, the most critical issue of life and eternity is one's relationship with Jesus Christ. We
believe that Jesus is the only way of salvation and that we have a
responsibility to share the gospel with everyone. We believe that
people are eternally lost without Jesus. Therefore the ultimate issue is
not whether you are pro-life or pro-abortion; the ultimate issue is
whether you know Jesus personally. The ultimate issue is not whether
you are pro-gay or anti-gay; the ultimate issue is whether you know
Jesus. The ultimate issue is not whether you are a Democrat or a
Republican; the ultimate issue is whether you know Jesus. The ultimate issue is not whether you are pro-Clinton or anti-Clinton; the
ultimate issue is whether you know Jesus. The ultimate issue is not
whether you are a capitalist or a socialist; the ultimate issue is whether
you know Jesus.

I am not saying that these issues and choices are not important
or that the Bible does not address them. I am saying that none is the
most important issue. The most important issue for Christians is living godly lives in the culture and maintaining focus on the main
thing: getting out the gospel of Jesus.

Upon reflection, I think the leaders of the Religious Right have
made several critical mistakes. First, they have expectations of the
government that God never intended. They expect the government

to reflect their religious values, but it was not instituted by God to do so. It was instituted to restrain evil and promote good so that the values of God could be reflected in the lives of the people who claim to follow God. Second, the Religious Right has abandoned the greater priority of communicating the gospel for the lesser priority of sanctifying the state. The net result is that they have accomplished neither very well. They have failed to impact people with the gospel, and they have failed to sanctify the state.

3. *Christians have a God-ordained responsibility to government.*

We have looked at what we should expect out of the government and at the temptation to expect more than God expects. But what should the government expect of us? Again, the Bible speaks to this issue and gives specific admonitions.

a. We are to pray for government leaders. The words we have cited from 1 Timothy were written while Paul was in prison in Rome—the center of political power in the ancient world. He was calling for thanksgiving and prayer for the emperor Nero. It was Nero who condemned Paul to die—yet Paul asked for prayers and thanksgiving on his behalf. We are to pray for those in political power in our country as well. I have heard all sorts of crude jokes about President Clinton and the First Lady. I have heard him called all sorts of names. I have heard him berated, attacked, maligned, and preached against as the very embodiment of the Antichrist. But I do not recall hearing one leader of the Religious Right offer a prayer on his behalf, not one word of thanks to God for placing him in power.

The only person I recall hearing give thanks to God for Bill Clinton was an African-American minister from Baltimore. There were fifteen of us at a breakfast meeting with President Clinton and Vice President Gore, and the subject was the pandemic of HIV/AIDS. Early in the conversation, the woman minister explained with delight, "Mr. President, I was so excited the night you were elected to office! I jumped around and said, 'Thank you, Jesus!'" I know that the night Bill Clinton was elected, the people in the Religious Right were saying, "Help us, Jesus!" But the black minister's prayer reflects better the counsel of Scripture.

Are we praying for the president and our political leaders? The Sunday after the story about the Monica Lewinsky affair broke early in 1998, I knew that I needed to pray for the president and the country during our church services. So I prayed:

> Dear God, we give you thanks for the privilege of living in this land of freedom. We meet in this building this morning to pray, to read Scripture, to sing, to give, and to listen to your preached words. And we do it without fear of harassment, persecution, or imprisonment. For this religious freedom we give you thanks.
>
> Our hearts are saddened and our minds confused by the events in Washington, D.C., these last several days. First, we pray that the truth would be heard and known. In the midst of legal negotiations and political spin doctors, we ask for the whole truth to be revealed. We know that you know the truth and that only the truth can set us free from this dark cloud of cynicism and despair.
>
> Second, we pray that during these times we would turn to you. We know that in the crises of life you are speaking to us and you want us to pay attention to you.
>
> Third, we pray for our president. Give him wisdom in conducting the business of our country. Give him courage to deal with these circumstances forthrightly without undue attention to political expediency. Encourage his wife and daughter. Wrap your arms of love and grace around them. We pray that you would draw the president's family closer to you and closer to each other.
>
> For those of us who are quick to pick up stones, remind us again of the words of our Lord Jesus, "He who is without sin, let him cast the first stone." Remind us that the mess in Washington is a reflection of the mess in our own lives. Help us to see our own sin.

b. We are to submit to government leaders. Paul writes, "Everyone must submit himself to the governing authorities, for there is no authority except that which God has established" (Romans 13:1). If all political authority comes from God, then in submitting to it we are really submitting to God. The word *submit* is used frequently in the

New Testament, primarily to describe the relationship of the world to Christ: "For he [Jesus] must reign until he has put all his enemies under his feet" (1 Corinthians 15:25). Again, "And God placed all things under his feet and appointed him to be head over everything for the church" (Ephesians 1:22). Submitting to government authority involves recognizing that authority is from God and then willingly and completely subjecting ourselves to that authority.

c. *We are to honor government leaders.* In regard to political authorities, Paul writes, "Give everyone what you own him: If you owe taxes, pay taxes; if revenue, then revenue; if respect, then respect; if honor, then honor" (Romans 13:7). Because government leaders are the servants of God—whether they recognize it or not—we are to honor and respect them. The Greek verb translated "honor" means to value something as precious. In terms of human relationships it means to treat someone with dignity because of his or her value. This is how we are to treat political leaders.

Submitting and honoring political leaders is especially difficult when those leaders are anti-Christian. But this is what Paul asks. Remember that Paul wrote these words to believers in Rome. The Jewish believers of the day would have found this teaching to be bordering on heresy. The Jews believed, on the basis of the Old Testament, that the only person to whom they could willingly submit was another Jew: "Be sure to appoint over you the king the LORD your God chooses. He must be from among your own brothers. Do not place a foreigner over you, one who is not a brother Israelite" (Deuteronomy 17:15). Submission and honor are always easier when the person to whom we are submitting is one of us. But the Bible calls for submission and honor to those who may not be like us, or—as in the case of Paul with regard to Nero—even an enemy of the Christian faith.

The Religious Right found it convenient to submit to and honor Presidents Reagan and Bush, but not Presidents Carter and Clinton. Yet Paul offers no exceptions to the rule. Nero lived a life of unrestrained sexual addiction, surrounded by transvestites, homosexuals, prostitutes, and orgies. He also hated Christians and had many of them murdered. But Paul admonished fellow believers to honor Nero as the king. Honoring political leaders does not have an exemption clause based on character or personality. Nor is there an exemption on the basis of the type or quality of the political system.

When I ate breakfast with President Clinton, I sat on his left. During the first fifteen minutes, we talked as we ate. We talked about the Bible and about what it means to be a Christian politician who is responsible to represent all the people, Christians and non-Christians alike. The president expressed his great disappointment with some of the pastors he had invited to the White House. They would talk about moral issues (including abortion), and he would find the discussions informative, positive, and helpful. Then, back in their churches, they would be unkind toward him in what they said from the pulpit.

"The most difficult thing to accept," the president said, "are the things they said and the jokes they told about my wife. How can ministers say such things?" When I returned to my own pulpit the next Sunday, I recounted the president's words and related what the Bible says about honoring political leaders. Since then I have refused to listen to jokes or tell jokes that demean the president and his family.

Honoring and submitting to political leaders does not mean ignoring or denying any falsity or lack of honor in their actions or words. John the Baptist, the predecessor of Jesus, was a preacher of truth and righteousness. He preached a message of repentance from sin, and he was tough on everyone. When the religious leaders came out into the desert to hear him, John told them, "You brood of vipers! Who warned you to flee from the coming wrath? Produce fruit in keeping with repentance" (Matthew 3:7–8). John confronted the sin not only of the religious leaders, but of the political leaders. He told Herod that his marriage to his brother Philip's wife was illegal (Mark 6:18). Herod's wife, Herodias, eventually persuaded him to have John arrested. During his imprisonment John would often have conversations with Herod. Indeed, Herod protected John and was afraid of him because he was "a righteous and holy man" (v. 20).

Unfortunately, today's political leaders may fear the Religious Right, not because they are "righteous and holy" people, but because of their ability to deliver votes. John told the king the truth without regard for the consequences, and he did it face to face.

d. We are to pay our taxes. The issue of the relationship between religion and politics is not an issue of recent origin. It was discussed and debated when Jesus was on earth. The Pharisees and the Herodians together came to Jesus and asked, "Is it right to pay taxes to Caesar or not?" (Matthew 22:17). The Pharisees and Herodians were a most unlikely coalition. The Pharisees opposed the Roman occupation of Palestine and believed in paying taxes to the temple—not the Roman government. The Herodians favored cooperation with the Roman government and favored the paying of taxes to Caesar. Now these enemies came together to ask Jesus about paying taxes.

The question was intended to trick Jesus. If he favored paying taxes to Caesar, the Pharisees would accuse him of religious compromise. If he did not favor paying taxes to Caesar, the Herodians would accuse him of political rebellion. Jesus asked for a Roman coin.

"Whose portrait is this? And whose inscription?" Jesus asked.

"Caesar's," came the reply.

Then Jesus said, "Give to Caesar what is Caesar's, and to God what is God's."

Jesus was implying that the followers of God are citizens of two kingdoms. We are citizens of God's kingdom and have responsibilities to God. But we are also citizens of an earthly kingdom and have responsibilities to the state. Jesus did not exempt us from paying taxes. The Roman government, which was the occupying force in Palestine, was fundamentally anti-Jewish. It promoted Caesar as a god. Later on, it would persecute and kill Christians. Some groups in the United States advocate refusing to pay taxes because some of those revenues would support governmental programs that they disagree with in principle. But the Bible offers no such option. We are to pay taxes whether or not the government is friendly toward Christians.

4. *The Bible and civil disobedience.*

The scenes on the television screen have become familiar: Several dozen people are blocking the entrance to an abortion clinic. The protest starts quietly, but then the police arrive. The protesters are asked to move, but refuse to do so. Then the police begin to arrest the protesters, who go limp and have to be carried to the police vehicles. People start shouting. Chaos breaks out, with people screaming at the police. Finally, everyone is taken away to spend the night in jail. That night the leader or leaders of the protest are interviewed for the television news report.

"Are you not breaking the law?" the reporter asks.

"We believe that we are justified in breaking a small law in order to protest a larger law that allows the murder of innocent pre-born human beings," a leader responds. The leader's ultimate appeal is to God's law, which is considered more authoritative than human law.

If all political authority comes from God and if we are to obey that authority, then when is it justified to disobey that law? Operation Rescue makes a compelling argument that it is justified to disobey human law for the purpose of protecting human life from abortion. In the Bible there are three specific situations in which people of faith disregard human law so as to obey the higher law of God. Although the three situations are different outwardly, they have a common thread— namely, when we are asked to do something that would cause us to disobey God, we must refuse.

Case study A: The protection of human life. When the children of Israel were held in slavery in Egypt, their numbers multiplied to the point that the Egyptians were afraid they might ally themselves with Egypt's enemies. So Pharaoh gave instructions to the midwives to kill every male child at birth. The midwives refused. "The midwives, however, feared God and did not do what the king of Egypt had told them to do; they let the boys live" (Exodus 1:17). Then "God was kind to the midwives" who disregarded the law of the land (v. 20).

Case study B: The issue of worship. King Nebuchadnezzar of Babylon built a huge statue of gold and demanded that all his governmental officials bow down and worship this idol. There were three Hebrew slaves among the royal officials: Shadrach, Meshach, and Abednego. When the music played, everyone bowed down except the three Hebrews. They understood that such worship was a violation of the Ten Commandments. It would be a denial of their faith in the one and only God.

Nebuchadnezzar was furious with the Hebrews. He threatened them with death in a fiery furnace. But the three young men responded, "O Nebuchadnezzar, we do not need to defend ourselves before you in this matter. If we are thrown into the blazing furnace, the God we serve is able to save us from it, and he will rescue us from your hand, O king. But even if he does not, we want you to know, O king, that we will not serve your gods or worship the image of gold you have set up" (Daniel 3:16–18).

Case study C: The proclamation of the gospel. In the early days of the church, the apostles were given strict orders not to teach in the name of Jesus (Acts 4:18). But they disregarded this order and continued to teach in Jesus' name. Upon being brought before the authorities, they said, "We must obey God rather than men!" (Acts 5:29). The apostles knew that Jesus had given them the necessary authority to do this (Matthew 28:18–20). When they were commanded to stop, they refused.

So when is it appropriate to disobey human law? When is civil disobedience justified? First and foremost, civil disobedience is justified when we are personally asked to disobey God. At that moment our choice is clear: I will obey God, or I will obey man. I cannot do both. For the Christian, obedience to God is first and foremost.

But what about Operation Rescue? The people who picket and block access and disregard the law of assembling are not being asked to do something wrong. They are protesting the wrong of others and protecting the life of those who cannot speak for themselves. I confess my ambivalence on this issue. On the one hand, we could say that this civil disobedience lies outside the guidelines of Scripture. That is, the disobedience would be in order only if the protesters themselves were being required to have abortions. On the other hand, shouldn't someone be speaking up for the unborn, and if so, who should that be? Who will give them a chance at life?

One thing is certain from the teaching of the Bible: Civil disobedience is only for rare occasions. In the entire Bible there are only three examples. In each of the examples, people of faith were asked to do something that, through obedience to human authority, would cause them to disobey God. Any civil disobedience beyond these circumstances must be carefully approached and only exercised as a last resort when all other means have failed.

NINE

FOCUS ON THE FAMILY, NOT ON POLITICS

The ties linking evangelical Christians to political conservatism are so numerous and so persuasive that it is possible to say the two are "yoked together."

Richard V. Pierard, evangelical historian
As quoted in Jerome L. Himmelstein,
To the Right (University of California Press at Berkeley, 1990), 229

I hope you sense our zeal in proclaiming a better way to transform society. We wouldn't mind it if you described us as zealous. But please don't label us as zealots!

Confused?

It was the late philosopher-theologian Dr. Francis Schaeffer who taught me about definitions. He said to always define the words you use so that everyone will know what you're talking about. He once told me that if you get fifteen people from different backgrounds in a room and mention any word or name, you might get fifteen different definitions or observations; so if you begin by telling your audience or readers what you mean first, then everyone will know what you're talking about.

The definition of "zeal" that I use here is "eagerness and ardent interest in pursuit of something; fervor."

Likewise, the definition of "zealous" is "filled with or characterized by zeal." Missionaries come to mind as an example of zealous people.

But then there is the definition of "zealotry": "excess of zeal; fanatical devotion." Christians must always guard against letting their zeal

117

turn them into zealots. I recall hearing a sermon a number of years ago in which the preacher spoke of God having a will but also a way. The preacher said it is possible to be committed to the will of God, but to impede that will by appropriating methods and strategies that are not the way of God.

Jesus repeatedly rebuked the Pharisees, who were so zealous about the will of God that they became guilty of zealotry in attempting to achieve their objectives. Their zealotry obscured the way of God. They had focused so much on God's law that they completely missed his ultimate objective—which was not a legalism no person could live up to, but a redemption that God had stooped down to accomplish. So even God found another way when mankind could not live up to his expectations. Rather than sitting in heaven "high and exalted," as Isaiah saw him in a vision (Isaiah 6:1), God came down to redeem fallen man. While his will and holiness remained (and remain) uncompromised, he found another way—a better way—to reach man than through a legal process no person could fully obey.

In politics, zealotry is often seen as fanaticism. Politics is about compromise, and goals are mostly achieved in increments. Politics and faith are irreconcilable. The former cannot tolerate zealotry; the latter cannot tolerate compromise. This is the reason that the two, when combined, become highly combustible. So any disagreement with the tiniest word, strategy, or goal of a leader in the Religious Right puts one in danger of condemnation and under suspicion for being a compromiser. The goal, rather than the methods of obtaining the goal, becomes everything. It is a form of idolatry, obscuring the way of God.

I offer this example. Dr. James Dobson, president of Focus on the Family, delivered a fiery speech to a group known as the Council on National Policy (CNP), a virtually all-white club of wealthy Republicans who meet several times a year in beautiful places around the country. On two occasions I have spoken to this group.

In his February 1998 speech to a CNP meeting in Arizona, Dr. Dobson threatened to withdraw his support for the Republican party because it had "betrayed" conservative evangelical voters. He added that he "would do everything I can to take as many people with me as possible." Dr. Dobson accused the party of "being out of touch with the people I'm talking about." He said he might take a leave of absence from Focus on the Family to focus full-time on politics.

The response to Dr. Dobson, who mailed a cassette of his remarks and a press release to various people, including me, was instructive. Clifford May, communications director for the Republican National Committee, told the *New York Times,* "To the extent that conservative groups and movements want to keep the Republican party's feet to the fire, we welcome that. But we ask that they keep it constructive and understand that this is a political party, which is more than simply a movement or interest group or a lobbying group. Political parties win through communication, not through excommunication."[1]

Dr. Dobson has publicly criticized conservative senators John Ashcroft, a Missouri Republican and a church-going, committed Christian, and Rick Santorum, a Pennsylvania Republican and a devout Roman Catholic. Dr. Dobson said he doesn't think the two spoke out strongly enough against sex education in public schools.

It takes very little to raise Dr. Dobson's ire. When I wrote a column suggesting he was putting too much faith in the Republican party to bring revival to America, he criticized me both on his syndicated radio show and in a monthly letter he mails to supporters. That's okay—I can dish it out, and I can take it, too.

When we asked to interview Dr Dobson for this book and promised his remarks would not be edited except for space considerations, he scribbled on my typewritten letter, "Dear Cal, this kind note took me back a bit. After attacking me nationally, misrepresenting my views, and trying to make it look like I think revival can come from the Republican party—it seems wierd [*sic*] for you to ask me to help write your book—a book to be coauthored with a man whom I have disagreed with emphatically on the very topic you have chosen. It's a strange request. Thanks, but no thanks. Jim."

Earlier, in his monthly fund-raising letter, Dobson said of me that I favored all believers withdrawing entirely from the political arena, as if I had advocated a return to the catacombs—which was a misreading of my views, but a further confirmation of the danger of seeing everything and every opinion in black and white. We saw this so clearly in the eighties. It was as if only the Moral Majority had all of the truth. Anyone who disagreed with us, even in the remotest way, was suspect.

Only God has all the truth. To the extent that we quote him accurately, we are loaned this truth. But when we begin adding things to his agenda, we diminish his truth and are onto something else entirely. So the wagons are to be circled and the "compromisers" are to be denied even an effort at understanding, balance, and clarification, to say nothing of fellowship. This response is familiar to us because we have seen it before. "Christian leaders" were "God's anointed," and on more than one occasion we heard the warning that one was not to touch God's anointed. The problem with this thinking is that it puts the individuals who believe it and teach it out of the range of accountability and sets them up for the dangers that accompany pride. On numerous occasions we saw people afraid to challenge or hold leaders accountable such as Jim Bakker, Jimmy Swaggart, and a number of others. Perhaps the people feared for their jobs. Perhaps they were afraid of damaging "the cause of Christ." Perhaps they were afraid what would happen to them if they "touched God's anointed."

Underneath Dr. Dobson's highly commendable zeal is a potential zealotry that is eating away at the benefits that can come with rightly applied zeal. In other words, he is working against himself. His and others' increasing zealotry is hampering the very goals he—and we—seek. By threatening to marginalize himself into a fort occupied by only "true believers," he will ensure that he will never succeed in and through the political system. Again, 36 percent of the evangelical vote went to Bill Clinton in the 1996 election, according to a Wirthlin poll,[2] so Dr. Dobson is really leading a force that is a minority within a minority. If he cannot affect policy when associated with the Republican party, what makes him think he will be more effective outside of the GOP?

Zealotry can also divide the very people he seeks to unite. On one visit to Washington, Dr. Dobson spoke to a group of House Republican leaders. Press reports said he was highly critical of the GOP leadership for not doing more on the social issues his organization supports. He implied that these people were traitors to the cause and to their stated convictions.

The members responded defensively that they were doing the best they could, but with an eleven-vote House majority (five after the 1998 election) and President Clinton's huge popularity (well over 60 percent at the time), it was difficult. It was difficult to practice the kind of politics that would advance what the leaders said are their mutual concerns, and it was difficult to gain the necessary majority. The majority has to include Democrats because not all Republicans in that slim majority agree on the social issues. In order to gain those votes, compromises must sometimes be made.

Purists see all compromise as a sell-out, and Dr. Dobson's response to these Republican leaders carried the language of one who felt betrayed. According to a report in the *Washington Post,* House Majority Whip Tom DeLay (R-Texas) told reporters that Dr. Dobson had sent a letter which "deeply hurt my feelings. . . . Dr. Dobson, quite frankly, is one of the principal people that brought me back to Christ when I first came to Congress. Because I saw his video called 'Where's Dad?' and it convicted me because my priorities were with my job and not my family, and it turned me around. So I have the utmost respect for this man."[3]

DeLay said he has been fighting for conservative causes and pointed to a vote he cast shortly after meeting with Dr. Dobson on pro-life legislation. "I stood up and passed a very difficult provision that I think will save babies around the world. He [Dobson] chose to take a pass on that bill. . . . I'll let my Lord judge who is moral."

DeLay added that people who work outside the system should spend a little time inside to get a better understanding and appreciation for what elected people face. He suggested that GOP leaders "do what we did with some of our more aggressive members . . . and that is let them work within the process and see how difficult it is. . . . If we can get Dr. Dobson to come in and help us get the votes . . . I think he will understand what we go through every day."

But zealots frequently understand nothing but their own agendas and their own ways of achieving success. They would rather die in a failed attempt to win all at once than take often-slow steps to advance their cause incrementally. And die they will, as once again it appears that they will try to win it all in a presidential election. In 1998, James

Dobson's representative in Washington, Gary Bauer, was toying with the idea of running for president in 2000. He will be as successful as Pat Robertson was in 1988. It isn't the zeal of the candidate that counts. What counts are many other factors that zealots cannot embrace because all they see is the end and not the means. By not paying attention to what means work, they cannot reach their ultimate goals.

There are times when such zeal is appealing. But in politics it allows the zealot to be painted an extremist. The vast middle, which candidates for public office must win in order to prevail on election day, will not vote for such a person. No person or nation (or horse) can be led where he does not wish to go. As much as social and religious conservatives might wish that the mushy middle was as zealous as they are, it isn't. It is a truism in politics that 40 percent always vote Democrat, 40 percent always vote Republican, and the battle is for the middle 20 percent, who are rarely swayed by the incendiary language that has been used by religious conservatives. If decibel level alone were sufficient to swing this middle 20 percent, we would have done it in the eighties.

Dr. Dobson has also suggested that he may withdraw from the Republican party and take "as many people with me" as he can. The way of third parties or movements outside the established two parties does not have a record of either success or longevity, much less influence. In the twentieth century we have seen Teddy Roosevelt's short-lived Bull Moose Party, the State's Rights Party created to deny black Americans their civil rights, and more recently, the American Party, inspired by then-segregationist George Wallace. Howard Phillips's U.S. Taxpayer's Party, whose candidate Dr. Dobson says he voted for to protest Bob Dole's 1996 presidential candidacy, and Ross Perot's Reform Party are among other splinter groups that have had negligible impact on election results.

In the eighties, we at the Moral Majority were zealous enough to believe that we would do better than all of these because we weren't a party. We were a "movement," a majority that was moral. We believed at the time that we could sufficiently influence the Republican party to stop the social mudslide of immorality and shore up the foundations of the nation through the political process. One of my favorite bumper stickers dreamed up by our opponents was "The Moral Majority Is Neither." Nelson Keener, another Falwell associate, suggested a counter bumper sticker that would say "The Immoral Minority Is Both." The truth was, and is, that the immoral are a majority, including us, because "all have sinned and fall short of the glory of God" (Romans 3:23). Some just practice their immorality more publicly and less repentantly than others.

Author Charles Murray had some insightful thoughts on the idea that politicians and the political system can transform human beings from the top down. In a column for the *Wall Street Journal*, Murray wrote, "The Democrats of 1964 and the activist Republicans of 1998—shall we call them modern Republicans?—share the fatal conceit that lawmakers can engineer the incentives governing human behavior."[4]

Murray is writing about tax credits for stay-at-home mothers, but the principle works in other areas of "social legislation" when there is no clear consensus among the population due to a general moral decline. Critics of this observation—(we know, we were two of them in the eighties)—will point to the Supreme Court's 1954 *Brown vs. Board of Education* ruling that struck down the idea of "separate, but equal" in segregating the races in America's public schools. But as bad as segregation was, the court appealed to a moral code that no longer exists.[5] The justices appealed to that code in order that the American public might be brought back to it, which deep in their hearts they knew was right. The absence of a general acceptance of that code today makes it far more difficult to hold a generation accountable, especially since that generation grew up rejecting the very idea of accountability and personal responsibility.

Murray continues: "The power of incentives to affect behavior is not at issue, nor is the power of government to affect incentives. But just as the information needed to organize an economy is too complex for central economic planners to collect and use, so are the incentives that shape human behavior too complex for central planners to engineer."[6]

It isn't necessary to consider Murray's point about whether tax credits will encourage women to stay at home with their young children instead of working outside the home and putting their kids in daycare. He thinks it will ultimately come to be viewed as an "entitlement" and will have little or no power to achieve its stated goal. Murray's larger point is government's inability to force sufficient numbers of people to do what they don't want to do.

We know about the argument—which we used to make—that all laws are the imposition of someone's morality. While that is true, those laws are largely based on a society's initial, if not ultimate, desire to obey the law. Most people hate the tax code, but most still pay their taxes. If sufficient numbers rebelled against the tax code and against the income tax, there aren't enough jails to contain the violators, and so the laws would have to be changed.

We would like to see Dr. Dobson serve one term in the United States Senate. He says he will never run for elective office, but he should. In his current capacity he is free to hurl ideological lightning bolts. As a member of the Senate he would be forced to compromise— perhaps not his (and our) cherished beliefs—but he would have to adopt different tactics if he were ever to have any hope of reaching his goals. That's the difference between zealotry and zeal. The person engaged in zealotry sees the use of different tactics as spiritual and ideological compromise, which they define as the abandonment of principle. The principled politician (and far too many are not principled) sees compromise as a short-term tactic to reach the same long-term goal. And while he or she knows that some things are beyond compromise, it is important to know when to go to the wall and when not to, always keeping the objective in sight.

Dr. Dobson is critical of "the church" and "weak-kneed" preachers, which clearly reveals his frustrated hope that somehow, some way, the sleeping masses can be mobilized to impose righteousness from the top. *U. S. News and World Report* ran a cover story on Dr. Dobson in its issue of May 4, 1998. Responding to that article, Margie Wickham of Maple Valley, Washington, wrote in a Letter to the Editor, "James Dobson has done mighty things. I listen to his programs, purchase his materials, and generally agree with his position on issues. But I am somewhat frustrated with the ultimatum he gave to the Republican party—more specifically, to the House Republicans. Dobson's one vote is the only one needed to change things at Focus on the Family, but in the U.S. House it takes a majority of 435 votes. A very different situation. Is Dobson willing to throw away the progress—albeit slow to many of us— that the Republicans have made simply because he is impatient with the process? I pray not. Dobson can be most effective for the American people and his ministry by continuing his work to change hearts, one by one."

The shortfall of registered Christian, conservative voters who vote with the Religious Right has not deterred Dr. Dobson or the Christian Coalition, the inheritors of the Moral Majority mantle.

Frankly, the phrase "Christian Coalition" seems more arrogant than the "Moral Majority." At least at Moral Majority we claimed to appeal to a broad spectrum of people, regardless of religious beliefs (though the truth is that most members and all staff were evangelical or fundamental Christians). We could occasionally produce a token Jewish person for appearance's sake.

The problem for religious conservatives is that the numbers aren't there to achieve redemption from the top down. These groups don't have sufficient troops to impose their will. At Moral Majority we believed that there was a "sleeping giant out there" that had to be awakened and, when awake, could reverse the moral and cultural slide. It may be sleeping, but it's not a giant, at least not enough of a giant to be capable of mobilizing enough people to vote for certain candidates to ensure victory. Getting enough people who all believe in the same religious-political agenda and who would vote for a certain candidate and party is an exceedingly difficult task.

The idea of a majority that is moral or a decisive coalition *and* Christian is, and probably has always been, a myth. Many good people who wish America was something else than what it has become have sent money to evangelists and politicians who promise directly or indirectly that they can change things if they can just get another contribution and win the next election. Some enclose petitions that they promise to "take to the White House." Ours were usually left at the gate. Some made it to the White House mail room, where they probably ended up in the "round file" reserved for all such mail.

But no goal can be reached—including the goal of again recognizing the inalienable right to life, even of the unborn—unless the materialism and self-centeredness of the population is reversed. That is why Dr. Dobson's greatest power is not in his focus on politics, but in his Focus on the Family. By trolling for votes and politicians who agree with him, he settles for the good instead of the best. And while there is nothing wrong—and much that is good—about politics, it is not the best. "Why not the best?" Jimmy Carter once asked in a book.[7] Why not, indeed?

So, for Dr. Dobson's comments you will have to listen to his radio program or read his mailings, which will, no doubt, continue to be critical of us. In fact, should his agenda fail, we envision his blaming us because "religious leaders" find it difficult to admit they pursued the wrong strategy. One must always have enemies and excuses as justification for one's failure. It can never be the leader, because the leader always sees himself as right. It is the followers who are wrong, and if it hadn't been for people like us, he might have won. Do you see the destructiveness of this way of thinking? It leads to pride.

It would have been nice to have had a discussion with Dr. Dobson for this book so that all of us—ourselves included—might benefit from his considerable wisdom and experience and, perhaps, even to be held accountable ourselves in case we might have missed something he could have helped us see. It appears that Dr. Dobson has chosen to withdraw from dialogue with believers who disagree with his current political activism.

And so the circle grows smaller, and the number of true believers shrinks, and the last man dies convinced that only he knows and practices the truth, and the kingdom of God is thus diminished because the way of God has been ignored in the pursuit of the will of God by those who claim exclusive knowledge of it.

Our response to Dr. Dobson's political activism has been strong and emphatic. We believe that he and his organization, Focus on the Family, have done more than anyone else or any other organization to strengthen the family in our nation. It is our concern that his current focus on politics will derail and dilute the good he is doing through Focus on the Family. Furthermore, we fear that this focus on politics will help to obscure the central message of the gospel, which is about personal, not political, redemption.

No wonder some people occasionally explain their rejection of God because of the poor example many of us have been. Much of the world can't see Jesus because of what too many have constructed in his way. That any of us might be the cause of another's stumbling qualifies us for having a stone tied around our necks and being cast into the sea (see Mark 9:42). Before evil characteristics are attributed to Satan, he is first called "subtle" or "crafty." Could it be that the very strategy of Satan is to corrupt religious conservatives by luring them into the trap of focusing on political kingdoms instead of the eternal kingdom?

Dr. Robert Norris is the pastor of the Fourth Presbyterian Church in Bethesda, Maryland, a suburb of Washington, D.C. In a sermon on May 24, 1998, Dr. Norris spoke on the subject "When the Old Gods Fail." His text was 1 Samuel 5:1–4. As I re-read the text, I realized that politics has become for religious conservatives a false god. Dr. Norris called the biblical story one of the saddest moments in the long history of Israel. He related how the people of God had forgotten their God, and as a result, they had declined politically, militarily, and religiously. They had even been conquered by their old and traditional enemies, the Philistines. The Israelites finally resolved to rid themselves of the Philistine yoke, so they gathered an army and challenged the Philistines to battle.

In the ensuing battle, the children of Israel were defeated. They met together to hold a council of war to discover, if possible, the cause of their defeat. In the midst of that council, one suggested that the defeat had been brought about because they had rushed to attack the Philistines without taking the Ark of the Lord—which they regarded as a kind of mascot. Had they taken it with them, this man said, they would probably have had good luck and would have succeeded. That is what the Israelites proceeded to do the next time. They gathered another army, took the ark with them, and challenged the Philistines to a second battle. This time the Israelites' army was not only defeated but completely routed, and the Philistines captured the Ark of the Covenant and took it away with them.

> Then they carried the ark into Dagon's temple and set it beside Dagon. When the people of Ashdod rose early the next day, there was Dagon, fallen on his face on the ground before the ark of the LORD! They took Dagon and put him back in his place. But the following morning when they rose, there was Dagon, fallen on his face on the ground before the ark of the LORD! His head and hands had been broken off and were lying on the threshold; only his body remained. That is why to this day neither the priests of Dagon nor any others who enter Dagon's temple at Ashdod step on the threshold (1 Samuel 5:2–5).

The Philistines didn't destroy the Ark of the Lord after they captured it. Instead, they argued that it was valuable and had brought success to Israel on many occasions; therefore they determined that it might be of help to them in the future, so they decided to put it in the temple of their own god, Dagon. They paid a kind of compliment to the God of Israel, who they thought was in this box, so they placed it beside Dagon on the shelf. Having done this, they began to celebrate their great victory. They had conquered their traditional enemies, they had routed their army, and they had captured the god of their enemies. To them the world seemed to be perfect.

Then we read an extraordinary history. The next morning, the keeper of the temple of Dagon, while making the rounds, found to his astonishment that Dagon had fallen to the ground immediately beneath the Ark of the Lord. He couldn't understand this, so he took the image again and placed him back next to the ark of the Lord. The people turned once more to their victory celebration. The next day, Dagon had again fallen to the ground, but this time, both the hands and the head were cut off. Nothing was left of the image of Dagon except a stump of a torso.

This holds, I believe, a very important lesson for the Christian community, for it talks about the nature of true religion. Our world is a place where the God of the Christians is often seen defeated, routed by the enemy, and captured, his cause seemingly destroyed.

Why is it that God's people should ever thus be defeated by modern-day Philistines? If we focus more on the story of the children of Israel, we find that when they were defeated, it was never due to the strength of the enemy. It was due to their own internal weakness.

When the children of Israel were in a right relationship to God, they triumphed. The challenge comes to each of us that we must depend on the Lord as he calls us back to himself, and depend on his power. He calls us to end our self-reliance, no matter what form it takes.

Too many of us in the conservative Christian community are trying to fight the Philistines using the wrong weapons. It has resulted in our not only being defeated, but humiliated. Even as Gary Bauer publicly muses about the possibility of running for president, my journalism colleagues are snickering.

If we truly desire to transform the world in which we live, we must look to God, his power, and the might of his Holy Spirit. Otherwise, we will continue to bring dishonor and embarrassment on the high cause to which we claim allegiance.

TEN

LOSING WHERE WE OUGHT TO WIN

And so, in the end, the Rev. Jerry Falwell's Moral Majority showed us the short and tempestuous life span of a James River flood. It rose up suddenly, thrashed around for a while, and receded, leaving little tangible evidence of its passing.

Darrell Laurant, columnist
June 23, 1989

As conservative Christians wage their battle against political evil, we are losing perhaps the most important battle of them all: the battle for our own. Sadly, the faith that could transform a nation has become so diverted by our fascination with politics that our own children are being captured by the enemy.

Josh McDowell, in his book *Right from Wrong,* serves up some frightening statistics about our children. These are not "other people's children," but "church youth," those young people who should be hearing a standard for truth and order in their lives, but who no longer can discern right from wrong. McDowell writes,

> The reason, then, that youth who do not accept objective truth are more likely to lie, cheat, or get drunk, is that they are seeing their choices through faulty lenses; they have embraced a world view about truth that blinds them to the difference between right and wrong, the difference between the counterfeits and the real thing.[1]

McDowell cites figures from the liberal Children's Defense Fund and from the book *13th Generation* by Neil Howe and Bill Strauss to show what happens to young people who are not taught, and do not accept, an objective standard for truth: 36 percent are more likely to lie to their parents; 48 percent are more likely to cheat on an exam; 74 percent are more likely to watch MTV and ingest its daily diet of promiscuous sex, violence, and rebellion against authority.[2] They are two times more likely to try to physically hurt someone; two times more likely to watch a pornographic film; two times more likely to get drunk; two and one-quarter times more likely to steal; three times more likely to use illegal drugs; and six times more likely to attempt suicide, the number one cause of death among teens.[3]

McDowell has also observed that the behavior of children reared in Christian homes is shockingly similar to their non-Christian counterparts in matters of alcohol and drug use and premarital sex.[4]

It seems to us that the best way to ensure a future society that reflects Christian values is to make sure the next generation does not make the same mistakes as their parents. Instead of putting all our eggs in the politics basket, Christians ought to be taking a long look at what is going on in their homes and communities. While wrong decisions and rebellion can occur in any family, we have the power to improve the odds that the decisions will be the right ones if we seize the power and opportunities we currently have.

This power has nothing to do with government and even less to do with politics. We seem to be asking the government and politics to do for us what we should be doing for ourselves. If we succumb to the lure of a government "quick fix" and absolve ourselves of personal responsibility, we will be no better (and be no better off) than the big-government liberals we so often criticize for turning to government as a first resource and not a last resort.

If people who want to "reclaim America" or bring "revival" to the country try to do it on the cheap, they will never succeed. As long as it is someone else's problem, it will remain the problem of all of us. Radical personal action is called for, not radical action involving government.

The most important first step in reshaping our nation is that we must keep our marriages together. All the sociological research, including that conducted by "secular" sociologists, shows that the number one cause of many of our social problems, including overflowing prisons, is divorce. A child who learns conditional love from his parents will display the effects of that conditional love for the rest of his life.

Jimmy Carter believed, and often said, that the family is paramount and that it can be the beginning and end of many problems. Even though he later convened a "White House Conference on Families" in which gays and alternative "family" structures were considered alongside traditional families, the power of his initial statements rings true.

Carter's first campaign speech following his nomination dealt with this subject. On August 3, 1976, Carter told a crowd in Manchester, New Hampshire, "The family was the first church. The family was the first school. The family was the first government. If we want less government, we must have stronger families, for government steps in by necessity when families have failed."[5]

When Carter visited the Department of Housing and Urban Development, he told employees, "Those of you who are living in sin, I hope you will get married." The crowd laughed, but Carter added, "I think it's very important that we have stable family lives. I am serious about that."[6]

The one common denominator of a huge majority of prison inmates is that they came from broken homes. Other than Paul Harvey's salute to golden wedding anniversary "survivors," there is little in the culture that affirms those who stay together. We are far more likely to observe the multiple marriages of celebrities or observe people living together or having babies out of wedlock.

So, as simple as it may sound, we need to hear more preaching and more role modeling by those who claim that marriage is a one-time thing.

The second step, after keeping marriages together, is offering our children a sound education. None of us feeds a child a healthy breakfast and then sends him off to a public school that has a leaky roof, cracked walls, poor electrical wiring, and asbestos in the cafeteria food. Yet that is tantamount to what many of us do when we send our children to schools that teach them (by default or directly) that there is no God, that they are accidents in a random universe, that their nearest relative is down at the zoo and that's why they like bananas on their cereal, that sex is something to be enjoyed strictly for the pleasurable feelings it produces, and that there is no right or wrong about premarital, extramarital, or homosexual sex, and that there is nothing to be preferred about America's way of life, including her government, her economy, her history, or her religious freedom. In the multicultural, diverse nation that America has become, we are no better than any other nation on earth—but we may be worse.

In Ray Bradbury's book *Fahrenheit 451*, published in 1953, the fire captain explains the key to the establishment of a totalitarian state: "Heredity and environment are funny things. . . . The home environment can undo a lot you try to do at school. That's why we've lowered the kindergarten age year after year until now we're almost snatching them from the cradle."[7] More than forty-five years after the book was published, it can now be said that the school environment is undoing a lot of what is taught at home and at church.

In one way or another, many public school children are getting this profoundly secularized and politically driven message. They get it minimally through textbooks and maximally from films and visitors to schools whom parents may never hear about. Those visitors come from gay and lesbian organizations that tell the students that 10 percent of them are homosexual. They come from Planned Parenthood and similar groups that tell them how to use condoms and, should the girls get pregnant, where to have an abortion without their parents' knowledge or consent. The inference is that they cannot trust their parents and should confer with Planned Parenthood "counselors," or the school nurse or school counselor.[8]

All of this is happening with children at younger and younger ages. Some states have mandatory sex education classes beginning in kindergarten. The goal is to strip them of their innocence early so that by the time they reach puberty they will be more receptive to what the government educators want to teach them.

To those who say we need to be representatives, or "ambassadors," for our views and values in the government schools, I respond: How many child ambassadors do nations send out? They must first be trained and equipped. It is the same with the military. We don't send our basic trainees to other countries to learn their values and tactics;

we train them at our facilities. With respect to schools, why don't we who are church-going, value-conscious citizens see ourselves as upholding the standard of truth and bring the government school kids to our schools instead of sending our children to theirs?

What makes us think we are training and equipping the next generation to think and behave in ways that will benefit them and their country by sending them into "education camps" where they are taught lies? No nation can be reclaimed when the next generation is being taught the ideas and values that have brought us to our present predicament.

In practical terms we are calling for greater support of private and charter schools that will instill basic Judeo-Christian values in their students. Personally, every Christian parent needs to consider the possibility of sending his or her children to private schools, even if it means financial pain. Collectively, we can support legislation that makes vouchers available for parents who want to move their children from public to private schools.

Additionally, Christians with children in public schools need to play an active role in the local schools. This does not mean storming into a school with a list of demands, but having a winsome presence at PTA and school board meetings, volunteering to help with school activities, and developing relationships with the school's leaders. It also means making sure your children have regular religious instruction through your church and in your home. It is naïve—and therefore dangerous—to expect a public school to do your job as a parent.

The third "radical" action may be the hardest of all, but it is equally as critical as the others. Television, music, the Internet, and other forms of audio and video "entertainment" must be tightly controlled or dismissed altogether from the home. We confine fire to the fireplace so it will not burn the house down. The cultural fires spreading across America must also be contained and controlled if they are not to burn those dearest to us.

Here again, the temptation is to ask government to regulate the media. While we believe that the government has a responsibility to uphold generally accepted standards of decency, there is no assurance that government standards will be the same as your own. Furthermore, conservatives have rightly argued that government should interfere as little as possible with our lives, believing that individuals and their families should do the important work of teaching values. So when we say that entertainment should be controlled, we are challenging parents to make sure their homes are not infiltrated with material that will pollute the minds and souls of their children.

When it is possible, we need to avoid being a two-income family—at least in the early childhood years. Otherwise, children have to be cared for in day-care centers that, no matter how "good," can never substitute for a parent—usually the mother—in the home. This will require a radical restructuring in our thinking and a new perspective by men on the value of their wives working at home and helping to build parental values into their children.

In a background paper provided by the White House for its 1998 childcare proposals subsidizing day care, one page described with hard numbers the way Americans care for their children. Michael Kelly, a senior writer for the *National Journal*, described it as a "depressing document."

In the *Washington Post*, Kelly makes some profound points that should be seriously considered by those who believe it doesn't matter where children spend their days so long as they are receiving "quality care." He says, "In 1995, nearly 13 million—more than half—of the nation's 21 million preschool children were receiving child care from someone other than their parents. Of children under the age of one, 45 percent were under such care. And these infants and toddlers and preschoolers are, on the average, in child care for a large chunk of their little lives; a 1990 study found that more than half of child-care children were in child care for 35 hours a week or more. Of school-age kids, every week an estimated 5 million come home to empty houses."[9]

Our pursuit of wealth and material things is not bringing these children happiness and stability in their formative years, but anxiety that leads to depression and antisocial behavior in their adolescent years.

Kelly, who is no more a radical than his publication is radical, continues, "We are engaged in a vast and radical experiment on our children. We are betting, against the wisdom of the ages and the lessons of our own childhoods, that it does not matter if parents leave to others the quotidian business of raising their young. The increasing evidence is that this is wrong. While it may sometimes be necessary for both parents to work full-time, it is undeniably better for children that they be raised in their homes, mostly by their own parents."

Many nights on the television news we hear of outrages involving day-care centers. As the White House's own data sheet notes, children in child-care programs are not, in a large number of cases, well cared for. And what constitutes good care? Is it simply living up to safety and fire code regulations, or are we concerned about the stability of the child and the values and virtues (or lack of them) being worked into our children while we pursue the almighty dollar?

One four-year study of child-care centers rated only one out of seven as good quality. Poor children fare worse than other children. According to one report, their "health and safety" is often compromised.

If the federal government wants to do families a favor, it should tax them less so they won't feel the pressure to work to pay their taxes. Instead of throwing tax money at the day-care industry (which the industry lobbyists clearly want), families with young children should enjoy tax breaks to allow one of them to stay home and be with their own children.

In some homes both parents work out of "necessity," but for the sake of our children we need to redefine what is "necessary" and what are simply our "wants." Wants and needs are two different things. As former First Lady Barbara Bush observed at a speech at Wellesley College, "Mothers and fathers, if you have children, they must come first. Our success as a country, your success as a family, depends not on what happens in the White House, but on what happens in your house."[10]

We realize that two incomes are sometimes necessary and that single parents who do not want to accept welfare must find ways to care for their children while they work. If some Christian businesspeople wanted to do something profound and effective in transforming culture, they might consider developing a day-care center in their business for their single-parent employees, or offering flex-time or job-share opportunities so that single parents can be home when their children arrive from school. If churches want to help save the family while at the same time influencing a new generation, they could offer child care for single parents in their neighborhood.

It really becomes a question of how badly we want to reclaim our country. Redemption can't be achieved with a mail-in coupon or a contribution to a religious broadcaster, television evangelist, or hired staff person at church. It will cost us personally and profoundly. But the value of what we receive can be priceless.

ELEVEN

LEARNING FROM OUR MISTAKES

Why should quiet ruminants like you and I have been born in such a ghastly age? Let me palliate the apparent selfishness of this complaint by asserting that there *are* people who, while not of course liking actual suffering when it falls to their own share, *do* really like the "stir," the "sense of great issues." Lord! how I loathe great issues. "Dynamic," I think, is one of the words invented by this age which sums up what it likes and I abominate. Could one start a stagnation party—which at general elections would boast that during its term of office *no* event of the least importance had taken place?

C. S. Lewis, in a letter to his brother, Warren
March 22, 1940

 Most children learn after unsuccessful attempts to fit a square peg in a round hole that it isn't going to work, and *cal thomas* they either look for the round peg or direct their attention to another game. It appears that too many religious conservatives have not learned from twenty years of attempts to fit the square peg of the kingdom not of this world into the round hole that is the kingdom of this world.

A front-page story in the *New York Times* by religion editor Laurie Goodstein told of a meeting held earlier that month by "the Godfather of social conservatives," Paul Weyrich, and about twenty-five prominent leaders of the religious and political right. "They fume that they had been used and abused, like some cheap date," wrote Goodstein.[1]

What did they expect? They have been dealing with politicians, who take as much as they can get from every interest group and give back just enough to keep them on a string so that they might stay in power. Such behavior makes "cheap date" a perfect metaphor.

Those religious-political alchemists complained that they had been faithful foot-soldiers for the Republicans, doing the grunt work necessary to get any candidate elected, from knocking on doors to staffing phone banks. And what did they get for their efforts? They got nothing, or little more than lip service.

Frustration and cries of betrayal are what you hear coming from the camps of those who expected something far different from the Republicans. By now, they believed as recently as ten years ago, abortion should have been outlawed, pornography at least under control, and family relationships respected and embraced again.

Gary Bauer, president of the Family Research Council, an offshoot of James Dobson's Focus on the Family, also served in the Department of Education and the domestic policy office in the Reagan administration. Bauer told the *Times,* "There is virtually nothing to show for an 18-year commitment."[2]

Tom Jipping, who oversees federal court nominees for an organization called Judicial Watch, said, "What I hear these days is a huge dissatisfaction with the assumption made twenty years ago that the Republican Party was the best vehicle for achieving public policy goals."[3]

Although the Republican party has consistently adopted a socially conservative platform at every presidential nomination convention since 1980, and though increasing numbers of Republicans are promoting legislation to end late-term abortions, grant a $500-per-child tax credit to families, and control pornography on the Internet, it isn't enough for Christians who want politics to change the world.

Many believe the GOP is moving at glacier speed when it ought to be operating like a Japanese bullet train. While moderate Republicans scream about the Religious Right having too much power, leaders of the Religious Right complain that they have too little. Allowing their main concerns to be placed on the back burner, the conservatives believe, has led to the burning of the pan, and they are tired of it. Instead of using this futility and frustration as an indication that they are using the wrong strategy, they search instead for a new version of the strategy that has already failed and cannot succeed, given the moral condition of the nation.

In mid-1998, House Speaker Newt Gingrich was said to have struck a deal with several conservative leaders for a vote on three pieces of legislation. One was the Religious Freedom Amendment, which conservative Christians hoped would allow the reintroduction of prayer into public schools. The second was a measure that would allow parents to use vouchers to send their children to private schools, including religious institutions. The third was a bill that would eliminate funding for the National Endowment for the Arts. All these measures pressed by the Religious Right have failed in one form or another in the past, and the president has shown he has the votes to sustain any veto should anything emerge from Congress he doesn't like. The big issues, including abortion rights and gay rights, will not be addressed, or they will be addressed only at the edges, because the religious conservatives don't have the votes in Congress and don't have sufficient public opinion on their side to get legislation on these issues through Congress.

In an interview Gingrich indicated that it isn't just a matter of zeal on his part or on the part of those on the outside who wish he would do more. "[Conservatives] haven't taken the House," he noted. "This is a center-right House, not a hard-right House. To get what they want in life, the conservatives need 80 more conservative members and a conservative president. So they're naturally dissatisfied. Since I am the Speaker of the House, I am the legitimate target of their dissatisfaction."[4] But Gingrich is no longer the Speaker, resigning after the poor GOP showing in the 1998 election. The future of social issues in Congress is even more problematic, given the party's goal of sticking to issues that tend to unite rather than divide, leading up to the 2000 election.

The leaders outside the power structure have laid out a strategy to put aside their past rivalries and form what they call an "independent political force" that they hope will influence those on the inside. Their goal is to speak with one voice, line up behind one presidential candidate, and collaborate on finding state and local candidates to champion their agenda. The problem is that anyone acceptable to this group is likely to be branded an "extremist," a strategy that has worked quite well in the past for liberal Democrats.

Disgraced Clinton political adviser Dick Morris (but not disgraced enough to keep his toes out of the political waters) wrote in the conservative magazine *The Weekly Standard* that while he expected Republicans to pick up seats in the House and Senate in the 1998 congressional races (they didn't, as it turns out), "Al Gore will win handily in 2000. Voters want split government. They understand the need for the two parties to check and balance each other. Having seen the GOP try to slash Medicaid and the Democrats try to raise taxes, they understand that competition improves and disciplines politicians."[5] This prognosis could change with the impeachment of President Clinton as 1998 was drawing to a close.

That is a sobering thought. It means that after more than two decades of political activism, conservative Christians might be faced with a Gore administration that would name very liberal justices to the Supreme Court whose ideology in favor of abortion rights, gay rights, and environmental issues could dominate for forty years. Maybe that's what it will take before conservative Christians realize they are not going to enact their agendas through government alone, or even primarily through government.

Modern politics has become so corrupting that virtually every political movie coming out of Hollywood in recent years has viewed politics through a thick lens of cynicism. The film *Wag the Dog*[6] is about a marriage of convenience between a political spinner and a Hollywood producer who team up to get the public's attention off a sex scandal involving a president and a young girl. *Primary Colors*[7] traces a not-so-subtle retelling of the 1992 Clinton-Gore campaign. Both carry a simple message: Unless you play dirty, you can't win, and if you are a nice guy who plays by ethical rules, you will surely lose.

Is this the kind of process in which conservative Christians ought to immerse themselves? And if so—if they must descend to this level of politics—can they really be said to be serving a greater kingdom and a greater King? The answer to the biblical question, "When the foundations are being destroyed, what can the righteous do?"[8] is not to paint the house that has collapsed due to the destroyed foundation. The answer is to rebuild the foundation.

Legal changes are necessary, but history shows they often come after the transformation of a culture, not before. Not always, but usually. The change we seek is more deeply rooted than the legislative process. Organizing our will and our finances around politics is like a financial strategy that is based on high-risk investments such as junk bonds.

The way in which culture is changed is not by adopting new versions of a strategy that has not worked and cannot work. (If it could, we wouldn't need God, because we could do it all in our own strength.) The way a culture is reclaimed is through people living by different values. The challenge of those who claim to be followers of Jesus Christ is, first and foremost, to be visible evidence of the invisible kingdom of God in our midst. It is to act and think like the One we claim to follow. Did Jesus appeal to Caesar for power or favor?

Fellow syndicated columnist William Murchison of the *Dallas Morning News* wrote a piece in which he spoke of a strategy that has a proven record of success. Murchison wrote in the aftermath of the Promise Keepers event that drew an estimated (by some) one million men to Washington for repentance, reconciliation, and prayer in the fall of 1997.

He noted that the secular left believed there was a hidden political agenda and would not consider that Promise Keepers was exactly what it claimed to be—apolitical. Then he wrote, "The variety of life, outside its political expressions, is rich and infinite. The problem is getting the politically obsessed to understand as much. Among modernity's high crimes is that of pigeonholing people by their imputed relationship to the political order. This exasperating habit wrongly puts politics at the center of human affairs."[9]

Murchison then quoted approvingly a United Parcel Service driver, who told the *New York Times,* "We can't change people through politics. Our job is to have a lifestyle of integrity. I do it with my customers on my route, with my bosses. I can't call in sick if I'm not sick. My bosses know that."[10]

When you compare this attitude with the most committed political activity, which behavior do you think will have the greater impact? Favoring political activity over personal integrity as the best means for changing society "would have to rest on the assumption that human laws shape destiny, when the whole of human history refutes that proposition," wrote Murchison.

> Dr. Samuel Johnson's couplet comes powerfully to mind: "How small of all that human hearts endure / that part which kings or laws can cause or cure."
>
> Modernity sees politics as secular salvation. The Promise Keepers see right through that great heresy and moral imposition. They don't believe for a minute that the collective power of society is perpetually available for banishing human vexations.
>
> How many fewer problems has the United States—has the human race—got in the era of big government than back when, for inspiration and entertainment, we looked to preachers and poets rather than to wielders of state power? The sheer quantity of modern afflictions—centering on alienation and moral rot—is hardly less than ninety-odd years ago, when Theodore Roosevelt began battling economic inequalities through the instrumentality of government power.[11]

Harry Blamires begins an extraordinary book, *The Christian Mind,* with the simple statement: "There is no Christian mind." This, rather than failure of political organization and political strategies, is at the root of our difficulties. "As a thinking being," he writes, "the modern Christian has succumbed to secularization. He accepts religion—its morality, its worship; but he rejects the religious view of life, the view which sets all earthly issues within the context of the eternal."[12]

Too often believers treat their faith as just one of the many things competing for their attention. They take it seriously, but it is compartmentalized. It does not pervade every aspect of living. Yet, if the Bible they often cite as justification for their agenda and tactics is true, it must be more compelling, even more radical, than a guidebook for reaching a comfortable level of societal privilege and influence.

We do not pretend to virtue or pretend that we have the revealed word from God, other than what he has already revealed in Scripture. We speak out of our personal experience of trying to change society through the political process. Out of this experience have come some understanding and some recommendations. They are certainly not exhaustive, but we hope they will generate vigorous dialogue in churches and Christian organizations and homes around the nation.

First, more of us should shut up! In the whirl of busy days, and amid the flood of information, we must find time to be quiet.

During the fourth century in Egypt, a group of men known as the Desert Fathers went to the wilderness to confront themselves and worship God. Their first rule was simple: "Apply yourself to silence." Their motive was not escape, but reflection.

Stillness is the only tool we have to suffuse our activities with thought. It is the way we can step back from the whirl and understand rather than simply accept.

William Wilberforce, whose life and example has been discussed elsewhere, said he spent half an hour a day in prayer, reflection, and quiet. But he added that on days that were particularly busy and rushed—when he had no time at all—he needed to spend a full hour.

Those of us who consider ourselves conservative Christians—especially those who have leadership—need to spend less time talking and more time listening to the God we serve.

Second, we need to look back. We must recover lost respect for tradition, history, and the source of law. The past has much to teach us. We are not the first people to be shocked at declining cultural mores. How did others respond? Which strategies and behavior succeeded, and which failed? In commenting on the deplorable social conditions in Corinth, the apostle Paul wrote of purifying the church that was being polluted by the world's thinking and behavior patterns. His agenda had nothing to do with cleaning up the culture. He didn't form a group of "religious conservatives" to demand respect and new laws from the ruling authorities. He knew that followers of Christ would never shape their world if they weren't first shaped by their Master.

The technological society, by definition, values only the "new," though there is really nothing new under the sun (see Ecclesiastes 1). It accepts a sort of chronological snobbery that dismisses the past as pre-scientific and backward. But this attitude cuts us off from the only source of real insight that can bring us wisdom. The moral debates have not changed. To approach complex issues without the companionship of ideas from earlier times is an act of hubris. It is the arrogance of believing in the self-sufficiency of our own small stock of private rationality.

Then, the church must stand firm. If people who claim to follow Jesus are to act as rocks in the midst of swirling change—if they are to bring eternal perspectives to shifting debates—they must be sure of their identity, which is not rooted in politics or the power games of this world. And, by the way, that identity is not only about knowing who they are, but what the wider culture thinks when looking at them. Are they known for "loving one another" and obeying the commands of Jesus, or are they known as petitioners in the corridors of power, standing no higher than others with grievances they seek to have redressed by the state?

If they are but another voice in the crowd, their power comes only from the ability to shout down the others—and they shall never prevail, because after they shout them down, the others will assemble a larger crowd next time and shout them down. And the contest becomes a never-ending struggle for what is presumed to be "power," but is not.

The church as Jesus established it is not an institution, but a people in whom he lives and works. Instead of a channel through which he can flow, some have turned it into a reservoir that stores up water—or worse, an institution that must be preserved. What a cynic once said about marriage could easily be said of the contemporary church: "Marriage is a wonderful institution, but who wants to live in an institution?"

The church has a source of authority and standards beyond politics, beyond the tides of passing fashion. It bears witness to a transcendent vision. Its first purpose is not to change the world, but to obey its Author and Head. And this, paradoxically, is what the world most needs.

Is there a better strategy and a better way than the failed attempts of the past and present to force a political party to do our bidding?

There is, but those who adopt it must know they will have great difficulty raising money in support of such a strategy and will probably not be asked, initially at least, to appear on the Sunday talk shows or be quoted in the pages of the *New York Times*.

The agenda begins with justice—not a justice rooted in "just deserts," but a justice that comes from a radical redemption of society, which itself flows from a radical redemption of individuals. Flawed people with flawed thinking and flawed tactics cannot heal a flawed culture.

In the end, each of us finds that justice is not enough. In the end, everyone is forced to hope—not for what they deserve—but for a mercy they've never earned.

From the beginning, redemption was a Christian revolution and a Christian scandal. It turns our society's normal rules, conventions, and expectations upside down. It violates every form of rigid moralism. It offends every form of human pride.

So at the outset we must confront the awesome equality of sin and redemption. We are accustomed to sorting our sins. We put them in a comfortable ranking. Pride or avarice—these are the sins of polite company. Prostitution, drug abuse, abortion, and robbery—these are sins of a lower class. But in God's accounting, this division is false. There is no moral distinction between the sins of the bedroom and the sins of the boardroom; between the crimes of mean streets and the crimes of Wall Street; between someone who sells his or her body and someone who sells his or her soul.

The world knows through experience that most people are sinners, though they prefer less "judgmental" words. They prefer words that have been stripped of moral judgment and do not lead to accountability, confession of guilt, and repentance. The Bible teaches, with far more wisdom and authority, that all people are sinners, not "dysfunctional."

This leads to the most radical teaching of all—a teaching that produces a frontal assault on our moral sensibilities. That is, the repentant prostitute is more pure in God's eyes than the proud banker. The transformed drug addict is more pious than the self-righteous socialite.

A volunteer who works in some of New York's worst ghettoes made this point: "I work daily with those whose crimes are nauseating to any reasonable person. The stink of sin would be unbearable but for the historical reality, the moral reality, of the Cross, which reduces all of us to the common ground of sinners who are equally deserving of hell and equally needing the mercy of God. And in the Cross is redemption."

That moral reality forces us to descend from the commanding heights of self-righteous judgment. It puts us on the same moral level as those we condescend to serve. It makes us very uncomfortable. But comfort is not the goal. C. S. Lewis reminds us, "I didn't go to religion to make me happy. I always knew a bottle of port would do that. If you want a religion to make you feel really comfortable, I certainly don't recommend Christianity."[13]

A belief in redemption, rather than a faith in reformation of the existing order, requires us to see the world differently—to see beyond the cold demands of justice. John Wesley wrote, "A poor wretch cries to me for alms: I look and see him covered with dirt and rags. But through these rags I see that he has an immortal spirit, made to know, and love, and dwell with God to eternity. I see, through these rags, that he is purpled over with the blood of Christ. The courtesy, therefore, which I feel and show toward him is a mixture of the honor and love which I bear to the offspring of God; the purchase of his son's blood, and the candidate for immortality."

Every human soul that crosses our path—even those who violate our peace—is a candidate for immortality. We are given by God a definition of human dignity that cannot be destroyed by a drug, a disease, a lifestyle, or an ideology. It is an attitude that Christian ethicist Paul Ramsey summarized with bluntness: "Call no man vile for whom Christ died."

A few years ago, Mother Teresa visited Anacostia—one of the worst neighborhoods in Washington, D.C. It is, in some parts, a panorama of pain and squalor. She had come to build a shelter.

Walking through the neighborhood, she was surrounded by reporters. One reporter cynically asked her, "What do you really hope to accomplish here?"

Mother Teresa replied with a smile, "The joy of loving and being loved."

Another reporter suggested, "That takes a lot of money, doesn't it?"

She answered, "No . . . it takes a lot of sacrifice."

Mother Teresa went on to say, "Do something for someone else . . . something that goes beyond the realm of a gift, and into the category of a sacrifice."

One of the most difficult things to sacrifice is the division of race and class. But here we have an example. Jesus did not teach the ethics of the country club. He violated every social convention. He dined with prostitutes and tax collectors. He scandalized the religious leaders of his day. There is no record of his ever meeting with a government official, except at his illegal "trial" on trumped-up charges instigated by false witnesses. His righteousness was never self-righteous.

Jesus fathered a revolution that began with the forgotten, the outcast, and the despised—a revolution, after all, that started in a stable, not a palace—and he ended his earthly life in a borrowed tomb.

French theologian Jacques Ellul wrote, "Until we have really understood the actual plight of our contemporaries and we have heard their cry of anguish, until we have shared their suffering both physical and spiritual, and their despair and desolation, then we shall be able to proclaim the word of God, but not until then."

Is this the first image that comes to mind when the world looks at modern "Christians," that they care most for the outcast? Too often, it is an image of close association to the "in-cast" and a courting in the corridors of "power" of those who really have no power at all.

Charles Colson tells the disturbing story of a pastor who was involved for several years in counseling an inmate at a local prison. Unexpectedly, the prisoner gained an early release. His first call in freedom was to the pastor who had ministered to him. "You're out!" the pastor said. "Well, good luck—maybe we'll see you sometime."

The former inmate got one message: He wasn't welcome at the pastor's church. It was one thing to minister in a prison. It was something else to welcome him in a "respectable" congregation.

Consider a story that took place in New York City several years ago. During a hard winter, the city's homeless shelters became filled to overflowing. Then-Mayor Ed Koch appealed to the city's religious leaders for help. He estimated that if every house of worship would take just ten people, an emergency would be alleviated.

The reaction from many churches was to look for excuses. The spokesman for one denomination commented, "It is a very complex situation and the remedy will be complex." Another said, "There are problems of implementation in many churches and synagogues. During the winter, many turn their heat off at night." When the test came, many New York churches were not prepared. They wanted to help the poor—but they wanted to give a gift, not make a sacrifice.

I am reminded of a quote by teacher-preacher Warren Wiersbe: "We have too many people who have plenty of medals and no scars."

Certainly there is a cost involved. Sometimes it is a price that is never repaid. Sometimes this kind of sacrifice is rewarded with abuse and betrayal by those for whom it is made.

Our challenge is not to bring pressure through new strategies on the Republican party. Rather, it is to bring reflection, a respect for history, and the standards of faith to the whirl of information and the advance of technology. This is the way we can refuse to be swept along in a tide of mindless change. This is the gift we offer to a culture in need. This is the way to recover the wisdom we have lost in knowledge.

G. K. Chesterton wrote, "We often read nowadays of the valor or audacity with which some rebel attacks a hoary tyranny or an antiquated superstition. There is not really any courage at all in attacking hoary or antiquated things, any more than in offering to fight one's grandmother. The really courageous man is he who defies tyrannies young as the morning and superstitions fresh as the first flowers."

If things change for the better, they will not change because the Religious Right manages to out-muscle what I have called the pagan left. It will come, if it comes at all, "'Not by might nor by power, but by my Spirit,' says the LORD Almighty" (Zechariah 4:6).

TWELVE

LET THE CHURCH BE THE CHURCH

The court, apprehending that there is too great a neglect of discipline in the churches ... and does therefore solemnly recommend it unto the respective elders and brethren of the several churches throughout this jurisdiction to take effectual course for reformation herein.

Whereas there is manifest pride openly appearing amongst us in that long hair, like women's hair, is worn by some men ... and the County Courts are hereby authorized to proceed against such delinquents either by admonition, fine, or correction according to their good discretion.

General Court of Massachusetts, 1675
As quoted in Edmond S. Morgan, ed., *Puritan Political Ideas*
(Bobbs-Merrill, 1965), 227

ed dobson In the spring of 1987, I resigned from my positions at Liberty University, Moral Majority, and Thomas Road Baptist Church in Lynchburg, Virginia. I accepted the position of pastor of Calvary Church in Grand Rapids, Michigan. That April, I drove our family to Grand Rapids for the first time. After checking into the Holiday Inn, we drove over to the church. There, parked in front of the church, we sat in our 1978 Pontiac Bonneville and prayed together that God would bless our new ministry. Later that day I returned to the church alone and knelt at the steps of the platform for an extended time of personal prayer. I rededicated my life to the Lord and asked for wisdom as I assumed the responsibilities of pastor.

Over the next several months I reexamined my own life in light of what it meant to be a pastor and *only* a pastor. I was no longer the editor of a magazine. I was no longer a college administrator. I was no longer a board member of the Moral Majority. I was no longer a traveling speaker and lecturer on moral and political issues. For fourteen and a half years I had been an assistant to Jerry Falwell. I had worn many hats and had been involved in a broad range of ministries. But now I was "just" a pastor. "What does this really mean?" I asked.

The first decision I made was that I would avoid the press as much as possible. I wanted to go about the work of being a pastor without the glaring attention of the media spotlight. Second, I decided that political involvement would hinder my ministry as a pastor. Therefore I would avoid all political entanglements. I would not attend either Republican or Democrat events. I would not march for or against anything. I was convinced that as a pastor I was called to reach Republicans and Democrats and Independents with the gospel. I was called to reach pro-life people and pro-choice people. I was called to reach pro-gay and anti-gay people. If I engaged in public political activities, I ran the risk of alienating the very people I was called to reach.

Third, I decided to focus on teaching the Bible. I would not get off on tangents but would consistently teach the Bible verse by verse. Over the years I have tried to do this. In teaching the Bible one cannot avoid the moral issues of our day. So, for example, as I have taught, I have dealt with the fact that life is a gift from God and that it begins at conception. To abort a baby is the taking of a human life. Or again, sexuality is a gift from God and is to be enjoyed within the commitment of life-long heterosexual marriage, and all expressions of our sexuality outside this principle are sinful. Keeping the pulpit free of politics does not mean keeping it free of clear, biblical, moral teaching.

Fourth, I decided that we are to love people unconditionally just as God loved us. I decided that my ministry would not be one of condemnation. I sought to follow Jesus, who said, "For God did not send his Son into the world to condemn the world, but to save the world through him" (John 3:17). I longed to be known as one who preaches a message of love and forgiveness, not a message of hate and condemnation.

Throughout this ministry in Grand Rapids I have tried to be true to these ideas. In attempting to live by them I have had to face some critical questions: Questions about what it means to be a pastor and what it means to be a church. Questions about the matter of politics and what a Christian's role should be in that regard. Questions about some of the fundamental presuppositions of the Religious Right and how they are in conflict with the clear teaching of the Bible. These are the questions I want to explore in this chapter.

I was ordained to the gospel ministry on December 17, 1972. After being examined by a council of pastors in South River, New Jersey, I was officially ordained a few days later at my father's church in Riverside, New Jersey. At the end of the service, a small group of pastors laid their hands on my head as I knelt at the altar. They prayed over me and set me apart for ministry—specifically, a ministry of prayer and the Word. Eugene Peterson, in his book entitled *Working the Angles,* describes what is meant by ordained ministry.

> One more thing: We are going to ordain you to this ministry, and we want your vow that you will stick to it. This is not a temporary job assignment, but a way of life that we need lived out in our community. We know that you are launched on the same difficult belief venture in the same dangerous world as we are. We know that your emotions are as fickle as ours, and that your mind can play the same tricks on you as ours. That is why we are going to ordain you and why we are going to exact a vow from you.
>
> We know that there are going to be days and months, maybe even years, when we won't feel like we are believing anything and won't want to hear it from you. And we know that there will be days and weeks and maybe even years when you won't feel like saying it. It doesn't matter. Do it. You are ordained to this ministry, vowed to it. There may be times when we come to you as a committee or delegation and demand that you tell us something else than what we are telling you now. Promise right now that you won't give in to what we demand of you. You are not the minister of our changing desires, or our time-conditioned understanding of our needs, or our secularized hopes for something better. With these vows of ordination we are lashing you

fast to the mast of Word and Sacrament so that you will be unable to respond to the siren voices.

There are a lot of other things to be done in this wrecked world, and we are going to be doing at least some of them, but if we don't know the basic terms with which we are working, the foundational realities with which we are dealing—God, kingdom, gospel—we are going to end up living futile, fantasy lives. Your task is to keep telling the basic story, representing the presence of the Spirit, insisting on the priority of God, speaking the biblical words of command and promise and invitation.[1]

On that December evening I pledged that I would devote my life to preaching and teaching the Bible. My father, who had been a pastor in Belfast, Northern Ireland, where preaching and politics are often synonymous, was a powerful influence on my life and my thinking about ministry. In the politically charged religious conditions of Northern Ireland, he had remained free of politics in his preaching and ministry. This was very much counter-cultural, but he would often remind me of the words of the apostle Paul to Timothy in this regard. Paul compared Christian ministry to being a soldier. "No one serving as a soldier gets involved in civilian affairs—he wants to please his commanding officer" (2 Timothy 2:4).

My father would always add, with a twinkle in his eye, "And if anything is a civilian affair—politics is." He believed that when you were ordained to pastoral ministry you were immediately exempted from political action, and when you were called to political service you were immediately exempted from pastoral ministry. That is not to say that a pastor gives up the rights of citizenship (including the right to vote), but it means that a pastor is called to minister independent of politics and political systems. My calling as a pastor in a free and democratic political system is the same as the call of a pastor in a tyrannical and nondemocratic system. We are both called upon to preach the Word without regard to politics.

I am not arguing for a complete withdrawal from politics. Some Christians believe that they should have nothing at all to do with politics or political parties and therefore do not vote or participate in any way. They believe that their objectives are exclusively committed to the heavenly kingdom and that this exempts them from any responsibility to an earthly kingdom. But as a pastor, I find that there are several areas in which politics cannot be ignored.

1. *We are to pray for political leaders.* In my pastoral prayers I often pray for our political leaders—local, state, and federal. My prayers transcend political parties.

On the Sunday after the 1992 election in which Mr. Clinton and Mr. Gore defeated Mr. Bush and Mr. Quayle, I prayed for all four politicians. I prayed that President Bush and Vice President Quayle would be encouraged and strengthened in the face of this recent defeat. I prayed for President-elect Clinton and Vice President-elect Gore that God would prepare them for the great responsibilities that lay ahead. I prayed for an orderly transition of government, and I prayed that the new leaders would pay attention to God and His Word.

After the service, one of the leaders of the church thanked me for praying for all four politicians. "Thank you for staying out of politics," he said. "You encouraged us to get informed about the issues and vote, but you did not endorse a candidate or even suggest a political party. Thanks! Not everyone in this church is a Republican, you know!"

Praying for political leaders who agree with us is relatively easy. Every Wednesday night at Thomas Road Baptist Church I would kneel on the platform and pray with Jerry Falwell. He would always pray for President Reagan and Vice President Bush. He would pray for their physical protection, for wisdom, for God-given advisors who knew and understood the Bible. They were compelling prayers. Yet, it is all too easy to pray for those who agree with us. What about President Clinton, who on the surface gives assent to the Bible but who in policy and action often contradicts what he claims to believe.

During the breakfast meeting I attended with President Clinton several years ago, he said he fully understood why many Christians disagreed with his politics but couldn't understand why pastors would preach against him by name from their pulpits. He was shocked that many of these pastors would castigate his wife and make fun of her from the pulpit. This kind of activity, along with selling anti-Clinton tapes or printing anti-Clinton literature, seems to be a clear violation of the biblical admonition to honor and pray for political leaders.

2. We are to preach the moral absolutes of the Bible. Many moral issues have unfortunately been politicized—issues like abortion and homosexuality. But the politicization of such matters does not exempt a pastor from giving clear biblical direction in regard to them. A pastor is obligated to preach truth—all the truth. If I ignore the moral issues of my day because they are unpopular or because they have been politicized, then I am failing in my responsibility to preach the truth.

In the continual moral decline of our culture, some people in the Religious Right have identified who is to blame. For some, the Democrats are to blame. For others President Clinton is to blame. For still others, the expulsion of God's name from public schools and the public square is to blame. Most recently, pastors have gotten the blame. We hear people say, "The pulpits of America are to blame. If preachers would stand up and be counted, then we could turn this country around." One national leader told me specifically that I was to blame because I refused to get involved politically: "It is people like you and your lack of moral preaching that is to blame."

I find this kind of blame fascinating. First, the person who questioned my preaching has never heard me preach. Second, those who blame the pulpits of America have never listened consistently to the faithful pastors who try to teach the Bible consistently week after week. We are not on national television or radio. We have no magazines and newspapers. We are virtually unknown outside our own communities. But we are preaching the Bible. And I resent outside organizations taking cheap shots at the faithful pastors of America because they do not march to the same drumbeat that the organizations do. Sometimes what we hear suggests that pastors and churches exist to serve national Christian organizations.

3. We are to exercise our rights as citizens. Being a pastor does not mean that we have no citizenship rights and privileges. We should vote, but we should not use our pulpit to influence the votes of others. We should seek to influence the political system, and I have chosen two ways to do this.

First, I have developed a friendship with our local state senator. We meet for lunch several times a year, and he occasionally attends our church. We discuss political and moral issues. On one occasion his assistant called me from the floor of the Senate to ask how I felt about a particular political (and moral) issue. But that is exceptional. My concern for this senator is more personal and spiritual than political. I pray for him, and I try to encourage him on his spiritual journey.

Second, I was appointed by Governor John Engler to serve on the board of the Children's Trust Fund for the State of Michigan, the board that deals with issues of child abuse and neglect. The charter requires that a person from the religious community serve on the nonpartisan board. At least once a month I spend most of a day in Lansing. I appreciate all the people of faith I have met who are seeking to influence the bureaucratic political system for good, for God, and for children.

The Bible teaches that there are three basic human institutions established by God: the family, government, and church. The family is the most basic of all institutions. It was created by God to provide companionship for a man and a woman and to provide care and nurture for children. God's creative intent was that the family would be a husband and a wife in intimate relationship with each other, with children reared by those parents in a loving and caring environment. Now, I recognize that in our broken world the ideal is not always possible. Divorce and premature death has led to broken families and single parents. Remarriage has led to blended families. Some couples cannot have children. We need to love and assist all these kinds of families as they struggle to deal with difficult circumstances.

The institution of human government was established after the Flood. Human beings decided to build a tower that would reach to heaven. God confused their languages and scattered them all over the earth. As a result, individual nations were established and each of these nations began governing their affairs (Genesis 10:32; 11:7–9). The Bible makes it clear that all political authority comes from God (Romans 13:1), yet the purpose of government is rather limited. It is to promote good and punish evil, and it has the right to collect taxes in order to do this (vv. 1–7).

The institution of the church was established by Jesus Christ. The purpose of the church in society was defined by Jesus himself.

> Then Jesus came to them and said, "All authority in heaven and on earth has been given to me. Therefore go and make disciples of all nations, baptizing them in the name of the Father and of the Son and of the Holy Spirit, and teaching them to obey everything I have commanded you. And surely I am with you always, to the very end of the age" (Matthew 28:18–20).

We should note several important factors about the church. First, its authority, or power, comes from above; it is not derived from the earth. Second, its mission transcends national boundaries and political authorities; Jesus told us to go to "all nations." Third, it is a ministry of the Word; we are to teach and disciple. Fourth, it is a ministry that is accompanied by the presence of Jesus.

Some of the confusion today about the role of the church and Christians in the body politic is the result of our changing the role of each of these institutions that God established. Consider the following chart:

THE INSTITUTION	ITS PRIMARY ROLE
The Family	Care and nurture of children
The Government	Ordered society
The Church	Spiritual transformation of individuals

Some people look to the church for the care and nurture of their children. They expect the Sunday school or the youth department to be the primary factor in molding the spiritual lives of the young. But this is a fundamental responsibility of parents. Others expect the government to be the primary agent in caring for and nurturing their children. In fact, many in government believe this to be one of their roles. But children do not belong to the government or the public schools; they belong to parents.

Both the church and the government derive their authority from God (Matthew 28:18; Romans 13:1), but for each it is a different kind of authority. The authority of the church is the power of the indwelling Holy Spirit, who transforms and changes people's lives through the message of the gospel. These changed people then become agents of change in their families and communities. The authority of the church is the power to change people and culture. By contrast, the authority of the government is the authority to punish wrongdoing and restrain evil. But the government has no power to change the hearts of evil-doers; it can only incarcerate or execute them. The authority of the government is very limited in that sense, whereas the authority of the church to change hearts is unlimited.

One of my concerns in regard to the Religious Right is that we are in danger of substituting our spiritual authority (the power to change lives and culture) for political authority (a lesser power that cannot change a single life). Have we not spent millions of dollars and immeasurable time to bring about political change? Even if we had been completely successful in bringing about that change, we would still not have changed a single life. Only the power of the church can transform within. Political authority, seductive as it is, is the lesser authority.

There are two factors worth noting in regard to the church's relationship to politics.

1. *Watch out for political involvement.* At Calvary Church we made the decision that we would be free of politics. We do not permit anyone to pass out petitions of any kind. We do not have voter registration drives. We do not distribute voter guides. We do not march for or against political issues. In other words, we avoid entanglement with political issues as much as possible.

Repeatedly, I feel the pressure to change the church's position. While writing this chapter I received a phone call and some literature asking us to get involved in gun control legislation. I also received a letter from Focus on the Family with petitions to distribute in our church to force the issue of casino gambling in Michigan to a public vote. The materials even included a suggested sermon to preach about the issue. Many of our people signed and passed out petitions—but not through the church.

Several years ago the Grand Rapids city council passed a gay rights ordinance that would protect homosexual people in the community. Immediately a coalition of pastors and concerned people formed and started a petition drive to put this issue to a public vote with the confidence that the community, which tends to be conservative, would reverse the decision of the city council. Many churches participated and had the petition available in their buildings. We did not participate as a church. When I was approached on this matter, I responded, "If you are asking me 'Are gays discriminated against in this community?' my answer is 'Absolutely!' If you are asking me, 'Is this the right way to correct discrimination?' my answer is 'No.' There are already laws to deal with this."

The petition drive fell short of the number of signatures needed. Some people blamed our church for this failure. I received many nasty phone calls and letters. I was accused of being a "gay sympathizer," promoting the gay rights movement, being duped by the gay community, being weak on moral issues, and lacking any moral courage. The tone of the conversations and letters was hateful. I am thankful I am not gay: Seeing the way other Christians treated me, I can only imagine how they would treat gay people.

Calvary Church held firm. We do not believe it is the role of the church to engage the political system through these means. I do not march against abortion clinics. I do not participate in the HIV/AIDS Walk. I do not march for hunger. I do not even march in the nonsectarian, nonpolitical March for Jesus. I believe in living my faith, not flaunting it.

Why are we so firm in our aversion to any kind of political involvement? First, when the church engages in the political system, using the weapons of that system, then it becomes another lobbying group and ceases to be the church. H. M. Kuitert makes this point in a most articulate way:

> So there are two kinds of power, power in the sociological
> sense (control of the means of controlling others) and power in

the spiritual sense (the light and power of the spirit of God), secular and spiritual power.

As we know today, both kinds of power are misused in what the church says: The worldly power of the church is used with an appeal to its spiritual power (the illumination of the Spirit) in order to help political and social standpoints to worldly power. As a church it knows no other power than faith and it can fight only with the sword of the Spirit. If it brings its spiritual power into worldly power-play, then it irrevocably becomes a political subject, as we now see, a party in politics, or a political party—and then it is no longer the church.[2]

Second, for a church to get involved in politics runs the risk of implying that there is a proper "Christian" position on every political issue. On some issues there is a clear and non-negotiable Christian position. For example, the matter of abortion allows little room for debate: The Bible clearly teaches that life begins at conception; human life is a gift from God and must be protected. But on many other issues there is not a clear, unequivocal Christian position. Good Christians disagree on such issues as the environment, nuclear weapons, gun control, capital punishment, and support of the State of Israel. Whenever the church or a group of Christians—such as the Christian Coalition—engages in the political system, it eventually takes a stand on a variety of issues. The danger is that this implies to others—Christians and non-Christians alike—that there is a correct "Christian" position on every political issue. The net result is that the understanding as to what it means to be an authentic Christian becomes contaminated.

This is why I object so strongly to the term "Christian Coalition." It implies that there is only one correct Christian position on every political issue. Does that mean that if I disagree with a particular position, I am not a true Christian? The Christian Coalition reduces the Christian faith to a series of political positions, and that is the equivalent of theological heresy. But whether it is the Christian Coalition or the church, neither has any business in the political system. Should we then ignore these issues? Absolutely not! These battles must be fought—but they must be fought by individual Christians, not the church or a group self-identified as Christian.

Politics is at times a nasty business. It is the struggle to gain power in order to accomplish one's goals. In every power struggle, one encounters opponents, or enemies. This is especially true in politics. Kuitert observes, "Politics is disputing with your enemies, since only in and through politics do you come to know who your enemies are." He argues that the danger of this struggle is that if "you do not share my political preference" you eventually "become like a tax collector and publican and one does not speak to him."[3] However, we are commanded to love our enemies and bless those who persecute us. We are to do good to our enemies (Matthew 5:43–48). If there is a role for the church and the Christian Coalition in politics, this would be it—loving your enemies and praying for those who persecute you. This is not a role I have seen the Christian Coalition adopt.

Is there ever a time when the church should get involved in the political process? Kuitert argues yes. He states that in a "situation in which the gaining of power through political position is forbidden or political parties do not exist," the church should become the voice of the ignored and oppressed.[4] Kuitert cites the church in South Africa as an example. The church became a voice for the blacks who had no voice in the political system. The same would hold true for the black church in America; it became the voice for a people who were, and to some degree still are, an ignored people. The same can be said of the church in Germany during the Nazi regime. The church had a moral obligation to speak up for and defend the Jewish people who were deprived of choice and freedom.

2. *The church can do what politics can never do.* I still believe in the basic political views of the Religious Right. In fact, I agree with nearly every position of the Christian Coalition. My values and beliefs have not changed. I am pro-life and pro-family. I am troubled by the smut on television, in the movies, and on the Internet. I am concerned about the erosion of our educational system. I am concerned about the entrenched racism in our country. I am troubled by the extremists in the gay community and their zealous commitment to a gay agenda.

I am concerned about the breakdown of the family and the ongoing spread of sexually transmitted diseases.

The list could go on. However, I do not believe that politics is capable of solving any of these problems. The transformation of our culture will come through the power of the gospel—one person at a time. I fear that in the Religious Right we have opted for a shortcut to cultural change—namely, legislation. But laws do not change people's lives. The church possesses the power to transform America and the world, but it is in danger of trading it for Republican or Democratic influence. In the process, we are distracting people from the ultimate solution: Jesus Christ.

So what can the church do, for example, about abortion? First, the church can faithfully preach the Scriptures and declare the uniqueness of human life, that it begins at conception, that it must be valued and protected. Second, the church can offer assistance to those who have had abortions and suffer from guilt and depression. Calvary Church has a support group for such women. It is an extended Bible study taught by women who have had abortions.

At the end of the Bible study we conduct a memorial service to honor the memory of these babies who were never born but who now live in heaven. During the service we sing, pray, and read Scripture. At the front of the chapel is a baby casket. Each woman lights a candle to honor the memory of the baby she aborted. She also places a rose on the casket. After a brief meditation, I stand in front of each women and take her hands and offer a blessing. I want each one to know that she is affirmed by God and the church.

Third, the church can offer alternatives to abortion. Calvary Church supports the local Alpha Women's Center, which offers an alternative to Planned Parenthood counseling. Many women in the church volunteer as counselors and helpers. We believe that these are legitimate and biblical responses to the issue of abortion.

What is true with regard to abortion holds true with every other issue: The church can make a difference. David Conklin passed away in 1998 after a long and courageous battle with HIV/AIDS. He contracted the disease in a bathhouse in Chicago when he lived a gay lifestyle. He was an activist. He threw eggs at Jerry Falwell and conservative activist

Anita Bryant. He was loud and proud to be gay. But then he met Jesus Christ, and Jesus forever altered his life. David left the gay lifestyle and eventually married and had children. We walked with his family through his decline in health, and I was with him the day before he died.

David is proof that any people, including gays, can change through the power of the gospel. Gays can be delivered from practicing homosexuality. Maybe, instead of fighting and hating gays, we should build relationships with them and care for them. Maybe we should listen to their struggles. I have done this, and doing so makes me weep. But the good news is that Jesus can forgive and heal. Have we forgotten this message? Have we abandoned our mission? Are we so obsessed with stopping TV actress Ellen DeGeneres and others who promote the "gay agenda" that we have forgotten that God loves Ellen as much as he loves us? Have we forgotten Jesus, who did not come to condemn but to save?

I am not suggesting that the practice of homosexuality is acceptable to God. It is not. It is sin—like gossip and pride and premarital sex and extramarital sex. But homosexuality is a complex lifestyle choice, and those who have accepted it need our love and the message of hope and deliverance that we bring.

We could transform our culture through the power of the gospel and the power of love. Kuitert says it well:

> To sum up, the features of the Christian church are determined by its saving message of God, who makes himself known as Creator, Reconciler, and Redeemer; *through its instruction,* by which it provides a search pattern with the help of which people can find the one whom they sought deliberately or unconsciously; *through prayer and intervention* for all human beings, especially for those who suffer under the violence of their fellowman; *through meditation and stillness; through the inward and outward working of love.*[5]

What is the role of the church? To present the saving message of Christ to a dying world. What are the methods? Instruction, prayer and intercession, meditation and stillness, and the inward and out-ward working of love. Let the church be the church.

It puzzles me that the leaders of the Religious Right, who are most careful and precise in their theology when they speak in the church, are most careless and loose in their theology when they deal with pol-itics. Many of their favorite ideas and statements are, at best, partially true and at worst, completely untrue. What they say about the cul-ture and our responsibility to it is often a contradiction to their avowed theology. They complain that the government does not reflect their theologically based values while at the same time they them-selves do not reflect them. My advice is, Be careful about your theol-ogy. As I have listened carefully to and have been engaged in the Religious Right over the last twenty years, I have developed a Top Ten list of its theologically flawed statements.

1. *America has a Most Favored Nation status with God.* I am a United States citizen by choice and am proud to be an American. I was born and raised in Northern Ireland and for most of my life main-tained my British citizenship. I can sing "God Save the Queen" with gusto. But I am most proud of my new home in America. There is no country quite like the USA.

National pride is good. I have traveled to many places in the world, and everywhere I go, people are proud of their country even if they do not like its political system. But in the Religious Right, national pride takes on spiritual proportions. It is as if America is God's favorite nation. The Religious Right argues that, given its rich European and Christian heritage, America has been blessed by God because of its adherence to Judeo-Christian values. They set America apart and above all other nations. This is heresy. God is God of all the nations, and all the nations (including the USA) are but a drop of water in the bucket. We are no more favored by God than Russia, Cuba, or Brazil. Such thinking is idolatrous.

2. *America was a Christian nation.* Leaders in the Religious Right have waxed eloquent on their belief that America was founded as a "Christian" nation. It is true that America was founded on a set of

moral principles that were deeply influenced by the Bible and Christian thinking, but America never was, is not now, and very likely never will be a Christian nation. If it were, how could it have justified slavery for so long?

3. *We must reclaim America for Christ.* D. James Kennedy, pastor of Coral Ridge Presbyterian Church in Fort Lauderdale, Florida, holds annual conferences entitled "Reclaiming America for Christ." This presupposes that America was thoroughly Christian at one time and that Christ wants it back. Both presuppositions are wrong. America was never thoroughly Christian, and Jesus does not want to reclaim it for himself. After they sinned, Adam and Eve were barred from paradise. The entrance of sin made the idea of paradise on earth an impossibility. No nation, including America, will ever regain paradise.

Study the teachings of Jesus, and you will discover that he never intended his disciples to claim or reclaim nations for himself. He wanted them to go into all the nations and preach the gospel and teach those who responded in faith. His mission was people-focused, not nation-focused. In fact, Jesus predicted that his disciples would be persecuted, imprisoned, and killed. That is, the nations would not be friendly toward the gospel. They would be gospel-hostile, and as we approached the end of the age, the conditions would get worse and not better (2 Timothy 3:1–9).

4. *We need to return prayer to the public schools.* One of the passions of the leaders of the Religious Right is to "return God and prayer" to the public schools. Many of these leaders have their own private Christian schools. None of their children and few of their parishioners' children attend public schools. I suggest that if they are truly concerned about public education, they should enroll their children in the public schools and do volunteer service there to make a difference.

Did we really keep prayer out of the public schools? Absolutely not! Christian students are free to pray before each class, each meal, and any other event, provided they do not do so out loud. And there is no need to pray aloud, because they are praying to God, not to teachers or other students. Do we really want public prayers returned to the classroom? If so, what prayers and to whom? If my children were in the Detroit public system, where many teachers and students are Muslim, would I welcome public prayers?

The proponents of public prayer contend that it would help correct the moral and educational decline of the public schools. But consider the effect—or lack of effect—of public prayer on Congress. Each day Congress begins it session with prayer, but then operates through the rest of the day with little regard for God. Public prayer in Congress (which I support) tends to confine God to a few preliminary moments. In many ways it is a disservice to God and the meaning of prayer.

5. *We kicked God out of the public schools.* When spoken prayer was barred from the public schools, there was the feeling that we had "kicked God out" and that all our social problems are directly connected to this one act of expulsion. Yet the very idea of "kicking God out" is theological heresy. Carl Jung, the renowned psychiatrist and therapist, had a saying engraved on his tombstone that was the central value of his life: "Bidden, or not bidden, God is present." Whether we are aware of God or not, he is there. We call this the omnipresence of God. It means that God is present everywhere. God never left the public schools or any other place on the globe.

I also believe that the idea of blaming our current problems on God's expulsion is simplistic and in error. It presupposes that when we prayed in the public schools, teachers and students really paid attention to God. When I attended high school in Philadelphia, we began each day with prayer over the intercom. That prayer made little if any difference in the way people lived and conducted themselves. Most of the people blatantly ignored God and his moral principles. It was my experience that prayer made no measurable difference for good in the public school I attended.

About the same time that prayer was barred, the Christian school movement began to grow at a dynamic rate. There was a mass exodus of teachers and children from public schools to private Christian schools. Could it be that the moral and educational decline of American public schools is in part due to this exodus of people of faith? What if we shut down every Christian school in America and the students, teachers, and administrators returned to the public schools—

would that have a positive effect? Would it begin to reverse the moral and educational decline in society?

6. *Our government must reflect our Christian values.* The Christians in Uzbekistan do not expect their government to reflect their values. The believers in Egypt and elsewhere do not expect their government to reflect their values. The only people who expect their government to reflect their religious values are countries where religion and politics are synonymous. In Iran, the religious zealots expect the government to reflect Muslim values. But in America, where there is no systemic connection between religion and the state, believers somehow expect the government to reflect their values. Are we looking for the Christian equivalent of a Muslim state? Do we want religious clerics dictating what we wear and what we do?

Jesus did not expect the world to reflect his values or the values of his disciples. In fact, he predicted the opposite.

> If the world hates you, keep in mind that it hated me first. If you belonged to the world, it would love you as its own. As it is, you do not belong to the world, but I have chosen you out of the world. That is why the world hates you. Remember the words I spoke to you: "No servant is greater than his master." If they persecuted me, they will persecute you also. If they obeyed my teaching, they will obey yours also. They will treat you this way because of my name, for they do not know the One who sent me (John 15:18–21).

While we should seek to influence our politicians to make decisions based on biblical values, we should never expect our government to reflect our values. We should expect them to be hostile. This is what Jesus predicted.

7. *The problem with America rests with its pulpits.* I have been accused on numerous occasions of being weak on moral issues. I am called "soft on sin" because Calvary Church cares for people with HIV/AIDS and welcomes them into the congregation. I have been accused of being weak on abortion because I refuse to line up in front of an abortion clinic or march in a parade. I have been called soft on the family because the church offers divorce recovery workshops and

LET THE CHURCH BE THE CHURCH 169

a variety of single-parent support groups. I have been accused of being soft on gambling because we refused to pass out petitions in our church. Many of these accusations have been accompanied by hostility and anger. In fact, I have been deeply hurt by some of the things that have been said.

But the most hurtful accusation is that I do not preach the Bible. And this accusation is hurled at many pastors in America. "If the conservative pastors of America would stand up and be counted and start preaching against sin, then we could turn this country around," politically conservative leaders have said. Well, I'm tired of being beat up. I'm tired of being accused of weak preaching by those who have never heard me preach. And so are thousands of pastors across America who are faithfully—even if not perfectly—teaching the Bible and trying to make a difference for God in their communities.

8. The answer is the Christian Coalition. The Christian Coalition, which engaged in the aftermath of the Moral Majority, is a national, grassroots organization with a lot of money, people, and influence. It is a political force to be reckoned with. But the idea of a "Christian" political entity is a somewhat flawed idea. First, the only institution in Scripture tantamount to a coalition of Christians is the church. The Christian Coalition as we know it is not the church. Second, there has to be room for differences of opinion on political issues. The Christian Coalition has a series of positions, but does that mean there is only one true Christian political position on every issue? Can I disagree and still be a Christian? Third, if one has to believe all the political positions in order to be a Christian, then we have reduced the Christian faith to political positions. Fourth, whenever we attach the word *Christian* to any political party, we are in danger of destroying the essential meaning of what it means to be a Christian. We run the risk of turning people who disagree with us away from the gospel and Jesus. These are risks I am not willing to take.

9. Structural change equals real change. People in the Religious Right get all charged up about structural and symbolic changes. We are passionate in our defense of the judge in Alabama who refuses to remove a copy of the Ten Commandments from the wall of his courtroom. He has become a hero to the Religious Right. I recently received a fund-raising letter from an organization not even connected to the judge that was asking me to contribute to a fund to fight for the rights of this judge and Christian people everywhere.

What difference does a copy of the Ten Commandments make hanging on a judge's wall? Will criminals be less likely to violate the commandments? Will jurors be able to make better judgments? The truth is that the Ten Commandments hanging on a wall is only symbolic and structural. Whether they hang there or not makes little permanent difference in that courtroom. We would be better served as Christians to teach the Ten Commandments to our children and live them out in our communities and at our work. This is what ultimately matters. Symbols, while they have their place, do not matter all that much.

10. Politicians are genuinely concerned about our issues. Several years ago I wrote an editorial for *Christianity Today* entitled "Keep the Pulpit Politics Free." The editorial upset Dr. James Dobson, and he subsequently attacked it—and indirectly, me—in his newsletter and on his radio program. We discussed our differences of opinion over the telephone and agreed to disagree. Sometime later, I received a taped copy of the speech by Dr. Dobson that set off a chain of media events, as related in chapter 9. I was eager to hear the tape in light of our expressed disagreements. But after I listened to the speech, I found myself in agreement with him.

Dr. Dobson contended that the Republican party had abandoned its previous pro-life and pro-family stance, that the people advocating these positions had been rebuked and betrayed by the Republican establishment, and that if the party didn't respond, then maybe it is time to make a change. I agree with all these ideas. Moreover, the speech led to a series of talks with Republican leaders and assurances to Dr. Dobson that things would change. And at this point I have deep concerns for Dr. Dobson. When the Moral Majority was at the height of its popularity, its leaders likewise met with the politicians and received their own assurances. But these assurances were never realized—and I predict that neither will those that were given to Dr. Dobson. Why not? Because politicians are politicians. Some genuinely care about our issues because they share our values. Most do not.

They are more concerned about the next election and about keeping power; they are inclined to use anyone, including sincere people of faith, to ensure that they maintain power.

———

Politics is a necessary evil. It is necessary because we live in a fallen world filled with broken people. The propensity of humans to do evil and to hurt each other is immense. Therefore government has the responsibility to establish laws that will restrain evil behavior as much as possible and prevent its citizens from hurting and taking advantage of each other. Consequently, we have laws about stealing, cheating, killing, abusing, and so on. These laws are necessary; without them we would have anarchy.

So politics is necessary—but it is also evil. It is not perfect, and never will be, because it is a human institution. There are no perfect politicians or perfect political platforms or perfect political systems. There never have been and never will be until God establishes his kingdom on earth.

Politics includes two important factors: ideals and power. Politics is about ideals. The Moral Majority was started because millions of Christians believed that their ideals were not adequately represented. Pat Robertson ran for president because his ideals were not well represented by other candidates. James Dobson has threatened to leave the Republican party because his ideals are not being adequately represented.

So politics is about ideals—but it is also about power. It is about the power to enact your ideals into law. In its purest form, politics is about using power wisely in order to accomplish noble ideals. In its less pure form, it is about using and keeping power at the expense of your ideals. From my experience, politics in America today is more about power than it is about ideals. During the height of the Moral Majority, we had an open door to the White House and the power brokers of politics. While they gave lip service to some of our ideals, I believe that we were used and, in some cases, even duped by them. Of course, we used them as well. It was affirming to us to be able to report our meetings with the president, the vice president, and others in the administration.

If we are going to engage in political power, we must understand that politicians are often more interested in keeping power than they are in standing up for principle. But there are exceptions. The late Paul Henry, a congressman from western Michigan, was a man of principle. I will never forget my last conversation with him, shortly before he was diagnosed with the brain cancer that caused his death. I unexpectedly encountered Paul at the Pittsburgh airport, where we were both to board a plane for Grand Rapids. He talked about the various issues he was confronting. Then I mentioned that I had seen his family in our church on a Sunday morning even though he was a member of another church in town.

"Yes," Paul said, "and we enjoyed the service. I like to take my family to other churches in the community from time to time. But I always do so in an off-election year. I would not do it leading up to an election for fear that people would see it as an attempt to get votes." I was caught off guard by his statement. Here was a man of principle. Here was a man who refused to use his Christian faith as a means to get votes. I will never understand why God took him home to heaven at such a young age when we desperately need more Paul Henrys in the corridors of political power.

William Wilberforce was another politician who lived by principle. Wilberforce was born in Yorkshire, England, in 1759. He was the son of a wealthy merchant and graduated from Cambridge. He then won a seat in the House of Commons. Wilberforce was a committed evangelical Christian. He joined the Clapham Sect, which was an evangelical group "intent on revealing Christianity by what they got done within the limits of the actually possible."[6] Their group had a twofold objective: the redemption of individuals and the improvement of human conditions.

Wilberforce's chief contribution to society was his lifelong opposition to the slave trade and his constant political pressure to get rid of it. It took Wilberforce twenty years of speaking and working before Parliament passed a law to abolish the slave trade.

Although Wilberforce devoted his entire life to making a difference in the human condition through political involvement, he understood that the lasting hope for humans lay not in politics, but in the church and true Christian religion. He considered his most important work the publication of his book *A Practical View of Christianity.*

> Let true Christians, then, with becoming earnestness, strive in all things to recommend their profession, and to put to silence the vain scoffs of ignorant objectors. Let them boldly assert the cause of Christ in an age when so many who bear the name of Christians are ashamed of Him: and let them consider as devolved [passed down] on them the important duty of suspending for a while the fall of their country, and, perhaps, of performing a still more extensive service to society at large; not by busy interference in politics, in which it cannot but be confessed there is much uncertainty, but rather by that sure and radical benefit of restoring the influence of Religion, and of raising the standard of morality. . . .
>
> But it would be an instance in myself of that very false shame which I have condemned in others, if I were not boldly to avow my firm persuasion, that to the decline of Religion and morality our national difficulties must both directly and indirectly be chiefly ascribed; and that the only solid hope for the well-being of my country depends not so much on her fleets and armies, not so much on the wisdom of her rulers or the spirit of her people, as on the persuasion that she still contains many, who, in a degenerate age, love and obey the Gospel of Christ, on the humble trust that the intercession of these may still be prevalent, that for the sake of these, Heaven may still look upon us with an eye of favour.[7]

We have much to learn from Wilberforce. Consider this:

—Changing moral issues in the realm of politics takes time.

—Changing moral issues in the realm of politics takes persistence. Withdrawing from the process will ultimately spell defeat.

—Changing moral issues in the realm of politics means dealing with the opposition and eventually convincing them of truth.

—The ultimate hope for society is not in politics; it is in the church and individual Christians.

THIRTEEN

A NEW AGENDA

My kingdom is not of this world. If it were, my servants would fight to prevent my arrest by the Jews. But now my kingdom is from another place.

Jesus Christ (John 18:36)

At the 1994 National Prayer Breakfast in Washington, U.S. Sen. Sam Nunn, a Georgia Democrat, spoke to an audience that included President Clinton and three thousand leaders of various political and philosophical persuasions. In his address, Nunn cut to the heart of how and where to solve America's deeper problems.

"Our problems in America today," he noted, "are primarily problems of the heart. The soul of our nation is the sum of our individual characters. Yes, we must balance the federal budget, and there are a lot of other things we need to do at the federal level. But unless we change our hearts, we will still have a deficit of the soul.

"The human inclination to seek political solutions for problems of the heart is nothing new. It is natural. Two thousand years ago, another society found itself in deeper trouble than our own. An oppressive empire strangled liberties. Violence and corruption were pervasive. Many of the people of the day hoped for the triumphant coming of a political savior, a long-expected king to establish a new, righteous government. Instead, God sent his Son, a baby, born in a stable. Jesus grew up to become a peasant carpenter in a backwater town called Nazareth. He condemned sin, but made it clear that he loved the sinner. He befriended beggars and prostitutes and even tax collectors while condemning the hypocrisy of those in power. He treated every individual with love and dignity and taught that we should do the same. He also put the role of government in proper perspective when he said, 'Render unto Caesar that which is Caesar's and unto God that which is God's.'"

Nunn's remarks, which even attracted the attention of the *Washington Post,* recognized the rightful role of government in bringing about a transformation of culture: "Government at every level must play a role in these challenges, but I do not believe that it will be the decisive role. I believe that the example we set, particularly for our young people, may be the most important responsibility of public service. We must demonstrate with our daily lives that it is possible to be involved in politics and still retain intellectual honesty and moral and ethical behavior.

"May we who would be leaders always be aware that we must first be servants. May we who compete in the arena of government and politics remember that we are commanded to love our enemies and pray for those who persecute us. I can't find any exception for the news media or our opponents.

"May we who seek to be admired by others remember that when we practice our piety before men in order to be seen by them, we will have no reward in heaven. May we who have large egos and great ambitions recall that the kingdom of heaven is promised to those who are humble and poor in spirit.

"May we who depend on publicity as our daily bread recall that when we do a secret kindness to others, our Father, who knows all secrets, will reward us.

"May the citizens whom we serve as stewards of government be sensitive to the fact that we are human beings subject to error and that while we need their critiques, we also desperately need their prayers. May we never forget that the final judgment of our tenure here on earth will not be decided by a majority vote, and that an election is not required to bring us home."

These are powerful words from an influential leader who understands the distinction between earthly powers and the power of integrity and faith.

The history of the past twenty years shows that while conservative Christian activists were effectively promising to end the moral slide, stop the gay rights agenda, and do other wondrous things, we never did achieve them. We did not achieve them because we lacked the power, but many people were willing to send money in the belief we possessed that power.

In fact, it was the people who sent the money who had the real power, or access to the real power. But they were robbed of their opportunity to exercise that power right where they lived, by living out their faith for all to see in their own neighborhoods and communities. In a high-powered political and media-driven world, that strategy may sound hopeless, ineffective, and irrelevant. Yet, that was what was thought about Jesus and his teachings. Many of the religious leaders and even his disciples were looking for a political deliverer to break the grip of Roman rule. They wanted a Messiah who would give them heaven on earth, end their oppression, and put them in charge. But Jesus would have none of it. His kingdom, he said, "is not of this world" (John 18:36).

On my passport is a notice from the State Department. It says that one of my options is to become a dual citizen. But there is also a warning. If I elect dual citizenship, I am advised that I might have to serve in the military of another country and might have to pay taxes to that other country as well as this one. Followers of Jesus are "dual citizens," with responsibilities to both kingdoms, but with only one clear priority.

We will never have "trickle-down" morality in America. We can only hope for "bubble-up" morality, and we may not get that. Scripture tells of a world that is winding down. Our response has been the equivalent of painting the house of a dying man, or performing CPR on a corpse. The reason there are problems in America is that we are sinners and are going our own way, becoming our own gods. You can't make people want something they don't want. That is a lesson politicians and others who espouse "family values" need to learn.

A seven-part series called "American Values: 1968–1998" ran in the *Washington Post* late in 1998. It said that things are not different at the visible top (politics, entertainment, law, education, marriage) because "the values environment has changed." The problem is not at the top, but among the citizens, so any restored sense of virtue will come, not from the top, but from the bottom. It will be noticed after millions of unseen decisions are made to live differently. This is the proper role for clergy and other moralists. Government can affirm right decisions. It cannot make them for people.

Politicians can't fix that condition—only God can. And he promises to do this by his Spirit, not through the Republican or Democratic party; and only through individual human hearts, not through human institutions, and most especially not through those representing the kingdoms of this world. If politicians could bring revival, we wouldn't need God.

Still, as temporary citizens of a temporary kingdom on this temporary earth, we do have certain responsibilities. The first is to vote and to do so intelligently. Not everyone who calls himself or herself by a party label necessarily believes in the things that party supposedly stands for. In the 1996 presidential race, Bob Dole said he would not be bound by the party platform. U.S. Rep. Tony Hall, an Ohio Democrat, is consistently pro-life while his party is not. Our responsibility is to vote for our principles and convictions, regardless of party affiliation.

After casting informed votes (not just for national office, but for state and local offices, where many who go to national office start out), we are commanded to pray for those in authority. These prayers are not limited only for those with whom we agree. The Bible makes clear that God is the source of all authority, and he placed even Bill Clinton in office for his own purposes (perhaps to disabuse religious conservatives of the notion that they have the ultimate power!). Probably the most powerful resource conservative Christians had as they wrung their hands about the president was prayer. What might have happened if more of us had prayed for him?

Our third opportunity as citizens is to pay attention to what elected officials are doing after the election. The Internet allows us to read bills soon after they are introduced and to comment by e-mail directly to members of Congress. How many of us with computers have done this? This is a marvelous tool that can influence policy if we are not too lazy to use it. If we are, others will use it in our place.

We can write letters to the editors of newspapers, supporting columnists and ideas with which we agree and critiquing those with which we disagree. Surveys have shown that large numbers of people read these letters—sometimes more people read the letters than the columns that inspired them. One faithful citizen, Michigan business-man Jim Russell, has formed a network of church writing groups whose primary purpose is to write letters to their local newspapers in ways that glorify Christ. A winsome letter commending a city council for courageous action can make as big a statement as picketing city hall.

The greatest power of all is the power we have to invest ourselves in the lives of others. Ask yourself which approach will have the great-est impact: (a) sending twenty-five dollars to a "prison ministry," and letting others visit the prison, or (b) visiting a prison in your area and building a relationship with an inmate so that when he gets out he is unlikely to return to crime? (a) and (b) together are good. But (a) without (b) will only build a bigger ministry. That is not necessarily bad, but it falls back into the world's way of trying to solve problems.

Do we reduce the number of welfare recipients by sending more money to government, or by involving ourselves directly or through our churches with people trying to help find welfare recipients a job and caring for their small children until they get on their feet?

Which is the best way to reduce the number of abortions (realiz-ing we will never end them all)? Sending money to an organization vowing to pass legislation that would restrict the practice, or volun-teering at a local crisis pregnancy center and telling a young woman the truth about the life growing within her and the positive alterna-tives available? Again, selecting both options would be best.

Perhaps most important, we really need to have a happier coun-tenance. Too many religious leaders and religious people appear in public with expressions and comments that make it look as if they are on the losing side. That not only encourages their political adver-saries, but discourages others from wanting to have anything to do with them. Who wants to hang out with whiners and complainers?

While many are now praying for an "awakening," we ought to be waking up. Instead of wishing for things to return to the way we thought they were, the new theological diversity that has led to the loss of a Christian consensus means that those who claim to be followers of Jesus have the opportunity to re-enter the arena and compete with everyone else on an equal playing field to win the hearts, minds, and—eventually—the souls of the masses.

But this will not and cannot be done using the old tools of power politics and slick direct-mail campaigns. Nor will we gain a hearing if we come across as a bunch of moralizers who want to force a worldview down someone's throat. As Paul writes in 1 Corinthians 13, we can have every gift and every experience imaginable, but if we have not love—even if we believe all the "right things"—we will be "as sounding brass, or a tinkling cymbal" (v. 1 KJV).

People need to see faith acted out before they are willing to hear the reason for it. Too many contemporary Christians have it reversed. They want to tell people about a cure for a disease the people don't know they have and about a God they don't believe they need, if he exists.

Faith should be *displayed* in the world, not placed in a museum for theological tourists to admire. At a time when a hurting world needs what Christians can offer, much of the church is fighting the wrong battle on the wrong field with the wrong weapons.

Separation—a biblical concept that means not thinking or behaving like everybody else—does not mean disengagement. Only a minority continue to believe that Christians have no responsibility in or to the world in which we live. To retreat or withdraw from engaging culture is to disobey Christ's instructions and to ignore his concern for justice for the poor. While apathy helped create the current spiritual condition, apathy isn't the sole cause of our national predicament.

The word *world* is used repeatedly in Scripture. Psalm 9:8 says, "He will judge the world in righteousness." Psalm 50:12 says, "For the world is mine, and all that is in it." Isaiah 13:11 says, "I will punish the world for its evil." But in Matthew 5:14, Jesus says, "You are the light of the world." And the disciple John says that the Lamb of God—Jesus—"takes away the sin of the world" (John 1:29).

In a most powerful passage of Scripture, John 3:16 says, "For God so loved the world that he gave his one and only Son, that whoever believes in him shall not perish but have eternal life." But there is a continuation of that statement on which few people meditate: "For God did not send his Son into the world to condemn the world, but to save the world through him."

When the average Christmas-and-Easter churchgoers look at modern believers, what do they see? They see criticism, condemnation, and a holier-than-thou attitude. They will see people, who they think are Christians who are supposed to represent God, condemning others. No wonder many are turned off and feel justified in not darkening the door of a church or seeking God.

If we are to impact culture, we can never do it from outside. If boycotting television networks and sponsors was an effective strategy, wouldn't television be better by now? While there have been marginal victories from some of these efforts, television's direction continues downward. And, it should be noted, so does its market share—the percentage of people who watch.

We stand in wholehearted agreement with conservative leaders who decry the condition of this country. We just think it's time to admit that because we are using the wrong weapons, we are losing the battle. Instead of modeling the message of Jesus, we model the message of political parties and interest groups and compete for a share of the power. The louder voice usually prevails, and we just aren't loud enough.

What was the first witness of the church shortly after the crucifixion, burial, and resurrection of Jesus? Did anyone say, "Let's get an army together and charge Rome so we can overthrow Caesar for what he allowed to happen"?

No, the first witness was that they loved each other and pooled their possessions (Acts 4:32). It was love, not criticism or condemnation, that persuaded others to learn more about Jesus and to ultimately follow him. It wasn't the purity of doctrine that attracted people. It was the purity of action in the form of observable love.

Jesus said to love our enemies (he loved his enemies), to pray for those who persecute us (as he did on the cross) because in doing so we will heap coals of fire on their heads (see Matthew 5:43–44; Romans 12:20).

We don't know many people who visibly love their enemies or pray for those who persecute them. We don't do it enough, but when we do, we find that it changes us even before it changes them—and if it doesn't eventually change them, it still changes us.

And that, perhaps, is the best message with which to end this book. We may never change the world, despite our good intentions. God in his infinite wisdom knows what is happening to America and has everything under control. In fact, we have seen the end of the story, and we know that eventually he wins. So why don't we start acting as if we're on the winning side?

EPILOGUE

LET'S DO IT HIS WAY

In the more virtuous days of the Roman Empire the Roman citizens feared harm only from their enemies, but when those days had become degenerate, they had to endure greater misery from their fellow citizens.

St. Augustine, *The City of God*
5th century A.D.

The "off-year" election on November 3, 1998, demonstrated the problematic, even declining, power of the Religious Right. Republicans, who at one time were expected to gain as many as five seats in the U.S. Senate, giving them a filibuster-proof majority, could not add to their fifty-five seats. In the House, the GOP lost five seats, giving it the smallest majority (five) since the first Eisenhower administration.

The biggest prize of all, California, found a twenty-three-year veteran of state government, Lt. Gov. Gray Davis, easily defeating Atty. Gen. Dan Lundgren (a lifelong Catholic who is pro-life). Lundgren had been hailed by some political and religious conservatives as "the next Ronald Reagan." As governor, the pro-choice, pro-gay rights Davis not only will manage the world's seventh largest economy, but will also oversee the redistricting of his state following the year 2000 census. That means a sizable number of Democrats could be elected to Congress after 2000, further blocking the objectives of religious conservatives.

Also defeated in California was Matt Fong, a "moderate" Republican who for most of the campaign was ahead of U.S. Sen. Barbara Boxer. Pollsters said Boxer was among the most vulnerable Democrats up for re-election, but she won anyway.

A comparison between the last off-year election and the 1998 election offers further proof of the decline of the Religious Right. In 1994, about two-thirds of religious conservatives voted Republican, and about one-fourth voted for Democrats, according to a poll commissioned by the Christian Coalition. But in the 1998 election, only 54 percent of religious conservatives voted Republican, while 31 percent voted for Democrats. Since most religious conservatives are perceived as being Republicans, these numbers indicate that the Religious Right is further away than ever from achieving its objectives.

Instead of acknowledging their own failures, the Religious Right blamed the Republican party for focusing too much on President Clinton and the Monica Lewinsky scandal. But that is precisely what they did in their direct-mail pieces, which regularly begged for money while deploring what the President and Lewinsky did in the White House and his admitted lying about it.

The day after the 1998 election, Dr. James Dobson issued a statement calling on Speaker of the House Newt Gingrich and Senate Majority Leader Trent Lott to step down. But religious conservatives were supposed to be the force that would put Republicans in a majority position with great power and influence to reverse the moral slide. Given the election results and evidence of their waning influence, perhaps it is the religious leaders who should resign from the political pulpits and devote themselves to their primary calling and what the Bible calls a Christian's "first love": the person and work and example of Jesus Christ (see Revelation 2:4).

It isn't just election results that seem to be affecting the tactics and goals of religious conservatives. The country itself is changing so that it no longer looks like the *Ozzie and Harriet* stereotype of the 1950s. We no longer look like that America, and while looks and beliefs are often separate, the new Americans are bringing with them a faith and political outlook that do not always, or even mostly, look like that fifties white-bread America.

In the influential *New York Times Sunday Magazine* just before the election, Nicholas Lemann, the national correspondent for the *Atlantic Monthly,* wrote about "The New American Consensus: Government of, by and for the Comfortable." In the article he noted,

All over the country, Republicans and Democrats seem to be racing for the center. In New York, the two major-party Senate candidates, Charles Schumer and Alfonse D'Amato, are presenting themselves as pragmatists [Schumer decisively beat incumbent Al D'Amato]. Jeb Bush, who lost the Florida governor's race four years ago, is running again this year as a distinctly more moderate Republican [Bush won]. Even Lauch Faircloth of North Carolina, one of the two or three most conservative members of the United States Senate, is stressing his support for environmentalism and health care reform in his re-election campaign [Faircloth lost].

Wedge issues aren't cutting the way they used to. Democrats are now against high taxes, welfare, crime and big government. Republicans are for public education, environmentalism, Social Security, Medicare—and, in most cases, legal abortion. The new consensus has been forged through the heavy (even by the standards of modern American politics) use of public-opinion polling.[1]

Writing in the *New York Times* just two days after the election, the libertarian columnist William Safire may have signaled what's ahead:

> The Religious Right would be wise to let economic conservatives take the G.O.P. wheel. The statehouse victories of the Bush boys in Texas and Florida and George Pataki in New York suggest that tax cuts and attention to local schools butter more political parsnips than an aggressive assertion of traditional values. . . . There's a respected place for moralists and religionists in the Republican vehicle; their principled resistance to the corrupting gambling epidemic will, I hope, shame G.O.P. fat cats greedy for casino bucks. But if races in 2000 are to be won, social conservatives cannot be in the driver's seat.[2]

In addition to this course correction within the two major parties is another trend that promises to trump all the political efforts and voters the Religious Right can muster. The *Washington Post* published a series of articles on "American Values: Fractured Parties" the week of October 4, 1998. The series documented the growing ideological and religious diversity of the United States.

No one group any longer has a monopoly, even a majority, on opinion. No single group can claim ultimate persuasive or electoral power when it comes to politics. The *Post* series chronicled the political, ethical, and religious views of five Democratic and four Republican belief groups. They referred to these clusters as "the parties within the party." Within the Republican party and under the "Religious Conservatives" category—which the *Post* found accounts for about 29 percent of all Republicans—there was this quote from forty-year-old David DeHaas, a real estate marketing entrepreneur from Boise, Idaho: "When I was a kid in school we got up and saluted the flag and we said a prayer before class. I think that today, if everybody did that in America, there would be a lot more peace in the land. . . . It hasn't gotten better; it's gotten worse since we put religion out of the schools and out of our lives."[3]

This is a common lament among religious conservatives. For many of them, the problem is easily understood. There being no prayer in school and no flag salutes has not only contributed to, but has been primarily responsible for, undermining the moral foundation of the country. And the solution is also easily understood: Put prayer back in the public schools and make saluting the flag mandatory again. If regular brushing can halt tooth decay, they seem to be arguing, why, then, can't regular praying and saluting the flag halt moral decay?

The *Post* says of these religious conservatives, "Their numbers, voting history and commitment to the GOP combine to give them political muscle. But their extreme positions on many issues isolate them from other Republicans as well as Democrats."[4]

Religious conservatives could credibly argue that their positions aren't extreme, but that more liberal people, who favor abortion on demand, same-sex marriage, and the rest of the socially liberal agenda, are the real extremists and that religious conservatives are merely trying to restore the previous moral order.

In view of the changing face, nature, and beliefs of many Americans, religious conservatives have an important decision to make. After twenty years of political activism and millions of dollars spent on various religious-political movements, how much longer are they willing to pursue their strategy and agenda before they realize it not only *has not* worked, but *cannot* work? Pragmatically, the numbers aren't there, and they are perceived as being so "extreme" that coalition building is difficult because their views do not attract people of other persuasions who must be included in any political alliance or coalition, Christian or otherwise. Politically, the primary objective of religious conservatives has been to change things at the top, hoping that will repair the moral foundation. This is a common error, not unique to religious conservatives, as we've pointed out elsewhere. It is easier to believe our problems are about the things we see, rather than the things that are invisible. So abortion becomes a problem of courts, who occupies the White House, and which political party controls the Congress, rather than of a materialistic philosophy that has contributed to the devaluing of human life and human relationships at all levels.

"We've forgotten God," said Abraham Lincoln in his unsophisticated but profound explanation of why brother fought against brother in the American Civil War. We at the end of the twentieth century have also largely forgotten God, including many people who claim to labor in Jesus' name. We have confused political power with God's power. We think that if we can organize enough of the "right kind" of people, we can reverse what we perceive as evidence of a moral slide.

But what if "we," not "they," are the problem? Suppose God has chosen not to bless the efforts of religious conservatives because they are not implementing his strategy and his agenda in his way? Does that sound heretical? What, then, is meant by the prophet Zechariah's statement, "This is the word of the LORD to Zerubbabel: 'Not by might nor by power, but by my Spirit,' says the LORD Almighty" (Zechariah 4:6)?

Too many religious conservatives seem to have lost sight of the process, preferring to focus only on the objective. But if the process is right, the objective will be attained. Apple trees must produce apples; they can never produce pears, because they are designed to produce apples. Christians can produce a more righteous nation if they focus on what righteous behavior and obedience to God's Word and God's methods look like. Focusing solely on the objective, however, will mean it is never attained—or, if attained, never sustained—because of the unpersuasiveness of political power. Consider the failure of the Soviet Union to eradicate the church. If the Soviets could not kill the church, what makes American religious conservatives think our government can restore it?

But one can't raise money for one's organization on the basis of "process." Only an often oversimplified objective can bring in the money, and this is the major reason why the so-called Religious Right doesn't have a voluntary prayer at implementing its agenda by political means alone. Our primary problems are not economic and political. They are moral and spiritual and cannot be resolved solely through politics.

So it is easier to ask for money for petitions to send to a president, or videotapes that contain "proof" of a president's lawbreaking, or questionnaires to be filled out by people whose views are already known by the one sending them, than to call people to feed the hungry, clothe the naked, visit those in prison, love their enemies, and pray for those who persecute them.

But this latter process produces the objectives that are pleasing to both God and man. Petitions, videos, questionnaires, and voting guides change little and reduce the power of our moral arguments to political warfare and not persuasion by example. Just because you have won an election doesn't mean you have persuaded a nation of your point of view. Ask the Republicans, who overreached after the 1994 election and thought they had a mandate to launch a "revolution."

Consider your own experience. Have you ever brought a person to your point of view by force? Even if the person for whom you voted beats the person for whom your friend voted, have you changed your friend's mind because the election did not turn out the way he or she wanted?

It is the same way with faith. No one is brow-beaten into the kingdom of God. More people can be persuaded through a gentle spirit and consistent living than by condemnation, triumphalism, and judgmentalism (which is not to be confused with legitimate judgments about right and wrong—there is a difference).

Religious conservatives have heard sermons that man's ways are not God's ways (Isaiah 55:8). In politics they have fused the two, causing damage to both church and state. The damage to church is caused by those who appear to the "unchurched" to be interested in ushering in the kingdom of God by force. The damage to the state is that at the precise moment when government needs the moral principles the church can offer, too many in both the conservative and liberal wings of the church have deserted their primary territory and gone lusting after the temporal power associated with the kingdom of this world. The church then becomes an appendage of the state rather than its moral conscience. It is transformed from a force not of this world into one that deserves to be treated as just one more competitor for earthly power. It is seen as just another lobbying group to which politicians can toss an occasional bone to ensure loyalty.

We don't have a shortage of leaders, but a shortage of followers of the one Leader who can transform lives and nations. We don't need to enlarge our vision, but make it smaller and more focused. We don't need more numbers, but more quality and consistency among the numbers we already have. We need more people who will do things God's way and fewer people doing things man's way.

Religious conservatives won't raise much money by doing things God's way, but they are more likely to get the results they seek. In this way the kingdoms are not confused, and each fulfills the purpose for which it was established.

Religious conservatives, no matter how well organized, can't save America. Only God can. But he will only consider doing it if God's people get out of the way and give him room. That's the better way. It is also the only way.

THE INTERVIEWS

We have tried to build a strong case for the church to lay down its impotent weapons of political activism in exchange for the greatest force we have to change the world: the gospel of Jesus Christ. We hope that our challenge generates a lively and serious dialogue about how people of faith should behave in the public square. The interviews excerpted here were conducted with people whom I respect and who have legitimate viewpoints on the concerns raised in this book. Some were our "enemies" in the 1980s. I am grateful to them for agreeing to be interviewed, for it is in this spirit of mutual respect— if not always mutual agreement—that we see hope for the future.

Cal Thomas

FORMER U.S. SENATOR WILLIAM ARMSTRONG (R-COLORADO)

Thomas: What is the role of the believer—that is to say, the follower of Christ—as an individual, and what is the role of the church when it is perceived as an institution in our constitutional republic?

Sen. Armstrong: I think believers are obligated to be deeply involved in the political process as individuals. First of all, Scripture tells us to do that. When the Pharisees came to Jesus and said, "Is it lawful for us to pay our taxes?" his response was, "Show me a coin." Then he asked, "Whose picture is on there?" They thought they had trapped him, but of course, Jesus used the occasion to teach a great lesson. They said, "Well, on the coin is the picture of Caesar." He said, "Fine, then render unto Caesar what is Caesar's and unto God what is God's." This is well understood to mean that there is a line beyond which the government may not interfere in the affairs of the church.

What is less well understood, I think, is that on that occasion, Jesus invested the political process with a status and a dignity it never previously had. He said, "Render unto Caesar what is Caesar's," and I don't think that just means paying taxes. I think it means obeying the traffic laws. I think it means participating actively in the process of civil government. This notion of participation was held by John Calvin, and it's been held by men and women of faith all through the ages right down to the present time, and I think it's pretty well understood by most thoughtful Christians. Regrettably, however, there is a huge number of Christians who are not registered to vote, which I think is a minimum duty. And they ought to be well informed before they vote. It drives me crazy when people fail to get informed before voting.

I think many Christians ought to take a more active role in supporting candidates. They ought to write a check to candidates of their choice. Many Christians could participate by being on talk shows and writing letters to the editor and being active in the political life of their community. I think some Christians are called to run for office—not all, but many are. As we do participate, we need to be on guard not to give people the impression that our ultimate reliance is on politics any more than it is on medicine or economics. Our reliance is first and foremost on Jesus Christ, but within that context and under his Lordship, we have some other responsibilities, of which political life is one.

Also, we should never position the church as a power bloc. While individual Christians have a responsibility, the church—the organized church—needs to be very careful that it does not set itself up as a power broker or pressure group. The members of the church ought to play that role on their own; the church itself, it seems to me, needs to be very cautious about that.

Thomas: What do you see as the primary cause of what is generally referred to as moral decline in America?

Sen. Armstrong: The history of human nature is very repetitive. The moral decline we're seeing in America is not new. There have been waves of decline and decadence and renewal in the past. You remember that when the Pilgrims arrived here in the winter of 1620, there was a brief period of great holiness and great faith on the North

American continent, which produced the attributes of character and thrift and hard work that led to prosperity. And as soon as we became prosperous, our forebears began to forget God and lapsed into decadence, and they quit going to church. They forgot the standards and values which were ingrained in them; they began to think that they were responsible for their own prosperity.

In the eighth chapter of Deuteronomy, that's exactly what happened. The people of Israel were warned, "We're taking you into a land of peace and prosperity and plenty, with agricultural and mineral abundance, and when you've built your house and field and your flocks multiply, then is your time of greatest danger, because if you forget God and say to yourself, 'I have done this, I have created my own wealth,' then the Lord says, 'I will destroy your nation as I have destroyed others.'"

Well, that's what happened here. The pilgrims got here, endured incredible hardship. Out of their character and their reliance upon God came an incredible system of economics which produced wealth—and they promptly forgot God and lapsed into decadence. By the late 1600s the situation got so bad that the government of Massachusetts actually appointed a commission to look into why God had withdrawn favor from the people, because they had enormous shipping losses, the crops were failing, they had all kinds of problems, and then there was an Indian uprising which finally shocked the people so much that everybody got back on their knees and began to pray, and they put down the Indian uprising and everybody thanked God and prosperity returned.

And then the process started again. At the beginning of the eighteenth century there were terrible demonstrations of decadence—wife beating, drunkenness, and so on—and that in turn sparked the renewal in the 1740s, '50s, and '60s that led up to the preaching of George Whitfield, and that sparked the American Revolution. Then the same thing happened. After the Revolution, at the beginning of the nineteenth century, we again had a period of decline. So I don't think what we're going through in this country now is unique in the slightest. I think we've been through it before—the cycle of faith, prosperity, indifference, decadence, poverty, disaster, faith.

Evidently the lesson of history is that most human beings do not respond well to prosperity, that character seems to thrive most, be strengthened most, in times of adversity. What we're seeing now is appalling, but it is not unusual in human history.

Thomas: The National Council and World Council of Churches have been very much involved in politics in this century. Some of that involvement has been good. Civil rights for blacks comes to mind, and the protest against the Vietnam War. But in their churches, doctrine was compromised, the people got messages on the United Nations and low-cost housing instead of the gospel, and a lot of those people who cared about the "good stuff" went to evangelical churches instead. How should pastors see their roles, and what limitations should they impose on themselves?

Sen. Armstrong: I think pastors ought to ask themselves, when they are thinking about political participation, how will this affect the ability of people in my flock to experience the love of Christ? How will some proposed stand I am taking affect my ability to minister to people who have a different political view? I think it is important to distinguish the pastoral role from other religious functions. If I were a pastor, I probably would wish to attenuate my own political participation unless there were people in my church who had different views who are also in positions of leadership. I'm a conservative, and yet if I were a pastor, I would want to be very careful not to do something that would make it hard for a liberal to know Jesus and worship in my church. I don't know exactly where the line is, but I think clergymen need to be very careful.

Over the last twenty-five years, I have from time to time met with some religious leaders who have sought my advice about this. In almost every case I have counseled people whose primary mission was pastoral care or evangelism to keep their political opinions to themselves, even if they were in agreement with my own. Not because I thought it was wrong or improper for them to express their political views, but because I didn't think it advanced their main ministry. A moment ago I said Christians should be involved politically, and now I'm saying that some Christians ought to be cautious in how they exercise this. But I think it's quite different for me as a Christian lay-man than it is for the leader of the church.

Thomas: As a believer you have had a set of principles, but others did not always share them in and out of Congress. How do you advance an ideal without compromising your principles when you have the power and authority and you're inside the system?

Sen. Armstrong: One of my colleagues made the point that when it comes to changing men's lives, personal example is not the *main* thing, it's the *only* thing. There's a lot of wisdom in that. I find personally that, on the most important issues, people are not much influenced by what you *say*, but are very much influenced by what you *are*. The weight that is accorded a person's arguments depends entirely on the credi-bility of the person himself or herself. I'm not sure if it was Lincoln or somebody else who made the point that if you're going to influence someone, you must first be that person's friend. I think that it is not very effective in Congress or anyplace else to run around lecturing people on moral issues. It is far more important to establish the cred-ibility and the platform from which they can draw conclusions.

Thomas: You often spoke out about the two hot political-social issues, abortion and homosexuality, when you were in the Senate.

Sen. Armstrong: Yes. I didn't seek to be a spokesman on either of those issues. In fact, I made some effort to avoid becoming a spokesman on them because those are issues on which, if you touch them, you expose yourself to a lot of risk. But the point is that I think people are very quick to detect hypocrisy. They're very quick to detect self-serving statements. So I think, particularly on moral issues, that both in Congress and outside—but particularly in Congress where you're dealing with the same group of people all the time and get to know each other very well—the people who really are effective in dealing with their colleagues on these sensitive issues are ones that their colleagues trust and believe. And that's more a reflection of who they are than of what they say.

Thomas: The reason for my question is that there's increasing clamor outside of Congress from various groups expressing frustra-tion that the Republican majority (you were only in a majority for part of your time as a member of Congress) isn't, can't, or won't do more to advance the "conservative agenda," particularly on these moral issues. In the Senate you're one of 100, and when you were in the House you were one of 435. Yet some people expect you to never compromise.

Sen. Armstrong: Let me give you an example of someone who I believe has been very effective in dealing with some really tough issues. That's Frank Wolf, a congressman from Virginia. As we're speaking, the bill on religious persecution has not yet passed the House, but it will very shortly. One of the reasons it's going to pass is that nobody thinks that Frank Wolf is behind it for self-serving reasons. They believe, correctly, that Congressman Wolf is pursuing this legislation because of his genuine compassion for people who are persecuted for their religious beliefs, Christians and others as well. So he has a credibility and a stature in dealing with this issue because it's not self-serving.

Now, if he were to say, "I want to make this apply to all the countries in the world except for such and such a country where my Commonwealth of Virginia happens to import a certain product that we need or export a certain product to the country"—in other words, if there were self-serving elements in that legislation—his credibility would evaporate in an instant.

I do think that in a lot of cases people outside the Congress are frustrated about how slow the process is and about how unyielding it is to changing public opinion. I share that to a large extent. I'm very frustrated, for example, that the Republican majority has not yet abolished the National Endowment for the Arts. That's something about which there was a very strong general agreement. It is something that, in my opinion, is within the power of Congress to do, even without the support of the president. I think that's something that they could have done.

But in a lot of cases the larger goals—particularly of the Religious Right, in which I include myself—are simply beyond the capability of members of Congress to do right now. There are some things that we ought to do. I agree with those outside the Congress who are disappointed at some of the things we've neglected to do. I am honestly disappointed at the tremendous inertia on the matter of the persecution of Christians. That legislation, which I believe will be enacted in 1998 [it was], should have whistled through, and instead it has taken a very strong concerted effort to get it through, much more than I would have thought was necessary.

On the other hand, since I believe that government is the chief threat to human liberty, in general the fact that it is difficult to legislate, to change the law, is a good thing. So balancing my natural impatience with how slow it is to get good legislation passed is the realization that the checks and balances that make it hard to pass good legislation have repeatedly saved us from the enactment of very bad legislation. People criticize the filibuster, but the reason the filibuster process is retained in the Senate is that at some time or another, every Senator feels called upon to make use of it. So we don't legislate quickly—and given the propensity of the government to do that which it shouldn't—it's a good thing.

Thomas: Christians are a minority of the population. Even the most liberal view, taken by George Gallup in '76 during the Carter phenomenon, found only 50 million people who claimed to be born again. Even if you accept that—which I think is way too high—it was still, at that time, only 20 percent of the population. Then, within that 50 million you don't have all Republican conservatives. So you have a minority within a minority, and it could be argued that the number who are serious believers, actively conservative, and Republican is still a smaller minority. So does this smallest of the minorities have a right to demand its way in and through government?

Sen. Armstrong: I think "demand" is a pretty loaded verb. And I don't want to quibble about the math. I don't think that relatively conservative Christians are in quite as small a minority as your question suggests. But I would admit that certainly we don't constitute a majority or anything close to it. However, having said that, I do believe that the traditions and culture and government and society of America basically come out of our experience in colonial times, which was the Puritans. Now, the Puritans are the most underrated and maligned group of people that can be imagined. They were thought to be grim and lacking in humor and so on—not true. The Puritans were thrifty, they were brave, they were holy—they were, in fact, very good role models. Their thoughts—not only about religious matters, but about government, about culture, about learning, about hard work, grit, industry, self-restraint—really have formed the cultural context in which this country has developed and in which it still exists. Now it's pretty frayed around the edges, but it still exists.

I would say that even in this decadent time, the conservative Christian consensus continues to be the dominant cultural—and even to some extent, political—theme of our country. It is really the glue that holds us together; it is the vital essence that makes America what it is. I would quickly add that it's not just the Puritans, but a lot of other contributing cultures that have made America what it is. But the bedrock comes out of the colonial experience.

Thomas: You spoke earlier about history having a cycle. Do we have to wait until the Baby Boomers move out of the picture before we see a restoration, or at least a hope of restoration, of that which went before? How do you see the battle between morality and immorality, if you will, turning out in the short term?

Sen. Armstrong: In economics, the leading indicators tell us, according to economists, what's likely to happen nine months from now or two years from now. If you look at the cultural indicators that are the portents of where we will be five or ten years from now, there is much cause for optimism. If you look only at what's happening now, it appears that the situation is getting worse and, in my opinion, will continue to get worse for a while.

Consider some of the leading indicators that tell me things are going to be better in a few years. One is the crisis pregnancy center movement that you're so familiar with. Those centers didn't exist twenty years ago. Now they are everywhere! Second is the home-school movement: 1,200,000 kids in America are in home schools. I don't think home schools are for everybody, but I think that suggests that there are probably at least 2.4 million adults who are interested enough in their kids to make that kind of an extraordinary invest-ment. I think the charter school movement, which is catching on like a prairie fire, is going to be one of the great social and cultural trends of the twenty-first century. In my opinion, it is just ready to explode across America.

Then there's the Promise Keepers movement. I was one of the group—which has not been officially estimated, but which I estimate at 1,400,000 people—who gathered on the Mall in Washington in the fall of 1987. My son and I both were there. That is a movement of enormous significance. I would say that the prayer-and-fasting movement is significant. There are thousands—I can't say if it's tens of thousands or hundreds of thousands, but there is a very large number—of people who are undertaking prolonged fasts and a larger number that are taking on shorter fasts.

We see the development of new churches with a vitality that is really beyond my experience. That has not crested yet; that's still growing. At the very time when the so-called mainline churches are continuing to decline, there is a renewed vitality in evangelical churches and in the Catholic Church. What's going on in the Catholic Church in this country and in Latin America, at least, and maybe elsewhere, is absolutely remarkable.

So there's all these things happening, and I could cite many other things. Is that going to have an effect on our culture? Of course it is! Not a political effect, but a cultural effect.

Thomas: I'm struck by the fact that everything you've just mentioned does not involve the government, with the exception of the charter schools.

Sen. Armstrong: That's right. But let me also say this: I really do believe that God is calling Christians to be involved in the political process, because many of the questions that God cares about involve government. Does he care whether or not innocent lives are taken through abortion? He does care. Does he care whether or not people are forced to have their children associate with homosexuals? I think he does care. Does he care, for example, whether or not religious schools in the District of Columbia are forced to give status to homosexuals? I think God cares about that. National defense—does God care about that? I think he does, and I think he expects us to. I think God cares about prosperity. I don't think he always gives prosperity to his children, but I think he does care whether it is possible for individuals and families to provide for their own economic well-being, to provide for their retirement and so on, and whether they have good job opportunities.

Those are all the kinds of things which, in a free society, get settled through the political process. If Christians don't fulfill their responsibilities, I think we're failing our faith. I want to add one more caveat. I said we shouldn't give the opinion that we're relying chiefly on the political process because our chief faith is in Christ. The church shouldn't be a power bloc. But we also should never give the impression that this is an exclusive process, that somehow only Christians can do this, because, you know, God was able to make sons of Abraham out of a stone. Certainly that means he can make a good legislator out of somebody who isn't necessarily a member of our church or maybe not even a Christian or maybe an atheist. So I don't think we ought to limit God by saying "only Christians" deserve our support politically. I would even say that the number of men and women in public life—starting in modern times with Jimmy Carter—who have honored Christ and who have been open about that is a sign of cultural renewal. It's been controversial, but these people are in both parties—men like John Ashcroft [former governor and now a senator from Missouri] and Sam Nunn [former U.S. senator from Georgia]. Jimmy Carter was the first megapolitician in recent years to really demonstrate that faith.

FORMER U.S. SENATOR AND 1972 PRESIDENTIAL NOMINEE GEORGE MCGOVERN (D-SOUTH DAKOTA)

Thomas: There is a lot of evidence of moral decline in America. What do you think is the chief cause of it?

Sen. McGovern: I think there's a deterioration in some areas in terms of the moral tone of our society, but not across the board. I think you can make a pretty strong case that we've made progress in the United States in some areas. Even the bare-bones crime statistics have improved. In most cities there is less murder and less aggravated assault than there was ten years ago. We have even made some progress in reducing the incidence of hard drugs in our culture. We've made some progress in the way we treat other human beings—civil rights comes to mind. Even people that we used to brand as "queers" we treat with a greater measure of Christian and religious tolerance than we used to.

I think the status of women has been elevated somewhat in recent years, but on the other side of that we are freer and sometimes less disciplined regarding sexual responsibility—easier relationships, promiscuity, and undisciplined sex. We see even on the great campuses of this country the phenomenon of weekend binge drinking. It was there when I was in college, too—fifty-five or sixty years ago—but not to the extent it is today.

So I would say it's too simple to say that we're living in a society in moral decline. We're living in a society that in some cases exercised the influence of progressive politics and progressive religion to make certain changes that I think have been pretty good. But we paid a price for that with less discipline over the more orthodox standards of morality.

Thomas: You note that sexual morality has been lost and there is less commitment to marriage and easy divorce.

Sen. McGovern: Those things concern me, and they do represent a decline in my opinion.

Thomas: How do we "get that back"?

Sen. McGovern: I think it's a long, slow process that societies have been grappling with, with inconsistent results from the beginning. It all started in my religious tradition with the Garden of Eden, the fact that even at the beginning people couldn't maintain certain God-given standards. And we can't transform the moral behavior of any society by doing it through edicts from the top; it has to be a slow progression of moral and spiritual improvement across the society. That's why, for example, I think the concept of what we used to call the Moral Majority comes at it the wrong way. The Moral Majority assumed that the kingdom of God is a Moral Majority. That's neither scripturally nor politically sound.

The Bible and other great religious scriptures talk about a "saving remnant." They don't talk about a Moral Majority; they talk about that remnant working within society to bring about the kingdom of God. It is made up of a small number of believers and faithful practitioners of good. They've probably never been a majority. God knows whether we'll see it in our lifetime. We certainly didn't see it in the twentieth century, which is one of the most violent and turbulent and bloody god-awful centuries in human history. One thinks of the Holocaust as perhaps the most extreme example of that, but it's been a hundred years of slaughter and violence and discrimination and a long battle even to establish minimum rights for children in the workplace and elsewhere.

My own view is that we work towards the kingdom of God, not necessarily by trying to capture control of Congress through a certain political agenda—although I have participated in those efforts and will probably continue to do so. But it's unlikely that you're going to achieve it by capturing the Congress or capturing a moral majority or capturing those on the left or the right who think that they have a special formula that's going to transform society. You do it by struggling with people who may have differing views than you. You do it through political action, through the church and other organized religious efforts, through education, and perhaps most of all, through the family and the effort to rear your children according to certain basic moral and spiritual precepts. But this is a long, slow, uncertain process.

Thomas: Prior to the emergence of the so-called Religious Right, there were many years of liberal religious activism in this country, some of it quite good—such as civil rights, which you've already brought up. But as we look at some of the mistakes the Religious Right has made in trying to impose a righteousness from the top down, what, if any, shortcomings do you see that the Religious Left made—not only in that period preceding 1979, but subsequently?

Sen. McGovern: One mistake the liberal left made about political activism is assuming they should have a monopoly on it. Some of the great movements of religious and political activism over the nineteenth century took place around the issue of slavery, which split the churches down the middle, including my own Methodist denomination. That was not so much a case of liberals verses conservatives; they broke on moral grounds, but they also took political action to achieve their end. Then came the great surge around Prohibition after World War I, which, again, wasn't so much a liberal-versus-conservative issue as it was one fought out on moral grounds—but they used political means to achieve it.

Then came the great struggle over civil rights, in which the churches were certainly the spawning ground of the movement, especially the black churches, but also the liberal white churches. Martin Luther King appealed to the white conscience as well as the liberal conscience. Then the great anti-war movement, which was identified sometimes with my role in politics in the '60's and '70's. I think all those movements had a strong religious, spiritual basis to them. I would have supported all of them—and did support all of them except the ones that preceded me, slavery and Prohibition.

But liberals were too defensive and too antagonistic—and paradoxically, so, too, I think are the Religious Right, the fundamentalists (of which my father was one), when they take up political activism. I don't think anybody ever heard me say, as a liberal, that the Religious Right didn't have a right to speak. The Religious Left also had a right to oppose them. I always quickly added that, but certainly people on the Religious Right had every right to speak out and to use political means to achieve their goals unless it was in open violation to some tax considerations. I think that was the biggest mistake that we liberals made: relentlessly and unfairly criticizing the Religious Right when they became politically active.

Thomas: Should ministers be involved in politics?

Sen. McGovern: I think they should stay away from direct partisan endorsement. I don't think a minister of the gospel should proclaim from the pulpit that we need a Democratic or Republican victory, or that we need to defeat Jesse Helms or elect George McGovern. I think that's going too far. But I think that clergymen, on the left and the right, are perfectly within their rights in interpreting what they regard to be the great moral challenges within our society and to speak to those challenges. Where ministers get into trouble, I think, is when they beat the drums for a particular party or a particular candidate.

The Judeo-Christian ethic transcends both political parties and all candidates, and I think that that's where the line ought to be drawn.

Thomas: Let me pursue that point, because James Dobson is now complaining that the Republican leadership in Congress either is not doing what it promised it would in order to get their votes, or is abandoning the principles it claims to uphold. Even though he's not ordained—he's a psychologist—he still speaks for a lot of conservative, religious people on the radio and in his publications. Is that what you mean by a too-close association?

Sen. McGovern: Maybe, because I don't think the agenda for America came out of the Ten Commandments or the New Testament. I think it's a mistake when one asserts that Newt Gingrich is disobeying his moral obligations when he doesn't fight for every last provision in that ten-point agenda of his. First of all, Newt knows as the Speaker of the House [since resigned] that, while it's one thing to stand up on a political podium and lay out a program, it's quite another thing to figure out the mix of compromises and adjustments that will get even part of that approved. He may lose all of it if he isn't willing to make some kind of concessions to people who disagree with all of it—but he might be willing to compromise on certain aspects of it. For example, he got the line-item veto, he got the balanced budget, he got the reform of the welfare system as it used to be. He's achieved certain things. He's maintained a fairly strong posture on national defense. Those are achievements within the framework of the Contract with America. But some of the other things that he's pressed for, he's found it's unrealistic to demand right now.

Thomas: If you were advising young people who love God and want to serve Him and want their lives to count for something, what would you say to them?

Sen. McGovern: I would try to convince them, first of all, that politics can be a noble calling, worthy of their participation. Whether they approach it from my perspective or from Jerry Falwell's is important— that's an important decision. Politics doesn't have to be a seamy, rotten game. I would try to convince them that, next to loyalty to their church or their spiritual principles and their family, a consistent participation in government and politics is a very high responsibility, and one they should take seriously. They should vote after they're well informed, they should take that vote seriously, they should take the discussion of public issues seriously, and they should, if they're so inclined, talk to members of Congress and talk to the press about their views.

Those actions are worthy of the most devout Christian—to participate actively in politics. That would be the first thing I'd tell people. I would say that I don't agree with Jerry Falwell on a number of things, but he has the right, as he has demonstrated, to participate in politics.

Thomas: Has Jerry done some good things in terms of reawakening a lot of the fundamentalist community to their civic responsibility? Before this, they didn't vote at all. Politics was dirty.

Sen. McGovern: He definitely has done so—so has Pat Robertson, so have others. Now, Billy Graham hasn't gone in too much for political action, but he shows up at inaugurals and shows up at receptions for senators and congressmen. He's on good terms with political leaders of both parties. He sets an example, not of a religious leader who is necessarily trying to advance the program of the Moral Majority, or Newt Gingrich's ten points, but an example that it's okay to be a friend of Lyndon Johnson and Richard Nixon and George McGovern, I think that's good. And in his own way, while I think he sometimes carried it to excess, Jerry Falwell and his Moral Majority have sent the message that it's okay to be a Christian and be active in politics.

I would also have a second message: It's okay to be a liberal. A good Christian can be a liberal. And it's okay to be a conservative, and I can make a case for that—perfectly respectable to be a Christian and be a conservative or a liberal. I can make the case either way.

Thomas: But what do you do, then, when you get into matters of right and wrong? I mean, if you say it's okay to be a liberal—

Sen. McGovern: Then you battle it out. It's the competition of ideas and the creative tension that moves our democratic society. That's what makes it move. It's the fact that there's always that creative tension between the liberals here and the conservatives there, between the modernists here and the fundamentalists there, that I think makes all of them better.

Thomas: Good answer. You wouldn't suggest that—I was tempted to get back to the debate mode we used to do, but we're doing a book, not a debate. But you wouldn't suggest that there are not some things that are not always right and other things that are not always wrong.

Sen. McGovern: No, I would not. I don't believe in that kind of moral nihilism. I think that some things are right or wrong. It's always wrong to discriminate against human beings because they're women or because they're brown or yellow or black. That's always wrong. It's always wrong to steal from the public treasury. It's wrong to steal from the private treasury, too, although it's even worse from the public treasury since we're all involved in that.

I think it's always wrong to go to war and kill people unless all other efforts have failed and the wrongdoing of the people you go after, or the ones who attack you, is so clear that you have no alternative. But we never ought to commit a young life to the battlefield unless we are sure that that's the only reasonable course. If you can achieve the same thing by diplomacy—what people sometimes call appeasement—then go ahead and do it. If you can avoid the killing of human life, it's worth some humility and some risk on the diplomatic front.

It's always wrong, in my opinion, to exploit somebody else's labor unfairly, to make people work for wages that are an insult to human dignity, or to make them work under conditions that are unnecessarily dangerous. It's going to be dangerous sometimes to fly an airplane, but you at least can require the airplane be inspected—that's the kind of thing I mean. It's always wrong to sell polluted food if you can prevent it. That's government with a moral tone. I would say this just as a general rule: Politics without some kind of a moral underpinning can be a very destructive and negative enterprise.

Thomas: Can the Religious Right as we've know it succeed with their agenda by changing tactics?

Sen. McGovern: I hope not, because I think they're wrong substantively. But I do think tactics are tremendously important. I must say that in the early stages of my career I tended probably to ignore them too much and to just assume that if I bought five minutes' time on television and sat down and talked reasonably about my views on agriculture or education or foreign policy, that was all there is to it. I later learned that that's not enough. You can be cut to pieces on television by cleverly devised negative advertising from the other side. It has to be answered. You can't assume that people are going to watch a blizzard of negative ads on television, adequately funded and kept up on a sustained basis, and still arrive at a victory at the end of the campaign.

I think I underestimated that in my presidential race. We had almost no negative advertising at all, and we didn't answer negative advertising. We took what I now think is a somewhat naive assumption that the attacks on me would bounce off, that no one would really believe I was weak on national defense, that no one would really believe I wanted to put everybody on welfare or that I wanted to turn my back on threats to America from Communism. I now realize that a lot of people believed that then and believe it now because of the probably-300-million-dollar campaign that was directed largely at negative advertising.

So what I'm saying is that tactics count. President Clinton understands that—he understands tactics. He may sometimes compromise conviction on a major issue, but he understands tactics so well that even in the face of an enormous opposition to him, he was re-elected easier than he was elected the first time. I think he stands higher today than ever in that regard, and it's partly because of tactics.

Thomas: Do you have to be dirty to do good?

Sen. McGovern: I don't think so, but I think you have to be shrewd and aggressive and opportunistic to achieve a victory at the polls today. Big money is a factor more so today than it ever has been in politics. It's very difficult to get into office today just on good will and candor and common sense, because information can be so easily distorted. You have to have the resources and the money and the "smarts" to see where you are vulnerable to those attacks.

Thomas: One of the slanders against you in the '70s was that because you were a liberal you must be Godless. Just tell me straight up what you believe about God, about Christ, about eternal life, about salvation.

Sen. McGovern: Well, I'm primarily a believer in what is called "the social gospel." But don't forget that that includes the word "gospel" as well as "social." I believe in the teachings of Christ that the central commandment is to love God and to love our neighbors. The second is likened to it: love our neighbors as we love ourselves. At a later point Jesus said, "How can you love God, whom you have not seen, if you can't love your fellow (humans), whom you have seen?" I take that as an invitation to make sure that we love our fellow human beings first and foremost. I think that may help lead us to an understanding of God.

My father would say that you first have to have what he would have called instantaneous salvation, instantaneous commitment—being saved and then later being sanctified. That was his route. I took a different route—one that I think is consistent with the New Testament and the Old Testament prophets. That is, putting the emphasis on justice and decency and love and kindness towards our fellow humans, always keeping in mind that we believe that each human being is a dignified, precious person who's worthy of that kind of respect and concern. The underlying assumption there is that we must have been created by some spiritual force across this universe that's worth preserving and worth protecting, worth admiring and worth loving.

I think probably we all have a different view of God. Some people have in their minds an old man with a white beard sitting on a throne. That was my view in childhood; I thought he was a male, obviously, and something like my grandfather—sitting on a throne somewhere way up in the heavens, and someday we would see him—but always watching us. That made me a little nervous, but I thought that if you were lucky, you could communicate with him through prayer and in other ways. I heard an awful lot more people say "God _____" than I heard say "help us God," but in any event, I've always had an unfinished view of what God is—whether God is a "he," whether God is a personal being, whether God is a spiritual force that goes beyond personal characteristics.

I know about theology, but I keep room in my spiritual and theological and religious philosophy for a broad interpretation of God. I think the central commandment is to love each other as we love ourselves.

Thomas: Now, it sounds as if you've elevated the second commandment to the first. Jesus said you should love the Lord your God with all your heart, soul, and mind.

Sen. McGovern: I suppose I've taken the excuse that Jesus is saying you can't love God, whom you haven't seen, if you don't love your neighbors, whom you have seen. A person confronted him late in life and thought he had screwed up everything and didn't serve God very well, and Jesus said to him, "No, inasmuch as you have done it unto the least of these, you've done it unto me." You may not have known it, but when you fed the hungry, cared for the sick, ministered to the homeless and those in prison, you were actually serving me. I take that on a leap of faith to mean that if I live a life that's humane and loving, with concern for other people, maybe if there is a judgment out there someday, I can stand up and say, "Well, God, I wasn't quite sure what you were like, or how best to communicate with you, but I've tried to be a decent human being, I've tried to be honest and loving and compassionate to my fellow humans, and sometimes I have been, and so I stand here with that as my only recommendation."

Thomas: You have just described salvation by works, yet Scripture says that salvation comes not by works, because man's righteousness before God is as "filthy rags" and we are saved only by grace through faith and not by works, "lest any man should boast." You are correct that there is a social application to the gospel, but it comes as a result of faith and, by itself, does not qualify one for heaven. So let me ask you a bottom-line question. The apostle Paul said that if we confess with our mouth that Jesus is Lord and believe in our hearts that God has raised him from the dead, we will be saved. Your father would want me to ask you, George, whether you can make that confession?

Sen. McGovern: Yes, I can. I believe that.

FORMER U.S. SENATOR MARK O. HATFIELD (R-OREGON)

Thomas: How do you see the relationship between a believer—a classic follower of Christ, a Christian—and the state in a free society like ours? What should it be?

Sen. Hatfield: First of all, a believer under our Constitution has every constitutional right that the nonbeliever has. If a group of believers wants to get together and organize a political cause or political issue, God bless them. That's their constitutional right. The history of the organized church has included times when it has become so politically involved that political power has corrupted its mission and message. The church—and I don't mean the institution as much as I mean the body of Christ, the spiritual church—has a priority of proclaiming the message of salvation. If the body does not do that, there's no other group or organization committed to do that.

Second, if there are people who desire to be leaders in a political realm, I think that's fine, too. But I do not believe that electing Christians to public office is going to redeem the government. I believe that the Christians' influence is, as the Scripture says, as light, salt, and leaven that transform the environment where they work and where they live. The church in Europe became corrupted when it created "Christian parties" to advance its agenda through government. These parties may be for rights and freedoms as we know them, but that doesn't make them Christian.

When you begin to put the label "Christian" on something, that's where I get a little uneasy. I don't care whether it's an elixir to prolong life or give you better health, or whether it's a product in the marketplace that deals with addresses and telephone numbers in a classified section. The word "Christian" can be very, very misapplied, or it can be so inclusive that it has lost any role in the redemption of individuals and of society. I think a kind of societal redemption is possible, and I think there is a personal redemption. People ask me, "Are you not concerned that the Christian right is taking over the Republican party?" And I say, "No, I'm not that concerned about it. The Democrats have had the Ku Klux Klan; we've had the John Birch Society. We've outlived those extremists, whether of the left or the right, who have taken over political parties or have had great influence from time to time."

Let me take off my political hat and put on my layman's hat. I'm more concerned as to what political activism is doing to the gospel. When you label something "Christian," if it is accompanied by an agenda of political action, does that mean that if you agree with the political items and the economic items on that agenda that that constitutes your Christianity? No. Christ asked Peter one question. It was not "who do others say I am," but "who do *you* say I am?" That is the basic question. People outside the faith get the wrong message. They think, "Well, if I believe in these political issues because they say this is the 'Christian' agenda, then I'm a Christian. And that to me is miscommunication. That is not biblical. The question is, who do you say Christ is?—not who agrees about abortion or school prayer.

Thomas: You seem to be suggesting, if I can refine it, that if one really wants to see government reflect "biblical values," God's people have to live by them and this will produce "bubble up" morality, not "trickle down." Is that a fair summation of what you said?

Sen. Hatfield: Yes. Not legislative morality, but from the heart. Exactly.

Thomas: So that if people are loving their enemies and clothing the naked and feeding the hungry out of their heart, this produces the kind of righteousness that is then reflected from the top. But if they seek to change unrighteous people from the top, they're going to be doomed to frustration and futility.

Sen. Hatfield: We have experienced the attempt to legislate morality often. Now, we always legislate morality in any legislative action, but to focus on what's immoral in society and believe somehow that passing a law against it will correct the problem is wrong. The cause of that immorality most generally speaking is sin. Government cannot redeem people from sin, nor can it transform them from committing sin. Only Christ can do that within the heart of the individual. You may want to use the law as a tutor, but law does not solve the issue. We have many laws against crime, but the prisons overflow.

Thomas: How did you sort this out as a senator? Everybody in Congress is "religious"; no one is listed in the Congressional Directory as an atheist. You were the first serious believer in public life that I knew. In the Senate, and when you were governor, when things seemed to conflict with your deeply held beliefs of right and wrong on a certain issue, how did you process this?

Sen. Hatfield: I suppose that in the political science profession, one of the basic issues that's debated early on is representing republican government. What is the obligation of the elected representative? Edmund Burke addressed that in the British Parliament years and years ago when he indicated that he felt the elected representative owes his best judgment, his convictions, his analysis, his study, and participation in the debate and then votes the best that he feels, contrary to whatever so-called signals or poll he may have heard from the constituents. You read the constituency, you understand the constituency, but there are times when you have to, in effect, lead and not follow.

I was preparing for public office by my education and my involvements, and I made it very clear that that was the kind of representation I would give. Now, that doesn't mean the constituents didn't rail on me in terms of the way I voted on a certain issue. If you should stop at that point, then it could be a sign of arrogance—I would be saying that I know more than the constituents and therefore I'm going to vote my thoughts and not consider them. You could hide, hoping that by the next election they would have forgotten. Instead, I would immediately go into the middle of my constituency and face my constituents in open meetings and explain why I had voted as I did, and share my basic thinking and what my vote represented. I found that even if people still disagreed with you, they would say, "Well, at least I know where he stands, and he's following convictions and not the 'wet finger in the air.' People, I found, admire that more than they resent it.

Thomas: You talked about the relationship between the believer and the state. What ought to be the relationship between the state and the believer? You hinted at it a moment ago that the state's obligation is to ensure religious freedom, freedom of conscience. Is there anything else?

Sen. Hatfield: I don't want the state involved economically or prescriptively to protect the church. The church really doesn't demand that much protection. I've often said that I believe the church should be taxed—at a different rate. Churches make a social contribution to the community, but they also receive services from the community— fire and police protection, sidewalks, and the like. I think the church is vulnerable in receiving special nontax status from the state. I would not want to see a detailed description of how the state acts toward the church, just let religion flow.

Thomas: Why has the Religious Right not succeeded in enacting their agenda?

Sen. Hatfield: They have tended to exclude certain people in our society. Some part of the community sees their political pronouncements reflecting a superior attitude and putting others in an inferior position. They baptize many of their issues with religious jargon or nomenclature that's strange to people outside the religious community, and therefore they convey the image that these outsiders are lesser citizens if they don't subscribe, or they are less religious or less spiritual. These outsiders perceive the Religious Right as attempting to impose their beliefs by law rather than create conditions in which their views are voluntarily accepted. The argument can be counterattacked to a great extent, but the point is, it's still the perception. In politics we're often dealing with imagery more than we are with substance.

Thomas: What about the "Religious Left" that has actively participated in public life? From conscientious objectors, like the Mennonites and Quakers, to the civil rights movement, which was born in black Baptist church basements and proceeded on a moral basis before it got into politics, to the unilateral disarmament crowd in the 1980s, to the environmental movement, the Religious Left has had a political voice. Has the Religious Left suffered from the same ailments now plaguing the Religious Right?

Sen. Hatfield: Many of the liberal, mainline churches have diminished in their numbers and potency. People went to church to hear spiritual encouragement and spiritual edification and received lectures on the United Nations, race relations, and low-cost housing. As a result, many of them gravitated to churches that have a message to preach on Sunday that not only related to God and Christ and was based on Scripture, but also showed how to appropriate that into daily life and personal relationships. So I think those churches' own history is showing that politics was not what people were really coming to church for.

In addition, I think you have to remember that the Civil Rights agenda really emanated from conservative churches. You look back at where the abolitionist movement started. Look at the writings of John Adams and the Constitutional Convention in terms of the black person.

Then, in terms of social outreach to the other less fortunate people, you find orphanages, you find education, and you find help for the poor. Really, the great movements came out of the evangelical church. The nation got to the point of the Civil War, and unfortunately, the first institution that divided between the South and the North was not the political parties. It was the church. As a consequence, churches in the South were defending the slavery issue. Later, the great coal mines had the union leaders—the "secular saints," as I call them—going in there to address the needs of the coal miners. The church was part of the ownership of the coal operator—he owned the church, the store, and the houses. So again, from the North came these evangelical people that were pointing out these social injustices. That's the rich heritage of the evangelical church. From my viewpoint—and I think from history—we let the liberal churches cut into our heritage and let it get away.

Thomas: Should ministers be involved in politics at any level?

Sen. Hatfield: Let's take generic politics. Anytime there's a community action or a group action to solve or address a social inequity, economic inequity, or racial inequity—whatever the issue—that is politics, and I think ministers should be involved.

Thomas: If it can be linked to justice, in other words.

Sen. Hatfield: Right! I would distinguish between the pulpit and the leadership of the flock. I think you can have in the church, away from the pulpit, a men's meeting, a women's meeting, Sunday school sessions, and so on, where an issue can be looked upon, looked at in a discussion arrangement from a biblical perspective: what does Scripture have to say about this? The pastor can be in that role as the leader of the flock, but his pulpit, I think, ought to be reserved for expounding the Word and preaching the message of salvation.

Thomas: When you opposed the war in Vietnam, you experienced some things personally that deeply affected your view of some evangelicals. Many expressed the view that our government is nearly always worthy of support. You received a lot of hate mail, some of which said that "you can't oppose President Johnson, because he's God's leader." They said if you oppose him, you're opposing God. And some questioned whether you were a legitimate Christian.

Sen. Hatfield: That is a deep concept, particularly among religious conservatives. They cite Scriptures such as "touch not God's anointed" and "the King's heart is in God's hand, and he turns it wherever he wills," and "God raises up leadership."

Thomas: How did the reaction of some Christians to your anti-war position change your thinking about the state, its power, and its function?

Sen. Hatfield: Well, I think going back to my student days, I found that in times of fear, a tribal instinct emerges and people rally around the chief. You read about various governments—not in the United States as much as perhaps in Europe—which focused on the threat from outside in order to unify people inside the state because their policies were not working. I don't think anybody would have felt that Hitler or Stalin was placed there by an act of God. We have God's permissive will and his directive will, but would you say that anybody who lied to protect Jews in the attic when the Gestapo rapped on the front door was guilty of a sin in the form of resistance to the Nazis? If you read Pastor Martin Niemöller and some of Dietrich Bonhoeffer's *Letters from Prison,* would anybody today, looking back, say, "Well, he should have bowed to the state?" I don't think so. I think when you consider the gospel universal, it can't be just taken as an American doctrine to apply only to an American system of government.

I don't believe, therefore, that we can say this is a "Christian" nation and the "New Jerusalem." Our Founding Fathers were men of vision, men of brilliance, men of commitment—the most noble characteristics we could ascribe to a group of men, we could ascribe to the gentlemen of the Constitutional Convention in Philadelphia, 1787. I don't think in history there has been a more committed group. Many of them sought God's leading as individuals, even though Benjamin Franklin was credited with saying, "If a sparrow cannot fall to earth without God's notice, is it possible that an empire can rise without his aid?" We have to remember that a number of them were deists—they weren't what we would call today "born again" Christians, evangelical believers—yet they knew the power of the Almighty in the affairs of people. They sensed it.

Having said that, I have never ascribed to the state this overall role to command people's lives, because we have protected the right of dissent in this country, unlike most other countries. You can stand on the street corner and you can say that the president of the United States is a lying so-and-so, and that's freedom of speech. On the other hand, you can say aspirin cures baldness and be arrested pretty quickly today for saying it. The point is simply that I hold the state in respect, but I'd never hold it in such reverence as to say it is infallible or does not deserve, at times, to be criticized.

Thomas: Would you say that the Republican party has almost become an idol for many conservative Christians?

Sen. Hatfield: And with Ronald Reagan, particularly, as high priest! I want to mention something else before I forget. It's very interesting that when Christ was here on earth, a lot of his associates did not understand the kingdom of God. After the resurrection, Jesus appeared to a number of people, and as they were trudging down the road, they asked him, "Are you now going to establish the kingdom of Israel?" The political! The political! Some say that Judas Iscariot was an insurrectionist and that in part he was trying to prod Jesus into action to bring about the new kingdom. I see a certain parallel there with the people today who think we're going to usher in the new kingdom by whatever you call it—the Moral Majority, or electing Republican conservatives to political office.

Thomas: Few would disagree, whatever their political labels, that the culture is suffering badly from a toleration and promotion of what we used to call "sin" before everybody became "dysfunctional." Where would believers be most effective in directing their energies to redress this problem?

Sen. Hatfield: First, the obvious. Start with redemption. It's very interesting that in redemption there is a double action. I think it was shown in the experience of the woman at the well. Christ said to the woman, "Give me a drink." Then he said, "Go fetch your husband." She could have lied and said, "Well, he's working." There had to be a response—an offer and an acceptance. He said to the blind man after putting the spittle on his eyes, "Go wash in the spring of Siloam." I think that very act of salvation teaches us that we have to accept something that is offered by God to us.

That flows right into loving God, but also loving our neighbor. In other words, it demands a response and accountability. Today the culture is ripped with ruptured relationships and the relational attitude of marriage has been replaced with the idea "well, let's live together and try it out." If it works, fine. If it doesn't, the female always is the one who suffers in the sense that she is either moved from or moved out. This happens because people are not really ready to make a commitment to a relationship. I believe in a relational religion as a doctrine, but I'm more concerned about validating humanity as humanity and validating humanity's need to be accountable to God and to each other. To me, that's the key to many of our social problems. You look at the divorce rate and the state of marriages and all these things. So a great social disintegration causes national disintegration. That disintegration starts with the individual and it gets repaired the same way. You can't just sit by and say, "I have no dog in that park" or "I could care less." Christ said in effect to people, "Here's the offer, here's an opportunity to make a response." I think you have to begin to build into people that need of response.

Thomas: What do you make of the contrast between President Clinton's high poll ratings in terms of his performance and other polls that show most people believe their own morals are higher than his and they don't believe he's telling the truth about extramarital affairs and other things? Should this matter?

Sen. Hatfield: Oh yes! It should matter, but it illustrates the materialism of our society, because if economic times were not good—the pocketbook nerve is the most reflective nerve in the political body— it would be a far different poll. Times are good—therefore they don't want to do anything to disturb them. As long as Clinton's president, he's going to get the credit for that, but if there is an economic downturn, you would find that totally reversed. People really are looking into a mirror, and they don't like what they see, and that's because Congress is reflective of people. Government should take a role of leadership and seek to change things by example, but they have not.

They see the debts—moral and ethical debts, which they have in their own family, their own neighborhood, their own country club—and conclude that maybe their own morals are not what they should be, so they don't want to be too critical.

Thomas: Are some conservative Christian leaders misleading their people by suggesting—actively or passively—that true moral change will come from the top?

Sen. Hatfield: I don't think that they're intentionally misleading people. We've always had people who believe that in one form or another. I just think they're wrong. Whether they have a ministerial degree or a political science degree, it is not the approach that's going to reform society or enhance society's moral character.

Thomas: So, if a Republican candidate, even one to the liking of the so-called Religious Right were elected in the year 2000, and Republicans held on to the Senate and the House, how much would change on their issues—abortion, gay rights, pornography, family values?

Sen. Hatfield: You would still have the Supreme Court. It is really to our political advantage in never being able to unite our government under one voice and one viewpoint. Under those circumstances, you would find some activity around the edges that if anything relates to sin, there's no way that a Republican government can change that vulnerability and bring force to some of our social problems—including abortion. I'm not saying now that to permit abortion isn't sin; I'm just saying that nobody I've heard speak feels it to be a sin—it's just a woman's right. So if it's not even in the field of theological discourse, you're not going to find government able to do that—the Supreme Court striking down such laws as unconstitutional. Even if Republicans could outlaw abortion and the Supreme Court didn't strike down the law, that is still dealing with the result of a cause that remains unattended. I don't see how morality can change in this country without a spiritual renaissance. We're looking for political, economic, and social solutions to basically a spiritual problem. And those solutions don't exist.

U.S. SENATOR JOHN ASHCROFT (R-MISSOURI)

Thomas: What do you see as the purpose of government?

Sen. Ashcroft: I think the purpose of government is to maintain an environment in which people reach the maximum of their God-given potential and to provide safety and security in which people flourish. There's a spiritual sense that goes along with it. As a Christian, I believe that Christ came because he didn't think people were doing well enough. They didn't have the kind of abundance in their lives they ought to have. The purpose of government is to try to set structural conditions in which people can do well. Christ comes because people are doing poorly, because things are wrong internally. Government's responsibility is to make sure that there is a hospitable set of externals that allow people to do well and to provide a framework in which people can grow. It shouldn't be growth of government; it should be growth of individuals. Unfortunately, I think too often we get into the situation of the government maintaining an environment in which the bureaucracy and government itself flourish at the expense of individuals and institutions.

Thomas: What do you see as the primary cause of moral decline in the country?

Sen. Ashcroft: Morality is a matter of choice. People make choices. The moral condition of a culture is an aggregation of the moral choices made by individuals. There is a variety of conditions in the culture that signal a disrespect for morals that have affected the kind of choices that are being made. I look at the impact that government has, and I think government has helped create an environment that is hostile to good, moral decision making. Moral choices are primarily shaped by the culture, and culture shapes behavior in an anticipatory or preventative way. Laws shape behavior by punishing after there's been an infraction. Our government of late has made it very difficult for the culture to operate by shaping behavior.

Incidentally, the culture shapes behavior with the "policeman" on the inside. The law shapes behavior with the policemen on the outside. The more you have the capacity to shape the behavior of a community with the policeman on the inside, the less you have to have the police on the outside. Another way of stating this is that the higher the level of morality, the lower the need for governmental legality. As we have destroyed the ability of culture to shape behavior, we have had to proliferate laws in an attempt to make up for the absence of the culture-shaping behavior. The proliferation of laws has never made up for it, but we keep adding more laws, and more laws, and more laws.

How has government expressed this hostility in the culture? It has done so by supporting the idea of moral parity—which is another way of saying that it has reinforced the concept that the only things that matter are laws.

It's a tragedy when the defining phrase of an administration is "there is no known controlling 'legal authority.'" The laws set the minimums for behavior in a culture. They are the thresholds. If you don't abide by them, you get thrown into jail. If everybody only does the minimums in a culture, the culture will be anemic; it cannot be a culture of leadership; it will not define the world as America traditionally has, for the last two hundred years, defined the globe as a place of increasing opportunity and freedom.

Our government has made our communities hostile to culture itself in two ways. That's because there are two ways in which culture shapes behavior—through stigma on the one hand, and affirmation on the other. We have devalued affirmation by giving everybody the "gold star" no matter what lifestyle, no matter what conduct they manifest. As long as it's legal, you get a gold star. So one thing that culture used to build—morality and moral decision making—has been devalued, made worthless. If you give everybody a gold star, the gold star means nothing.

The second way in which culture shapes and provides a good place for moral decision making is through stigma. We have outlawed stigma. We have outlawed it by saying that it's politically incorrect and inappropriate to say that certain things are wrong. We are no longer capable of identifying things as being wrong, and we are no longer capable of ranking, for affirmation, things that are legal. Once you devalue affirmation and you outlaw stigma, you make it impossible for the culture to shape moral choices.

Now, let's get back to the first part of my answer that the moral decline of the culture is the result of collective moral decisions that are not as good as they ought to be. I think government is related to that because the leadership in our culture has been too oriented to legalism and has unfortunately embraced this doctrine of moral parity. By doing so, it has implemented a strategy of devaluing affirmation and outlawing stigma.

Thomas: How do you turn this around? Certainly not by government alone.

Sen. Ashcroft: No. The idea of government being the source of goodness in the culture is a mistake. That probably reached its epitome in the 1960s, when Lyndon Johnson projected that greatness would come from Washington. He wanted to say that we could be a Great Society, but to be great we'll have to control it and orchestrate it and evoke it with policies in Washington, D.C. The genius of the American republic is not that the values of Washington be imposed on the people; the genius of the American republic is that the people's values be imposed on Washington, D.C. This reversal in value flow, which I think can be clearly traced to the Great Society era and to that mindset, is, I think—well, I'll just put it this way: We've all seen how "great" the arts have become since the National Endowment of the Arts was brought in to make art "great" in America since the '60's. And we brought in a lot of stuff to make the families of America "great" in the '60's—and we've seen the family devalued tax-wise, we've seen the family devalued with the suggestion that fathers can be replaced with welfare checks.

Thomas: If Washington isn't the answer, and if policies set in Washington are not the solution, then . . .

Sen. Ashcroft: Wait a second! You've made a fundamental mistake in your question. Once you say "the" answer and "the" solution, you've too narrowly set the stage. There are answers and solutions. While Washington isn't "the" answer, nothing else is "the" answer.

There are some things in Washington that are part of the answer, and there are other things that for pastors are the answer.

Thomas: What do you think ought to be the primary role of pastors in this process?

Sen. Ashcroft: I think leaders—be they pastors, community leaders, moms and dads, senators, or congressmen—have an opportunity to do things in their respective roles. There's one thing that you do in your governance role: We should take the hostility toward morality out of the system. And take the hostility toward faith out of the system. That's what the Charitable Choice Provision and the Welfare Reform Law were designed to do—to take away the hostility that's been expressed governmentally toward the values as expressed in the culture.

We've displaced a lot of cultural stuff with government once we thought that the values had to flow from government into the culture instead of vice versa. Pastors need to call people to their highest and best, not accommodate the culture at its lowest and least. Christ came to call people to their highest and best. At the risk of being grossly misinterpreted here, the president of the United States ought to call people to their highest and best.

Thomas: Misinterpreted, why?

Sen. Ashcroft: Because I juxtaposed those statements, and it will sound like "Uh-oh, he's come to Christianize everybody." The point is that governance is the process, by imposition and mandate, of compelling people to live at a level of the threshold of acceptability. If all a leader does is to govern, he's not a leader—he just mandates that people make it to the lowest possible level. We have an opportunity for everyone that's in government, and everyone that's in a pastoral role—pastoral roles really specialize in the other things. Instead of mandate and imposition, which are the currency of government, pastors should work by model and inspiration, which are the currency of leadership. We need people in Washington, we need mayors, community leaders, school teachers, and principals who not only impose by mandate and imposition the threshold rules of the society that are necessary for governance, but who, by model and inspiration, call the culture to its highest and best.

Thomas: The question I was asking about the pastor relates to the fact that we've had people on both sides, left and right, talking about what the limitations of a pastoral role should be. Should he preach politics from the pulpit, should he be perceived primarily by the unbelieving culture as organizing for the Republican party, or unilateral disarmament, or the environment? Should there be a demarcation line between the two kingdoms from a pastoral role point of view?

Sen. Ashcroft: I think pastors should speak the truth in love. This is what Christ did. And they should call people to their highest and best. I think they should work to inspire people to moral decision making and responsible behavior. My own view is that there's a catalytic power in the truth which will have an impact on the hearts and minds of people. I don't know of any area of truth that the pastor should be warned away from, or any area of reality that should be "off limits" to pastors.

Thomas: Let me refine that a bit. What would you say about a pastor who was involved in distributing the Clinton Chronicles and denouncing from the pulpit the president and vice president of the United States?

Sen. Ashcroft: I think that's a matter of conscience for that pastor. The way I read the Bible, there were various kinds of prophets. When I say I would ask pastors to speak the truth, I invite them to speak the truth as they see it. There are pastors who have been very critical of me, and frankly, on some occasions I have thanked them because sometimes they've been right and I needed criticism.

Thomas: How does this play, though, to unbelievers who think that conservative pastors are in the pocket of the Republican party and the result is to be known more for one's political position than for the gospel they are called to preach?

Sen. Ashcroft: I have enough trouble figuring out how I should act and trying to act properly as a politician rather than trying to tell all the pastors in America how and at what level they should express themselves. I think they should call people to their highest and best and call people to morally responsible decision making—and the best framework, in my judgment, for morally responsible decision making is expressed in God's Holy Word, the Bible. I think that's what a pastor should do. There will be disagreements about whether people have done it the way it ought to be done.

Thomas: You have been one of the favored few whom Dr. James Dobson has been mildly critical of for voting on one or two things that displeased him. Virtually everybody comes to Congress with a certain set of standards and principles and a lot of zeal that they're going to change things and make them better. But once they get on the inside, even as committed believers, they find in the Senate there are 99 other people and in the House there are 435 members, and you can't always have your way. So they sometimes compromise and are attacked for selling out their principles. You've heard all these things at one time or another in public life, I'm sure. For the benefit of those who are on the outside, how is it for a committed believer, when he becomes one of a hundred in the United States Senate, to impose his will or see his way enacted into law without compromise?

Sen. Ashcroft: It's very difficult to impose anything in a free society. We were very pleased to be able to get fifty-two senators to agree to a national, organic bloc ban on federal government testing in our schools. It was very difficult. We worked for a couple of years for that. We started out with thirteen votes in favor of our position and ended up with fifty-two, and if Senator Helms had been there, it would have been fifty-three. So it's very difficult. It's important for the public to understand that you're not in a position to just come in here and insist, yet the public is in a position to insist—so it ought to understand that it won't always get a full loaf. But that should not stop the public from demanding what is right. That's healthy in this democracy.

When the prophets of this culture criticize me, whether they be from the right or the left, I think that's important and they should continue to do so. They may expect me to have the ability to get exactly what they want when I don't, and they may expect me to believe exactly what they believe when I don't, but that doesn't mean they shouldn't expect it. One thing that's difficult here is to take on twenty or fifteen or maybe only a dozen issues and try to stay focused.

One of the models I have in life—the model I respect most—is Christ. Christ didn't address every evil all the time. I think we have to be careful that we don't expect those who are in public life to be on top of every battle all the time, because if we are not focused, we don't have the kind of penetrating capacity that comes when we line up all our resources and direct them toward a specific objective.

Thomas: George McGovern told me the idea of a Moral Majority, of a super Christian Coalition, is biblically false. He said, "God's people have always been a remnant, a minority within a larger structure and culture." I'm wondering if you think that individual believers are mistaken when they assert that their worldview is really in the majority, or ought to be, and that they should expect to see it reflected in government?

Sen. Ashcroft: I think that American history belies Mr. McGovern's position. There's been a substantial period of time when there was a worldview that was common to most Americans in the history of this country. So, while a specific worldview may be a remnant in one setting or another, it depends on how you define a community. Take a church, for example: Are we going to say that only a small fragment of those people can ever be true believers because the remnant is always a small part of any community, if a church is a community? I don't think so. I think there is a great deal of the American experience which has been defined by a unity of worldview.

There is a serious question about whether we have that kind of unity of worldview and the value of it in modern American culture. But to suggest that it can never have been and was never meant to be is wrong, I think. Unless I'm mistaken about my understanding of American history, there has been a significant period of time in which there was a substantial unity of worldview. I think that's what allowed documents like the Constitution, the Declaration of Independence, and the Federalist Papers. Sure, they had disagreements, but the kind of worldview expressed there had a coherency and unity which I think is to be valued.

There has been an adequately unified worldview to embrace a therapeutic kind of culture in which there was a constant stream of healing and a stream of progress and according greater rights and opportunities and a broader set of horizons to the population generally, moving us toward our highest and best, making the environment a stronger place for growth and opportunity on a consistent and continuing basis.

Let me just throw one little wrench into this machinery. Some people think you can never have unity unless you have uniformity. I think a profoundly important point about America is that this has been a culture which has never understood unity to require uniformity. I like to illustrate this with a musical analogy: Great orchestras are not uniform. They have different kinds of people, they carry vastly different instruments into the hall—some to blow into, some to be beaten upon, some of wood, some of metal, some of string and wood. They put the music on the stand and they play different notes, and this would appear to be a recipe for chaos. They don't have uniformity, but they do have unity, because they follow a common objective and they are directed by well-meaning, talented leaders. What is interesting about this is that when you have unity, the absence of uniformity doesn't become a liability. It becomes an incredible asset in that setting.

Thomas: You are the person we're interviewing who is considering running for president. If you decide to run and if you make it, what could you do, given the limitations of our Constitution, to restore affirmation and to stigmatize those things that we used to consider bad and wrong, not only for individuals who practice them, but also for the country? [Senator Ashcroft announced in January 1999 that he would not seek the presidency. Still, his thoughts are included because they are interesting.]

Sen. Ashcroft: I think the opportunity for real leadership is to speak the truth in love.

Thomas: Define that in specifics. President Carter told young people in his administration, "Those of you who are living together and not married ought to get married." Is that the kind of thing you're taking about?

Sen. Ashcroft: I commend Jimmy Carter for having done that.

Thomas: Is that what you're talking about? To make the "bully pulpit" more pulpit than bully?

Sen. Ashcroft: To make the bully pulpit an opportunity for the expression of a call to our highest and best.

Thomas: Would these be sermons? Are we going to have the Reverend President?

Sen. Ashcroft: I don't think we sermonize to people. We promote and elevate in the culture the things that elevate the community. Unfortunately, we have leadership now that has sought to elevate aspects of the culture that are detrimental to the community. My own view is that to come full circle on the moral climate and the tone of the country is a collective aggregation of choices, and I think the leadership choices have profound impact because they resonate throughout the culture. I would want to lead the public to choices that are focused on integrity, on the people's reaching their highest and best rather than accommodating culture at its lowest and least.

U.S. REPRESENTATIVE TONY HALL (D-OHIO)

Thomas: What do you see as the role of the believer—the serious Christian or Jew—and the role of the church when it's perceived as an institution, a denominational group in our constitutional republic?

Rep. Hall: I think the role of the believer and the church is to love God and to love others. I believe it's to love Him with all heart, soul, mind, and strength and to love others as you love yourself. That means a lot of different things to different people.

Thomas: The big debate over the last twenty years has been about the "proper" relationship between religious people and the state. The evangelicals and fundamentalists developed a catacomb mentality following the Scopes Trial in the 1920s. They were ridiculed for believing in Creation and not evolution. Many of them went AWOL in terms of any kind of political involvement. This belief in disengagement was preached in pulpits all over America for decades. It was said politics is dirty, it forces you to compromise, there is a higher kingdom that we ought to be focusing on and preparing for, and if you get involved in politics you're going to become tainted and dirty. Then, when the so-called Religious Right exploded on the scene twenty years ago, some of these people who had controlled the terms of the debate— even the religious terms of the debate—said, "No, no, get back where you belong. You shouldn't be here in the first place because you're violating the First Amendment." So I'm asking, from your perspective, is there a demarcation between faith and politics?

Rep. Hall: The genius of the Constitution is the separation of the church and state, which I believe in.

Thomas: What does that mean to you?

Rep. Hall: I look at Europe, and I see that the Church of England is the official government church, and it's dead. What has happened in many of the European nations is that they have not separated the church and state. Therefore the church, down through history, has said, "If we can get control of this situation, we can just change it." But the fact is, the church is one of the worst compromisers of all, because they get into something they don't understand and then they start thinking the way politicians think, and what happens is, they get compromised.

Now, I believe that there are very definite answers that Jesus and God speak to us about in the Scriptures. Whether it be abortion, whether it's homosexuality, whether it be lewd talk—a number of things. I think we can act on those in government, and I think they are direct orders from God. Another one is how we treat the poor. Whether it's the government doing it or the people doing it, the church doing it or the people doing it. There are 25,000 verses that say we're supposed to be involved with the poor, the hurting, the orphans, the widows. But God doesn't necessarily say—to take a current example—I want you to feed everybody in the world except those people in North Korea. He doesn't say that. He says, "You feed the people."

Thomas: Why do you think many religious conservatives have majored only on the volatile issues like abortion, gay rights, pornography, and bad TV and have ignored some of these other things you've talked about, including the poor, justice, even gossip and slander and bearing false witness, which are also listed in the Bible with other sins?

Rep. Hall: It's a mystery to me. I don't understand it, because it's as clear to me as those other issues. Abortion is as clear to me as speaking out about injustices and speaking out for the poor and the hurting. Maybe it has something to do with the history of the liberal church verses the conservative church that goes back to the Sermon of the Mount. The Sermon of the Mount was always looked upon as a very liberal theology. It was taught by liberal churches and therefore, for some reason, probably wasn't interpreted correctly—not only by the liberal churches, but by the conservative churches.

I think something happened there, which somebody who is a much better historian than I am could probably figure out. But I think that started it, and what's happened is that this evangelical right side (to the right of me and many people) has over the years represented a very judgmental attitude. And they hurt the cause of Christ rather than help it or promote it, because they judge. I mean, they say if you're a bad person, if you're a drunkard, if you're an adulterer, if you're whatever you are—you're this and you're that—and they slam a name and at the same time say how wonderful they are, how pious they are. They'll also say of the poor people—well, look at these poor people: They don't work, they're lazy, they're on welfare, they're fat—every time I see them they're driving a Cadillac. That's a strange thing. I spend a lot of time with poor people. Most of the poor today in the country are the working poor. These are the people who don't want to be on welfare, but they're hungry because they're working a couple jobs, their families are split, they're not "making it" two or three days out of every month and they are not able to make it. So there are the stereotypes that have been set up.

How they've been set up over the years, I don't have the slightest idea, but the other side has been very judgmental and has judged people who are not believers and they have judged believers. They have judged me. They have had people come into my district, into the churches in my district, and say that Tony Hall is not a believer because of the way he votes. I had a voting record approval rate from conservatives in 1997 of about 45 or 50 percent—probably the highest it's ever been. It normally is much lower that than. According to them, I have been "right" on pornography, abortion, and homosexuality, but when it came to budget matters, or voting for the Department of Education, or some kind of a tax consequence, my vote was anti-Moral Majority, anti-Christian Coalition. Therefore, how could I be a Christian in view of the way I voted?

I said, "You know, I look to and fro for what Jesus said about capital gains and could not find it." So when somebody arbitrarily says, like the Moral Majority or the Religious Right, "This is the voting record," these are the people who vote 100 percent of the time or 80 percent of the time and so they are the Christians. These are the kind of people we want to support." Two of the people had a 100 percent voting record for the Moral Majority—one was a homosexual, and another one I believe got into an affair with one of our pages over here.

Thomas: Are you sure this is the Moral Majority, or are you speaking generically?

Rep. Hall: Generically—Christian Coalition or whatever. All of the people who got "zero" might have been very, very good people. But they certainly must be anti-Christian, couldn't have been believers. I'm not saying that these critics don't have the right to say such things, but not only have I been the recipient of that, but I have also seen it turn people away from following God. That's the problem, because some of my colleagues whom I've tried to witness to say, "Tony, if you're part of the Moral Majority or that Christian Coalition, I don't want anything to do with it—these people are mean and they're vindictive and they're judgmental, so don't talk to me about God." A lot of people use a lot of excuses about why they don't come to Jesus, and that's a convenient excuse. We have all kinds of excuses, but nevertheless, I have seen people run because of the hypocritical nature of these kinds of groups that hurt people; they kill the cause of Christ, in my opinion.

The greatest example of the judgmental way, I think, is the story of Jesus and the adulterous woman. I think it's a wonderful example. Who are the people chasing her? They're the pious people. These people are going to stone her to death, and Jesus writes in the sand and says some wonderful words—and you know what he says about those who have not sinned. But the important thing is, they left—and he agreed with them, but he didn't say it publicly. He said, "Go and sin no more." He agreed that she was a sinner, but he didn't publicly condemn her. So she loved him, because she felt safe with him. That is the way we're supposed to be. I think if Jesus was here today, he would be doing what he did then! As you read the gospel, Jesus spent his time with three groups of people: the disciples (the twelve); the sinners, which are you and I and everybody else; and the poor. Those are the three groups. The fourth group drove him nuts! And that was the pious group and religious people. The only time he got mad was with those people.

Thomas: What do you see as the primary cause or causes of moral decline in America?

Rep. Hall: Bishop Fulton J. Sheen said it many years ago. He said we have the Statue of Liberty as we come into the country. On the other side of the country we ought to have a Statue of Responsibility. If you let democracy go unchecked, it will destroy you. You will eat your young, and you will be destroyed from within because there's too much freedom. With liberty, and with all the people who died for it so that you and I can say whatever we want to say, comes a responsibility to be people of character, people who care. I find that amazing.

It just drives me absolutely crazy that our parties, both Republican and Democrat, and the president attack the tobacco companies because it's an easy group to attack. At the same time they allow pornography on the Internet, they allow abortion, they allow 30- to 35,000 people to die every day in this world, they allow our working poor to not have enough food in our own country, and the list goes on—and yet they take the easy way. So there are a lot of reasons for the moral decline, including the fact that we have not taken responsibility. That's number one.

Number two, we have allowed things to creep into our society without stepping up and saying, "Wait a minute! Hold on!" For example, thirty years ago you could go to a movie and you never heard the "F" word. As a matter of fact, when they said "damn" in *Gone with the Wind,* everybody was shocked. Ever since then, it's gotten worse. We've allowed that to happen over time. And these people who have allowed it to creep in are so cool: They hide behind the First Amendment, which drives me nuts. So many abuses have been done under the banner of the First Amendment. I wish we could throw them in jail for a while. It's just amazing what has happened under the First Amendment.

I bet our Constitutional fathers would be rolling over in their graves if they knew exactly what we were doing. That has been allowed to happen. It's gone unchecked. Edmund Burke said, "All it takes for evil to prevail, is for good men to do nothing." Most people in this world and in this country are sheep. I don't say that in a derogatory way. Most people don't want to lead, and there are very few people who do lead. The rest want to be led by people of character. They will follow if you have something to say. But most people won't step up and lead, and when they do, they take the easy way out, they do the easy things. Tobacco? That's easy! They do the things that are popular, but the character things like pornography and abortion and all the garbage that goes on—they don't stop that. We've allowed our society to erode. I don't mean to be giving a political speech, but it just really makes me mad, because I believe that in our democracy we have responsibility. There ought to be a Statue of Responsibility.

Thomas: Virtually everyone, regardless of party label or religious label or political position, has mentioned materialism in one way or another, as you have just done. The focus on self, the consumption of more and more things, the bigger house, the bigger car, the nicer clothes, more money in the bank, and never having enough—these all help to blind you to the need of others.

Rep. Hall: We have too many freedoms. To hear a Democrat saying that is unbelievable. We have so many freedoms, it's stifling. As a result, people have so much from which to pick and choose, but there's no character, or moral direction, or vision among a lot of the leaders saying, "This is the way we should go." Everybody is doing the polls, everybody is afraid to step up.

In the first chapter of John, when John the Baptist sends his disciples over to him, Jesus asked questions. They are very interesting. Jesus practically said, "What do you guys want?"

"We want to follow you home," they replied.

He said, "Well, come and see."

Jesus already knows where we are. He wants to ask us the question as to where are we, and he wants us to say, "Well, what is it that you want?" Well, I want to be successful, I want to have a nice house, I want to have two cars. I think what he's saying to us is, What's the difference between you now at forty or fifty or sixty and when you were a little boy and you had your little cars? Is there any difference? You're still playing, but with your "big" cars now. There's no difference. And the difference among us as believers is, where's our foundation? Who makes things work? Jesus is the only one who can give us the foundation to start to change our lives.

Thomas: What do you think should be the role and limitation of pastors in our society?

Rep. Hall: They should teach Jesus and teach the Bible. I think that's the role of pastors. I think they should be very careful about supporting politicians in a partisan way. But I think that they should not refrain from taking a position. And if they're going to take a position because they're a pastor, they had better be able to support it with the Scriptures. On the other hand, the first role of a pastor is to teach Jesus, to teach the Word, to mentor us.

Thomas: You talked about some of your colleagues who were repulsed by the Religious Right and so want nothing to do with God. Accepting that at face value, at what point does the commenting on political issues become counterproductive and, in fact, become the primary message?

Rep. Hall: This is a difficult one. I've been reading the book about Billy Graham that he just wrote about himself.

Thomas: Just As I Am.

Rep. Hall: Right! He talks of the different relationships that he had with presidents, including Lyndon Johnson and Richard Nixon, and the turmoil that he got himself into and some of the problems that he had, and what he said about Clinton recently and stuff like that. I think the role of the pastor is really to not judge anybody in public. I think the role of the pastor is private. If you're going to be "in" with the President, or "in" with somebody like that to talk to him, be real honest with him, admonish him, teach him. And if you know he's done something wrong, I think you should tell him.

Thomas: To his face and not on television.

Rep. Hall: Not on television. I don't think you should do it publicly. People ask me what I think we should do about things, and I say, "The first thing to do is pray for them, because that's what God said to do."

He says in 1 Timothy to pray for the leaders—not because they're better, but because they have the ability to make things good or bad—so that the people can live peaceful and tranquil lives in all godliness and dignity.

There is a poignant saying in Africa: "When the elephants fight, the grass dies." That means when the big guys fight, people die. If all of us politicians all over the world fight all the time, people are going to perish.

There are a lot of civil wars and humanitarian crises. Even here at this particular time in this great democracy, we fight one another. And when we do that, while most of our people don't perish, they are not served, they don't live peaceful and tranquil lives. So the first thing we have to do is pray for our leaders.

The second thing is not to be afraid to go and see them, tell them you love them and are praying for them. Don't judge them. If you're going to say something harsh to them, you should know them a little bit better before you do that. I don't think you have the right to say that, because you're going to lose them. If you didn't know me and you heard I did something bad and you started to chew me out, you wouldn't last very long in my office. I wouldn't think much of you. If you came and spent a year with me and we really got to know each other and we became friends and then you came to talk to me, I'd listen to you. I think that's the way you do it. I think you do it behind the scenes. I think you do it quietly. I don't think you embarrass anybody or judge them in public. I think you love them. When you're friends with them, you admonish them and teach them and guide them. And I think you do it the way the Scriptures say: If they won't stop, you go get somebody else to come with you, and you try to follow the Scriptures.

Thomas: Where do you think we're likely to be twenty years from now as the Boomers move out of influencing every decade that they moved through?

Rep. Hall: I don't know. I'm not a prophet. I do know that there are isolated revivals that are breaking out. I think that our country is very prosperous, doing very well, but I think in this democracy we have so many freedoms that we are letting things go, and I think we're going to eat ourselves up here. I think we're in for some big trouble.

Thomas: What kind?

Rep. Hall: I think that morally we're allowing things to go to pot. The way that we pass over things and look the other way—what's happening on television and the Internet, what's happening with our acceptance of things that we shouldn't be accepting. You know, the lifestyles, the family styles, the homosexuals—we're saying we're accepting same-sex marriage. We're starting to do things that were never thought of or heard of thirty years ago.

Thomas: Who has the power to stop that?

Rep. Hall: I think the believers have the power to stop it. I think they have the power through prayer, through spiritual strength, and through revival, and it can only come from God. I think that we need to get down on our knees and start praying to God. We do need revival; we need to turn to him more. A lot of people say that a majority of this country are believers (in God). Whatever it is, it's a large number. But they're not committed. Billy Graham said, "I thought my job really was to bring people to God. Maybe my job was to bring Christians to Jesus."

U.S. SENATOR RICK SANTORUM (R-PENNSYLVANIA)

Thomas: What is the role of the believer in Jesus Christ as an individual and the role of the church when it is perceived as an institution in a constitutional republic?

Sen. Santorum: The role of the church is to help shape, mold, and restrain the individual. When I look at my two-and-a-half-year-old, I see that he is not naturally "good." He's wonderful, and he has a lot of great characteristics, but I don't know that any of my children are naturally good. They need parents and churches and faith to provide the kind of value structures necessary for people to be able not only to pursue their spiritual desires, but also to interact in a peaceful way with each other. So that's the role of a church, speaking solely from a utilitarian standpoint as far as our country is concerned. Obviously the pastors have their own role, which is to shepherd the people in their flock toward heaven. But in so doing, they create better citizens, so they have a very important role to play in providing, for the country and for the government, quality people with strong values and convictions who can then reflect those values in the laws that they pass.

Thomas: What do you see as the primary cause of moral decline in America?

Sen. Santorum: I go back to the deterioration of the family, and with it the deterioration of community and the overall moral relativism we see when there is no pursuit or truth, nor any desire to even understand what truth is—or that there is, in fact, "a truth." In a speech I gave the other day on Lincoln and Clinton I mentioned how Lincoln was an abolitionist. We had a civil war over it! There was, in fact "a truth" then, and there are, in fact, truths today that we choose to ignore. That's a rather frightening thing. I think that leads to the general breakdown.

If, because we're tolerant and accept other people's viewpoints, even though we know that they are not necessarily truthful, we have nothing to hold us together anymore. There's no common bond that keeps us in this nice level playing field which I talked about earlier, where we can interact. Our planes don't intercept, we just believe fundamentally different things, and therefore we have a lot more friction and problems within our society. Many people watch the evening news and just scratch their heads and say, "How can people think that way? How can people do those things?" And they insist that we must accept them. If you don't believe that a marriage is a meaningful union, one that is sworn under God that you have to maintain—it's just something that's convenient because you can sleep together and it's legal—the consequences of that are very severe for a country.

Thomas: What can government do to restore some of this lost sense of morality and truth?

Sen. Santorum: Get out of the way! I've been working on the renewal of lives, including the concept of not having the government solve problems in Washington or dictate solutions. Yes, government can help. We can allow families to keep the resources they've already earned so they can invest in their children, or we can provide tax credits so people will give money to nonprofit organizations that help those in need in our society. And most of those we hope, and we believe, will be faith-based nonprofit organizations that will teach values.

But what we've done historically in this country is create large government bureaucracies that act like buffers between individuals and the community instead of conduits to bring people together. These buffers are people who allow you to be independent (other than of government) of your neighbors—you don't need fathers, you don't need next-door neighbors, you don't need people down the street because government will be the umbilical cord for all you need. Therefore the only thing that makes you a community is a common mailing address. It's no longer a sense of connectedness, because there's no need to be connected. We only need to be connected to our federal umbilical cord and we are free to go about our own business. The effect is not only to destroy a sense of community, but to destroy the family.

Thomas: What should be the role and limitation of pastors, priests, rabbis—the clergy, the ordained in our society—particularly when they interact with government?

Sen. Santorum: I bounce all over the place on that. When I first ran for office, I would say, after the fact, "Why aren't these folks coming out and being supportive of me, and being more vocal?" Some were, even from the pulpit, but my faith is the Catholic religion, and my goodness, they wouldn't get within a ten-foot pole of me. I wondered why. If I was, in fact, pursuing most of their belief system as far as the government was concerned, why wouldn't they be supportive? Maybe I can say I've become somewhat more enlightened since I've gotten here and have seen the downside and the pitfalls of that.

I look at the Roman Catholic Church, and I think their framework is correct and it is this: You don't get personally involved in candidates and campaigns, but you get very involved in issues of importance and take very strong positions and stands and support anyone who will stand up for these particular values. That has its perils, too. I look at how the Catholic Church deals in the area of welfare, and it is a disaster, in my opinion, the way Catholic charities and other organizations have become the extension of the welfare state instead of a separate organization doing faith-based missions. Catholic charities have become completely co-opted by the state. So you have to be careful. You don't get too close, because if you get too close, then it's very easy to get co-opted.

And what a lot of the evangelical churches have done very, very well—with the gospel missions and the rescue missions and all the others, the Salvation Army—they have kept that distance from the government and in so doing have kept the integrity of what they have done and have been able to be much more responsible spokespeople. In fact, I found them to be somewhat uncomfortable when I approached them and asked them to give opinions as to how government should interact with them. They said, "Well, we just sort of like to stay away from it because of the corrupting influence of it."

So it is important to let your opinion be known and to fight for what you believe in, but not to the point where you become co-opted by the government.

Thomas: Let's talk a moment about those people outside of government who aren't running for elected office but have such zeal to fix what is wrong with America—abortion, gay rights, pornography, the rest. As a senator, as one inside the government, what would you say to people on the outside who think you should move faster and suggest you may be a compromiser because you don't?

Sen. Santorum: I understand the dynamic. I think part of the problem of people looking at Rick Santorum and others and saying, "They sold out," is that there is a general mistrust of politicians (even among people you consider friends), and President Clinton has been an outstanding example of why there should be. We rank right below used-car salesmen. The general attitude is, even if we like you, we still question you because you're involved in this. They think this is not noble work, even though it is, in fact, very noble work. Most of the people here in the Senate are doing their very best in trying to deal with the issues at hand. But I think there is an overall feeling by the public of distrust, or lack of confidence, or disdain, for elected officials.

Now, having said all that, people should read Catherine Brinkerbiddle's *Miracle in Philadelphia* and find out what our wonderful, astute, noble Founding Fathers did to compromise to get the Constitution of the United States, which now we hold up as a pure and principled document. You say, "But they were compromising on higher principles." I don't know that we are compromising on lower principles. We compromise on a variety of competing convictions that, depending on your perspective, can be very honorable and, in fact, quite moral. I don't question [Democratic Senator Daniel] "Pat" Moynihan's morality when he continues to support state-sponsored welfare. He believes that's very moral, that it's our common need to pull together and help. I just don't believe that it actually accomplishes what he hopes it will accomplish. That doesn't mean he's any less moral than I am.

I think the same can be said with various issues. Now, we get here and we run up against people who have very strong feelings the other way and we come up against something that's really a bugaboo, and that's the way it is. I'll never forget when I first got here, I was trying to get something done. I was walking back from the Senate chamber with [Republican Senator] Bob Packwood and lamenting all the problems I was having. He said, "It's funny—you remind me of me thirty years ago."

I said, "How so?"

He said, "Oh, I came here and I was going to do this and I was going to do that and I just couldn't get anything done. It was just horrible trying to move anything." And he said, "There was this one piece of legislation that I was working on and it was a great thing and I thought we were going to get this done and someone filibustered and then we lost it."

Packwood said he remembered walking back and seeing an old-time senator from the sixties, and he said he would never forget that man telling him that he used to feel the same way you do now. Still, for every good bill that is stopped, there are ten bad ones that we stop, too. But you know what, if it's really a good idea, in six or seven years it will pass, too. And Packwood said, "And things work out best that way."

By and large—not always—it has been the best way. It takes an incredible amount of patience. And recognize the fact that one-third of the Senate changes every six years. It takes the House ten years to turn over completely or almost completely. It will take the Senate three times that long to turn over. As a result, the passions of today will have cooled substantially by the time the Senate has changed, and we will have seen the wisdom of what the passion was for and those that were not so wise will have filtered out.

Thomas: Are you optimistic, as we see the social and moral problems today, that this is going to be turned around in five years, ten years, twenty years?

Sen. Santorum: Absolutely! I believe that as long as good people who have strong values and convictions continue to populate this country and live out those convictions in either public or private life, the United States of America will eventually solve all their problems. That's just a core belief in our communities and in our values and in our institutions. I think the federal government has done a fairly good job trying to snuff out a lot of those institutions. And I think we are seeing a general direction, a recognition from even the other side— from many of them, not all of them—that government is not the end-all answer and may even be a big part of the problem. We're seeing, not just a retreat, but a slow understanding that increasing freedom and putting more responsibility back out into the community, into the family, and into the churches is the right general approach. It is just a seed right now, but I can point to several things that have happened.

Back in the summer of 1994 I introduced a welfare reform bill. (I had also written the Contract with America provision for welfare reform.) I was blasted by Ted Kennedy, Pat Moynihan, and others. Radical! You know, people are going to be sleeping on crates and starving in the streets, and this was going to be the worst pullout of the federal government in history. It would be just awful. So what happened? A year-and-a-half later, I'm managing the Welfare Reform Act on the floor of the United States Senate, and this bill was dramatically different from mine—much more cost conservative, much more deregulatory, much more devolutionary than what I had put forward, which was so "outrageous." We're debating the bill, and after speaking on the floor of the Senate, Kennedy ambles up and says to me, "You know, my staff and I were doing a little research and we saw a bill that you introduced a year and a half ago." He said, "That's a good bill. If you introduce it, I'll co-sponsor it with you."

So when people say, "What are you guys doing up here?" I could say that what we are doing is, fundamentally, moving the goalpost. What the folks out there don't see is how far the goalposts have been moved. Yes, we're still far away from the goalposts that they've set, but I guarantee you it's not the same goalposts that they had a few years ago. The goalposts have, in fact, moved on a whole variety of issues. If Arlen Specter [R–PA] can support partial birth abortion at one time and then later call it infanticide—you can say, well, that's just a little thing, but look! Progress, that's what we have to look at.

For forty years the Democrats understood the game when they controlled Congress, and that's not to take big bites out of the loaf, but just take a crumb a time, make progress in time, and pretty soon—over time, in a way that the public will accept, in a very gradual fashion—the goalpost has been moved. The public doesn't realize that, in a sense, we're still twenty yards away. They don't realize that the goalpost has moved and that they moved, too. If you can do it in that way so as not to revolutionize anything ... Some of the people out there are saying, "What happened to the Republican revolution?" Well, thank God, the revolution has been silenced. But progress is being made.

Thomas: To unmix your metaphor: If you take a crumb at a time, sooner or later you end up owning the bakery.

NORMAN LEAR, PRODUCER, FOUNDER OF PEOPLE OF THE AMERICAN WAY

Thomas: Virtually everybody—left, right, Democrats, Republicans—regard the current social condition as being less than ideal, to put it charitably—whether we're talking of crime and drugs, family breakup, pornography, or abortion. Taking a broad view, what would you regard as the primary causes of moral decline in America?

Mr. Lear: I think about this a lot. I think the greatest reason for the decline of moral values has been the escalating short-term, bottom-line philosophy "give it to me now." That stems largely from the misuse of the free-enterprise system—for example, the need for a public company to have a profit statement this quarter larger than the last at the expense of every other value. One sees this in the way tabloidism has grown, in the kind of television we would all agree we don't want to see anymore. They are bought and paid for in the short-term thinking of people who need the ratings because they have to show that bottom-line profit statement. I think there are men and women with great "family values," to use that expression—religious-minded people—who run major American public companies and who, for the sake of those profit statements, feel they must put those values aside when they enter the workplace.

Thomas: I am amazed at how many people in the interviews I've done—with conservatives and liberals, Republicans and Democrats—have said the same thing. Materialism is the thread that runs through virtually everything else.

Mr. Lear: From what does that materialism derive? That's the key. Yes, the materialism, of course. We've become that kind of society. But I go back a lot of years when people were asking me what right I had to put a message into a television show. I wasn't thinking about message. I was a father and a husband and citizen, and we examined our lives, and we dealt with the problems of the world, and we had points of view—so it came out as having something to say. That's not what motivated it, but people used to think that. I would say that such a quick, brief message in any particular show was overwhelmed by the ten-to-sixteen commercial messages displayed in the course of the show. Wall-to-wall, floor-to-floor, you are what you own, you are what you drink, you are what you wear, you are how you smell, you are what you consume—talk about a message to American children, American families! That's the overwhelming message of American television. Overwhelmingly it's the commercial message: You are what you buy, buy, buy.

Thomas: What do you believe should be the role and the limitations of clergy in our society?

Mr. Lear: They have every right and an obligation, I think, as strong men and women to be citizens.

Thomas: To be citizens?

Mr. Lear: To be citizens, to lead.

Thomas: To lead?

Mr. Lear: To lead anywhere. They have the right and obligation to express themselves socially, culturally, and politically to some degree. Politically, I guess to any degree. I would say the right and the obligation.

Thomas: Even from the pulpit?

Mr. Lear: Yes, as a flat statement, but with caveats that would come later in a longer conversation.

Thomas: How do you see a believer's relationship—a person who seriously believes in God, tries to practice the tenets of the faith, the Ten Commandments, the Sermon on the Mount—to the state in a free society?

Mr. Lear: You're describing me.

Thomas: Well, describe you, then.

Mr. Lear: That's not hard to answer. I love this country. I fought in a war for this country. I flew a great many missions in World War II. I adore the Constitution, the Bill of Rights, the First Amendment. I would fight another war—if they would take me at my age—anytime for those values. I stand behind nobody in my affection for and belief in God. I'm not a church-going religious person—or, in my case, a synagogue-going religious person. I've not found my way that way. But I think you attended a National Press Club event a few years ago where I spoke to this.

Thomas: You did me the courtesy of inviting me to sit at your table—probably ruined your career.

Mr. Lear: I spoke then about what I believe. Most of us are groping—I mean, we're gropers, we're human beings, with all our faults and failings, and we're groping in all our different—God bless them— ways. God made this world, if you take it from the insects to the birds to the humans, in such infinite variety, and I don't believe any two people have the same relationship with God. I struggle for meaning, and I struggle for better understanding, and I will for the rest of my life. That's the journey I love the most, and most of us are on it.

Thomas: Where I was headed with this question relates to what you have done with People for the American Way and the questioning of the limitations of religious activism. Many of us are familiar with the quite proper relationship between the church and the civil rights movement and the anti-war movement, in which religious people—even pastors—demonstrated and petitioned their government for a redress of grievances. This was their political right, but also their moral and religious right. More recently, people who are at least partly motivated by religious faith address animal rights and the environment. So what I was trying to get you to articulate is whether there should be limitations for conservative religious people, when clearly there have not been for liberal religious people.

Mr. Lear: Well, when one's rights and values impinge upon another's, I think we have to stop and consider. At the beginning of all of this in terms of the last twenty years you're discussing in this book, we have any number of tapes on which Pat Robertson was referring to America as a Christian nation. I'm not sure, but I don't think he does that anymore. He's moved off that, and I think a number of others have. Falwell, too, has moved off this "Christian nation" thing. They came to realize, I assume, that you can't call a nation a Buddhist, Jewish, or Christian nation when it's so culturally multi-religious. By the same token, liberals, progressives, and People for the American Way members have always been too timid about voicing their religious and spiritual beliefs. I don't believe most Religious Right people would be so foolish as to think being liberal or progressive eschews belief in God. People can't really believe that because you're progressive you have no faith. But where the pressure and the movement from the Religious Right have been most effective is in moving liberals to the place where they are much more freely acknowledging their beliefs.

Thomas: Do you think that some people through court decisions and other means have gone too far in what has been perceived as hostility toward religious faith?

Mr. Lear: I don't know anybody who feels the courts have shown hostility to religious faith. Religious feeling is personal. It's personal, and at its essence it's something that fills the individual soul. I would never understand why it requires public expression if it means the discomfort of somebody else's soul.

Thomas: Why do you think the so-called Religious Right has not succeeded fully with its agenda?

Mr. Lear: I can't look at the Religious Right and not think it's successful. I think it's been enormously successful. It's very powerful. It exercises enormous influence in public policy and certainly in the direction of the Republican party and a number of Democrats. "Fully" successful—I think they haven't been fully successful because America is America. Because there are people like People for the American Way who can blow a whistle and say, "Hey, stop!" We can't have you folks succeeding in pushing your religious views on the rest of us, because that's not, in our view, the American way.

Thomas: Would it be equally a threat if some people in your organization were fully successful?

Mr. Lear: I don't think so, because I don't know what it is that we are struggling for that isn't among our bedrock Constitutional guarantees. We're not looking for another government or another belief in government. I don't know anything there that isn't constitutionally what we care about.

Thomas: Many in Hollywood are politically active, but you're the only one as far as I know to start a full-scale political organization. Was there anything in your life or background that led you to this decision?

Mr. Lear: I married early, I was married at almost twenty-one, I had a child at twenty-four, I have six children now. I love my country. Perhaps that was heightened by the fact that I was a Jewish kid growing up as Hitler came to power. As Father Coughlin ranted, as Carl McIntire ranted, I don't know why or how it came about that at age thirteen or fourteen on the radio I would listen to them. I didn't have any kids I could talk to about it, because they weren't listening. I can't explain it, but I felt the threat as a Jewish kid. I remember that when the war happened, I couldn't wait to get involved. Have I answered your question?.

Thomas: You're doing well.

Mr. Lear: I guess—seriously—I love getting up in the morning. I love this life. I love this country, and I'm serious.

Thomas: A funny man who is serious! I'm going to ask you a strange question. If through some error in a computer mailing list you were tomorrow named the head of a major religious, conservative organization—

Mr. Lear: Ha, ha, ha, ha—

Thomas: We know about those errors in the computer mailing list. We sent Ted Kennedy a Moral Majority membership card once. This started a wonderful friendship, by the way, which continues to this day. What would your strategy be? Take your tremendous skills and your insight on the side and perspective from which you come and apply them in a way that would make you successful as a religious conservative.

Mr. Lear: I would bring together, I would try to find, those leaders in the Religious Right movement who, despite political disagreements, really are lovers.

Thomas: Lovers?

Mr. Lear: Lovers! People who love—seriously love—people. I don't believe Pat Robertson when one second he calls me "anti-Christian" and the next is saying how he loves everyone.

Thomas: Really?

Mr. Lear: And other Hollywood people he has called anti-Christian, and then he talks about loving everybody, loving all of God's creatures. You can't love that way. But I think it would be a great benefit to bring together those people who do love that way, who disagree with me totally but clearly would love me, as I think I am capable of loving them. I couldn't love Falwell or Robertson because I detect too much insincerity and too much animus. I don't feel that, but I do see it in some places. It would be wonderful to bring all those people together to talk about those differences of opinion—prayer in school, for example—all of these things from people who basically are capable of truly loving one another as God's children, as Christ would have it, as the Sermon on the Mount would have it. I mean, who would wish to live any other way—if a human being could accomplish it—than to seriously resonate with the Sermon on the Mount?

Thomas: Moral Majority once sent out a fund-raising letter calling you the biggest threat to the American family.

Mr. Lear: Jerry Falwell called me the most dangerous threat to the American family in our generation, or something like that. At that time I was getting a number of death threats. But I got a couple of death threats from one source that really brought me up short. I had to show them to my wife and my partners, and all said I should get some protection. So I hired Gavin DeBecker, who's now a major name in the security field. He traced the guy who threatened me, because you know the FBI won't do that. You can get death threats, but unless there's some extortion involved where they say, "I'll kill you unless you send me a quarter," the FBI won't get involved.

But DeBecker found the guy, and he was twenty-some years old, still living with his parents in southern California, and he had a room full of things on his wall, including that Jerry Falwell quote, with a target around it. After a couple of weeks I thought having a bodyguard was ludicrous, and I stopped that. But we paid for surveillance on this young man for a couple of years just to be sure he didn't leave his town and so forth. His parents collaborated to let us know if he was going anywhere, because they were deeply concerned about their son. They didn't now why he was so apprehensive.

Thomas: That's fascinating!

Mr. Lear: Pat Robertson wrote me at one point and said, "Norman, you shouldn't be saying the things you say. Your arms are too short to box with God." Pat Robertson said, "I was a Golden Gloves boxer and you shouldn't be saying these things—because your arms are too short to box with God."

[The letter, dated May 13, 1982, ends this way: "Norman, though I am a former Golden Gloves boxer, I dislike fights. I seldom fight, but when I do I seldom lose. But regardless of my personal action, I want to warn you with all solemnity in the words of a Negro spiritual, 'Your arms are too short to box with God.' The suppression of the voice of God's servant is a terrible thing! God Himself will fight for me against you — and He will win."]

Thomas: You and People for the American Way have been perceived by some religious conservatives as being hostile to religion, especially in the public schools.

Mr. Lear: In 1984 we released "ten rules" of mixing religion and politics that were written by Jim Castelli, a former journalist. In 1986 we reviewed history textbooks and determined that, among other things, the textbooks did a poor job of teaching students about the importance of religion in American life, or the role that religious leaders had played in our country's history. In '87 we held a conference on values, pluralism, and public education. Our values can be promoted in public schools in ways that promote constitutional freedoms. We joined the broad coalition in Congress in calling for passage of the Religious Freedom Restoration Act. We were joined by a coalition of groups, such as Concerned Women for America and the U.S. Catholic Conference. In 1995, people you know served on the committee that drafted a document concerning religion in the public schools, a joint statement of current law.

Personally, I have spoken often about the need for a greater accent in public school on the role religion has played in our country's history—which is not the same as wishing to see any specific prayer mandated by the government in that school. Did I mention that there is nothing in our laws to prevent any child from praying all day in school—or carrying a Bible, or wearing a religious T-shirt, or holding specific religious events after school on school grounds?

PAT ROBERTSON, FOUNDER OF CBN TELEVISION NETWORK, REGENT UNIVERSITY, AND THE 700 CLUB

Thomas: What is the purpose of government, as you see it, in a constitutional republic like ours?

Mr. Robertson: I am a Jeffersonian, conservative by nature, who believes that government governs best that governs least. I think the role of government is to do for the people what they can't do for themselves; to maintain order and to defend a nation against its external foes; to regulate roads, commerce, and the business affairs of the people; to make an environment in which human beings can reach their own potential. So I am more of a laissez-faire type of conservative in terms of what the role of government is. I don't think government should be active in the lives of people and compel them to do things. I think it should make an environment where the people may pursue their own destiny and prosper accordingly.

Thomas: To follow up on that, I would like you to expand on the concept of government. Why do we need government? Jefferson wrote of the need to secure the rights that God has endowed, so governments are instituted among men. I guess I want you to expand on the "if men were angels theory."

Mr. Robertson: That was the Madison thing: If men were angels, we wouldn't need any laws. Government exists to keep safe the rights of its citizens so that they're not trampled upon by the mighty and they are not oppressed by overseas aggressors. And also to regulate their activities so that they don't hurt one another. For example, it's a nice thing to have a traffic light, which is merely an impartial arbiter that says, if you wait a few minutes you can go, and then you have to wait a few more minutes and let somebody else go at an intersection. That's a nice regulation. It is also good to have some larger body which can create a currency and regulate commerce with foreign nations and deal with weights and measures and standards.

Thomas: What do you see as the primary cause of moral decline in America? You have spoken a lot about it. Now, with twenty years or so of perspective, have you reached a conclusion? Is there a primary cause?

Mr. Robertson: Our nation is battered by several forces that came against it simultaneously. World War II was very disruptive. It took millions of men away from their homes and their families, took them overseas into battle. Many were killed. At the end of that time they were intent on forming families and getting some share of the American Dream financially. In the process, they had a huge crop of children, which set in motion centrifugal forces that exerted enormous pressures. Large numbers of homes were built, and families were formed and kids were going to school, and urban sprawl and so forth—all of which broke down the traditional bonds that we had in our nation. Then right on the heels of World War II came the Korean War and, shortly after that, the Vietnam War. They were some of the external forces at work in our culture. Internally, there was the introduction of the psychedelic type of music, rock and roll music, and excessive freedom in the creative community to bring more and more sensuality and hedonistic types of programs into television and radio.

Coupled with all this you had the assault on the Constitution by Madalyn Murray O'Hair and others and the Supreme Court becoming activist and actually destroying 175 years or so of our tradition by taking the Bible and prayer out of the schools and then allowing an assault on the religious beliefs of our marketplace. We began to experience the so-called naked public square. On top of *that* there was an assault on the family in the early 1970s, when the feminists and homosexuals lobbied incessantly for what is called no-fault divorce. Then in 1973 you had *Roe vs. Wade,* which cheapened the value of life, and it was as if we were hurling into an abyss. It was one shock after another. And then the laws were changing dramatically so that the people had no chance, at least in the public environment, to correct what was being done. They couldn't give their families the bulwarks they were used to. So it was a witches' brew that led to the situation we have right now.

Thomas: How many of these were causes, and how many were effects? We look at history, not only our own history and that of Europe, but also going back to biblical times when the church was strong, when the ancient Jewish people were strong and living according to God's precepts. They had strong leaders (of course, they had a theocracy back then), but when their hearts grew cold toward God, they got some nasty leadership that reflected the coldness of their hearts.

Mr. Robertson: Well, in the 1880s and '90s the higher criticism of the German theologians was seeping across the Atlantic into our theological seminaries. There was "the social gospel" in the early 1900s, with the main organized churches first swinging to a type of social gospel and social activism and then moving completely away from the fundamental truths of the Bible. So there was Gresham Machen in the 1920s leaving Princeton and organizing what's called Fundamentalism as a protest against this. But, indeed, the Protestant church was in a decline from the turn of the century until World War II. So when you have World War I, World War II, Korean War, and Vietnam War, the insidious nature of Communism tried to infiltrate all of the branches of our life and the assaults from the ACLU and various other Communist-leaning groups—I mean, we couldn't stand against it. You're right in a sense, the church was weakened first and then the other parts of society were weakened by these successive shocks.

Thomas: That's a good perspective. Let me turn to politics. You ran for president. You are the only one so far in the so-called Religious

Right to step out and put yourself on the line in that way. You have wide influence with a considerable segment of the Christian community through television. Where are you headed? Would you ever consider running again?

Mr. Robertson: No, Cal, I think one run is enough for a lifetime. I started in the '80s something called the Freedom Council, and that was a response to what I perceived as the failure by Jimmy Carter of the beliefs that he espoused. We were, frankly, shocked by the antics of Hamilton Jordan, Jody Powell, and some of the other types that came up there from Georgia. I think Carter had an impact by activating a lot of born-again Christians because he said he was born again. Therefore they began to be very interested in the political processes because they had a man who said, "I'm a born-again Christian." But when he seemingly betrayed them, in four years they turned against him and voted overwhelmingly for Ronald Reagan and at least 6 million evangelicals switched parties—went from the Democrat to the Republican Party—so there was a big swing.

It wasn't so much that I wanted to be president as that I wanted ideals and concepts to have a voice and to continue. So, in a sense, my campaign was a continuation of the Freedom Council, and then the Christian Coalition was a continuation of my campaign. It wasn't an ego thing for me per se. It was something, I thought, to enunciate the ideals that many of the evangelicals felt deeply in their hearts.

Thomas: Do you see in your lifetime, given the cultural conditions in the country, an evangelical Christian being elected president?

Mr. Robertson: It's been suggested—very rightly so—that Clinton may be setting us up for a Republican "Jimmy Carter"—somebody who talks about honesty and decency and morality and spiritual values, more than being "born again,"—that such a Christian would find a warm reception in the American electorate. I believe that if the Republican party's nominee were Senator John Ashcroft, he'd win the presidency and so would be a born-again president at the turn of the century, the beginning of the new millennium. I firmly believe that. I think that an honest man with a great deal of moral integrity, quite intelligent, very experienced, carrying with himself what would be called "Midwest heartland of America" values, would do very, very well all over this country. [As mentioned elsewhere, Senator Ashcroft announced in January 1999 that he would not be a candidate for president in 2000.]

Thomas: I take it from that answer you don't necessarily accept the polls that show a high popularity rating for President Clinton.

Mr. Robertson: Absolutely not. The country right now is very rich. People are enormously wealthy. At the higher end of the spectrum, the stock market has benefited over 50 million shareholders. People have low mortgage rates, low inflation, low gasoline prices, and rising profits in the stock market. Therefore they say, "I have a pretty good deal, I don't want to change it." However, exit polls that I saw taken after the 1996 election indicated that a vast majority of them did not like Clinton, but they said, "You Republicans gave us no alternative." A clear majority of them said, "Bob Dole gave me no reason to vote for him." Plus, he was perceived as an old man at seventy-three, even by his peer group: It's too big a job for us, we don't think Bob can do it. Had the Republican Party found a vigorous, attractive individual, he could have beaten Clinton. Clinton himself is not popular. The American people don't trust him. But what they're saying is, "I'm wealthy, and so as long as I'm wealthy, don't rock the boat." In 1973, '74, and '75 we were in the midst of a gripping, blinding recession. The stock market had crashed, many people had lost fortunes, real estate was in the tank, and it was an easy thing to throw the president out. If Nixon had had the same economy that Clinton has, he would never have been run out of office.

Thomas: Does it ever concern you that the average unbeliever who doesn't know the difference between an evangelical, a Pentecostal, a Catholic, and a Baptist—they're just "religious" or "Christian"— might be turned off to the gospel because of the perception of the political message that accompanies it?

Mr. Robertson: Very frankly, we have toned down some of the political rhetoric for that very reason. Our first job is obviously to serve God and to win people to his kingdom, not to establish the Republicans as the ruling party in America. I think that we as private individuals can help candidates, and we should do that. And there is certainly nothing wrong with the Christian Coalition being as strong as it is in the grassroots. I'm the leader of that organization, and I'm very proud and excited about what they're doing. But I think all of us must understand that our principal goal is "to serve God and to glorify him and enjoy him forever," as the Westminser Catechism says.

We should not let anything we do or say having to do with temporal issues turn people away from the gospel. That does not mean that Christians shouldn't be involved in politics in any way, shape, or form. Jesus said, "Render unto Caesar what is Caesar's and to God what is God's." The temporal realm is Caesar's and we are Caesar. It means that in a democracy such as we have, a republic, we are Caesar, we're the voters. So every Christian owes his "Caesar," his country, informed active citizenship. That means supporting good candidates and enunciating issues and, in fact, running for office if circumstances call for it. There's absolutely nothing wrong with it. I think statecraft is one of the highest callings that there is in this world. When you look in the Bible, you see Daniel, who ran a nation. You see Joseph, who was in charge of the biggest empire on earth. You see David, a spiritual man, the sweet psalmist of Israel, who was a general of great renown and also a very fine king.

Thomas: When you were deciding which issues to address in the Christian Coalition, how do you process that with the name "Christian" coming even before "coalition." Obviously, Scripture speaks about very relevant issues such as abortion and homosexuality. But when you get into budget matters and other things, some of the criticism of Christian Coalition—and Moral Majority before it—is that these organizations tend to get captured by economic and other forces that are not part of a biblical worldview. Give me a sense of how you process what to address and what to ignore.

Mr. Robertson: First of all, it's a misnomer to think the Christian Coalition is saying we're the only Christians and anybody that's not part of us isn't Christian. I think the threat of the Moral Majority was that everybody said, "Look, we're not part of it and therefore we're not moral and therefore they're trying to impose their so-called morality on us, and we don't like it. That is the biggest problem of religious people being involved in any kind of politics in America. The American people feel that anybody religious is trying to jam religion down their throats and use the government to do so. Because, you see, this is what the liberals do. The liberals use the government to jam their point of view down people's throats. They use the government oppressively.

And what the Christians want is freedom. They want the government away from their lives and off their backs and out of their schools and out of their churches. They essentially want to be left alone and free of government-controlled influence, whereas the liberals feel just the opposite. They want a major statist role in every part of people's lives. They assume the Christians must be like we are, and instead of imposing liberalism, they're going to impose "fundamentalist Christianity" on us. This is a problem. It's a communications problem that has not been solved. But what do you do?

First of all, as I said, the Christian Coalition isn't a coalition of Christians, period! It is open to anybody—we have Jews involved—but it's a coalition of those who embrace Judeo-Christian biblical concepts. It's not exclusive, it's just one organization that happens to have that name. But in my opinion the Christian Coalition as an entity should espouse those views that have some biblical impact; an impact of family, public order, decency, that type of thing that do not tend to destroy the family, disrupt the family or brutalize individual lives. That is the concept that I think we should embrace. Therefore we're pushing very hard at religious freedom amendments that wouldn't discriminate against anybody because of the way they worship God. I think that's a very important thing to put in our Constitution. We believe that a marriage penalty is unfair because it mitigates against intact families in favor of people who would live in companion relations instead of being married. We favor a child tax credit which would help mothers to stay at home who don't want to work, who want to care for their children. We think the nurturing of children is a very important thing. It's that kind of an issue that the Christian Coalition is most known for rather than just abortion and homosexual rights, etc.

Thomas: You have talked over the years to many theological students studying to be pastors. If you were giving advice now to a young pastor or a pastor with a young church (150–200 members), would you tell them that it is a good idea to get involved in the political life of their community. And if so, are there limits?

Mr. Robertson: I think it's a very tenuous line, and it's a skilled person who can stay on the line and not go one way or the other. I would certainly tell them to avoid extremism.

Thomas: How would you define that? Because that's often said of you, that you're extreme. What is an extremist?

Mr. Robertson: I would define extremism in religion and politics as equating a political party with a church, equating a political platform with a creedal statement of a church, equating any kind of temporal policy with the eternal values of salvation, grace, and God's kingdom. Once the kind of zealotry that would go into defending the Lord gets into politics, then people get to be very hard and unyielding and unreasonable, because politics is a question of give and take among people of good will—supposedly—who have different points of view. The way to consensus in a democracy is that through majority rule people work out their differences. But if that is placed in an eternal context, that this is God's will, then all of a sudden people can be killed because they stand in the way of God. You can have the fanaticism of the ayatollahs in Iran, or what we have in Libya, or people who would go to war over their points of view, like the Hezbollah or Hamas. Well, that kind of thing is just anathema for the Christian, we can't have that sort of thing. That to me is fanaticism, or extremism.

Thomas: Look back over the last twenty years. If you had been in charge of all of this beginning in 1979, with the benefit of hindsight, what might have been done differently to advance the agenda that most people on the so-called Christian Right believe in?

Mr. Robertson: I appreciate Ronald Reagan, and I don't in any way want to denigrate him, but the truth of the matter is that during Reagan's administration our budget—our total national debt—doubled and tripled. And I think we added another trillion under George Bush. There were some good initiatives put through such as tax cuts, some regulations were taken off, and the Cold War was won. That was the great achievement; we could be proud to be Americans. It's hard to realize how things were prior to 1989 and '90, with the monolithic

Soviet Union confronting us. So Ronald Reagan saw Communism as an evil empire, and he made it a policy goal to bring it down. It was very expensive, but he did it. That part was very good.

In terms of public morality, we missed a great opportunity to get a prayer amendment approved to the United States Constitution back, I think, in 1982. The administration did not fight for it at all. They gave lip service to it and allowed a cabal of liberal Republican senators to beat it, led by Lowell Weiker of Connecticut. In terms of putting people on the Supreme Court, they missed that opportunity. They appointed Sandra Day O'Connor, who has been a champion, I suppose, of abortion rights. She's been somewhat iffy on religious freedom. They put Anthony Kennedy on, and it turned out he wrote the *Lee vs. Weissman* decision, which was one of the strongest decisions against religion in the public arena that we've ever had. We had Antonin Scalia on, but they should have put Robert Bork in earlier, so the strategy was wrong. Then you look at Bush's appointee to the Supreme Court, David Souter, He's an absolute disaster. An earlier Republican president, Nixon, put in Harry Blackmun, and Blackmun is the one who wrote *Roe vs. Wade*.

In my opinion, the Supreme Court has been the driving force for the moral breakdown of America and the secularization of America. The decisions have been absolutely arbitrary, unconstitutional, unhistoric, and disastrous to the country. We've cheapened life, and we've taken away our moral moorings in a whole generation of young people. Now we wonder why kids are out there with guns shooting their fellow students when they won't even let them post the Ten Commandments on the walls for them to read. So what should Reagan have done? He should have fought for those conservative justices, and he, of course, should have had a Congress to go along with it.

Thomas: Have the last twenty years of political activism by conservative Christians been useful?

Mr. Robertson: I think as we stand right now, Cal, with the Congress in 1994 having switched to the Republicans and to a relatively conservative House and Senate, the groundwork that was laid over the years paid off in that regard. We have a sitting governor in Arkansas who's a Baptist preacher. We have another strong believer who is a senator from Arkansas. We have one from Kansas who is a strong born-again Christian. We have a couple of senators from Oklahoma, one a very devout Catholic, the other a very strong evangelical. So all over this nation—at the lower levels and the legislatures, and in the Senate and House of the United States, and in the governors' mansions—there are a number of people who are pro-life, pro-family, and pro-Christian in their values. So it was a slow, incremental thing that has come about.

Now, if you look at the country, it's hard to say that we have accomplished that much. The budget is bigger than ever, the deficit is finally cut down, but the amount of spending in the United States government on things like the Department of Education, and the increasing of power in Washington haven't slowed down, in my opinion, one bit. We haven't finished the job, but I do think that a foundation was laid if we don't quit, because after all, the liberals didn't take charge of this nation in just ten years or twenty years. There was the liberal theology back in 1880 and 1890 and then the ACLU in 1918 and various other groups like the Council on Foreign Relations in 1928. Year after year after year, these groups worked diligently for their agendas, and they didn't quit just because they lost a few battles. So, with an election coming up in the year 2000, if the evangelicals truly turn out and let their voices be heard, we could indeed see an evangelical, born-again president, a totally different Cabinet, a different style of appointments to the Supreme Court and other courts, coupled with a conservative Congress. If we had that, we could roll back many of the bad things that have been done in government.

I think the jury is still out as to whether all these years were effective, but I think at the end of this century we could say, yes, they were. Not as much as we had hoped, but we've moved the ball down the field a bit.

Thomas: Lincoln talked about the Civil War being a judgment for what he called our "presumptuous sins." He said that we had forgotten God, that's why all these things had happened to us. I'd like to have your opinion as to whether abortion, the advancement of the gay rights movement, pornography, drugs, overflowing prisons, and all of these other social problems are the cause of our decadence or a reflection of it. If they are a reflection of it, can they be fixed solely from the top?

Mr. Robertson: No, they can't. Lincoln said, "If it is God's will that every drop of blood that was drawn by the lash should be paid by blood that was shed on the battlefield, then His will be done." I frankly think that the United States of America stands on the brink of really terrible judgment. We have committed sins in our nation that are heinous. It must be close to 40 million children killed by abortion. Now we are moving into euthanasia. Recently there was a professor at the University of Colorado advocating infanticide of neonatal newborns. We lead the world in every known pathology except drunkenness, and we're second in that. There are more unwed pregnancies, there are more people incarcerated, there's a greater use of drugs in America, and on top of that we're spewing out pornography and sensuality in our movies, television, and other media. America is like Babylon, the Mother of Harlots. So that is cause, in my opinion, for a righteous God to bring His wrath against us.

On the other hand, America is right now experiencing a great spiritual revival. The churches are coming alive. There is fasting and prayer. There's great evangelism. There's a tremendous move for missions overseas. Everything that you really want to see begin to come from the church is starting to come, and people are getting very serious about God in the churches.

So we have this dichotomy in America. On the one hand, renewal and spiritual activity is unprecedented. On the other hand, you have moral decadence that probably is unprecedented in this nation. Where is it going to go? Will we, indeed, turn back from the abyss as a nation, or will we keep going forward? My current feeling is that we're going to move forward toward the abyss. I think that by the year 2005 or '06 or '07 or something like that, we're going to be in really serious, serious trouble. I don't know whether it will be external—terrorists with deadly anthrax or something like that—or whether it will be a financial collapse, or a war, or all those things, but I do think we're extremely vulnerable right now.

KAY JAMES, DEAN OF THE ROBERTSON SCHOOL OF GOVERNMENT, REGENT UNIVERSITY

Thomas: The perception of many conservative Christians is that things ought to go faster, and if they don't go faster then they're going to take their marbles and go home. You hear James Dobson threatening to leave the Republican Party, because Republicans aren't moving fast enough with his agenda.

Ms. James: I actually am coming to some different conclusions than I was even two weeks ago on that very subject because the bottom line is, you get more of what you reward. I applaud Jim in that he wants the same thing—we all want the same thing—and you know what, he's gonna get it! They're giving it to him. He's getting the meetings, he's getting the legislation on the agenda, and he's getting rewarded for that.

Thomas: You really think so?

Ms. James: Absolutely! Absolutely!

Thomas: He's getting the meetings? What legislation is he getting?

Ms. James: He apparently is. They're saying, what legislation do you want, what do you want moved, what do you want to go? I think what is happening is, they're sitting down and saying, "What is the most we can give? What is the most that we can do right now?" And something will happen. Something is going to happen that would not have happened had Jim not done that. Now, if you or I had gone in and sat down nicely and said, "This is what we want and we'd really like you to do this, please," they would have said, "Sure!" And nothing would have happened.

Thomas: Okay, we'll see whether these politicians keep their promises. [They mostly didn't.] I developed the term "trickle-down morality" to play off the disparaging "trickle-down economics line" used by Democrats. How much do you think that a change of leadership can heal the moral and spiritual brokenness of the nation?

Ms. James: None.

Thomas: None. And do you think that a nation that doesn't care about righteousness is likely to elect someone who does?

Ms. James: Not at all.

Thomas: So what are we doing all this for? The Moral Majority, the Christian Coalition, Focus on the Family—all these groups. Why are they bothering to change the—

Ms. James: Because it will do other things. I don't think that it will affect the moral base, but we can get good government, and I think that's important.

Thomas: What is good government?

Ms. James: I think Christians have a responsibility to be involved in government. I went to Washington with a very different perspective. I really thought I was going to help President Reagan take this nation into the next century. I really thought we were going there to advance the agenda, to advance the ball, and to help them with their vision of America. I mean, great sounding mighty words—and I left thinking that the purpose of Christians in government was to make sure that government did no harm. It was not to advance the ball.

I don't believe that it is appropriate for Christians to extract themselves from the process, to give up and go home. I believe that we're called to be salt and light. I think it is absolutely essential for us to be involved in all those spheres—in government, in politics, in the culture—to be involved in every aspect of American life. If we come as principled people of character and integrity, we will have a good benefit for the entire country. And so I believe that taking the principles that we believe in into government will help government to be better. If we believe in personal responsibility, if we believe in religious liberty, if we believe in mercy and justice and compassion, and we take those beliefs into government, government will be better. So I think it is important for us to be there.

Thomas: What about the role of pastors? You have described a proper function and role for individual citizens, individual believers. But one of the complaints about preachers in the last twenty years is that they've politicized the gospel and are in danger of diluting it to the point that the liberals did in the thirties, forties, and fifties through the National and World Council of Churches, the latter saying that the world's agenda is the church's agenda. Where does the danger lie? Where's the fault line there?

Ms. James: I'm not sure I see the danger, because I really do believe that it's important for pastors to encourage the people within their congregation to be good citizens. First of all, I believe we have a responsibility to be in this world.

Thomas: Sure, but what about pronouncements from the pulpit such as "you ought to vote for this guy" or "this guy is corrupt"? You have some pastors denouncing Clinton from the pulpit on Sunday mornings.

Ms. James: I think that they should be talking about principles, values, issues. It is entirely appropriate for a pastor to talk about the evils of abortion and to lift up the value and the dignity and the sanctity of human life. I would also say that it's important for pastors to help their congregations understand what it means to have a biblical worldview. In other words, your faith should have an impact on everything you do, not just what you do on Sunday morning between eleven and twelve (if you go to one of those kinds of churches), but when you think about whom you're going to vote for. You should apply those principles to the decisions you make—not just in politics, but in every decision. So in that sense, it would have an impact. In terms of denouncing an individual from the pulpit, I'm not sure that's entirely appropriate. I tell people when I speak that Bill Clinton didn't cause the problems in America, and Bill Clinton can't solve them.

Thomas: Or he's a reflection of them, as I say.

Ms. James: He's a reflection of us. We elected him. I wrote this little book called *Transforming America from the Inside Out*. I said in there that I believe that apart from any political strategy, there needs to be a cultural strategy. Everybody is crying for what America needs—a new president, a new Republican leadership—and if that doesn't work and we want to get real superspiritual, what we need is revival, because what that means is, if more of the people out there were like us "good Christians" then this whole thing would be resolved. And so we go out and save "those heathens," and this will all be great.

I've come to the conclusion, Cal, that it's none of the above, and it isn't even revival, but it's renewal within the church. I really believe that when we start demonstrating our faith in very real and practical ways, we will have far more credibility in the public policy process. Imagine what it would be like if Christians all across America started taking homosexuals into their homes, working in AIDS hospices, caring for the dying. If we started inviting abortionists to our churches, loving them—imagine what that would do! You know, I think we would have far more credibility in the pubic policy process when we say we really don't believe that special rights ought to be given to the homosexuals in our community if, in fact, we could be believed when we said we hate the sin, but love the sinner. But unfortunately, I believe that what we demonstrate to the world is that we hate the sin and we hate the sinner, with some notable exceptions.

I even go so far as to divide those issues up along racial lines. The banner issues in the black community are poverty and racism. In the white community they are abortion and homosexuality. You have to be out fighting those two issues if you're really saved, or your very salvation is in question. In the black community you cannot call yourself a Christian if you're not out doing something to fight poverty and racism. I, of course—being one of those people that gets walked on from all sides—believe that, at the point of the Cross, all of those issues are important, but I believe that we don't have credibility. How many major national conservative Christian organizations do you know that have as their mission fighting poverty and racism in the white, conservative community? How many major national organizations sponsored by the black church do you know that have as their mission fighting abortion or homosexuality?

For that reason, I tend to get in trouble with both sides, because I go to the black churches and talk about abortion and homosexuality, and go to the white churches and talk about racism and poverty—so then I get everybody mad.

_____

JERRY FALWELL, FOUNDER OF THE "OLD-TIME GOSPEL HOUR," LIBERTY UNIVERSITY, AND MORAL MAJORITY

Thomas: What do you see as the purpose of government?

Rev. Falwell: In it's purest form, a democratic government should defend the people from foreign aggression and from one another and should keep their mouths shut on just about everything else.

Thomas: It almost sounds like a Libertarian view.

Rev. Falwell: I do believe in regulations that are necessary for civilized society to function—speed limits, I do not oppose taxes within reason to fund necessary government, I believe in the military. I think we owe more to the soldier than we do to any preacher or journalist as far as our freedoms are concerned. I do believe in the maintenance of civil rights and the guarantee of civil rights—properly defined—as a role of government.

Thomas: Jefferson talked about the purpose of government being to secure the "inalienable rights" that God had endowed, and to secure these rights, governments are instituted among men. I'd like you to expound on the idea that we've abandoned the whole philosophy or biblical teaching of flawed human nature that needs to be controlled, either from within by the presence of God or from without by the state according to God's standard, or it becomes oppressive or dictatorial. That government has become oppressive and confiscatory in terms of taxes, and people are out of relationship to it as God has intended. I don't want to put the words in your mouth, but I'd like you to expound on why government has become dysfunctional in our day.

Rev. Falwell: American government is dysfunctional because it has forgotten—totally forgotten—who we are. Regardless of what the ACLU may feel and others like them, America was founded not, necessarily, by godly people (though many of them were), but on godly principles. I believe if an unsaved person practices tithing, for example, God will bless him for it. It's a principle, like gravity—it works for everybody. When the Judeo-Christian ethic in it's purest form was established in this country, although we still were not giving women the vote and we were still practicing slavery, we had the necessary foundation to build upon and daily improve to create what we did create, the greatest nation on earth.

The sanctity of human life, born and unborn, is a basic principle of the Judeo-Christian ethic. I believe that the Abrahamic covenant—the promise that God gave to Abraham that he would bless those who blessed him and curse those who cursed him—is a fundamental ethic for the success of any society and has certainly been one of the reasons why we have been blessed. The guarantee of civil rights to all persons, born and unborn, regardless of color or ethnic differences or religious differences, is very necessary.

I believe that America went wrong basically within the last generation. I think you could go back to about 1947, when the Supreme Court began to act independent of its commitment to the Judeo-Christian ethic. In 1962 they put it in concrete form for the first time. The Supreme Court and all of the courts under it since then, in this country, have generally been hostile to the ethic on which the nation was founded. As a Christian, I do not have the same privileges and rights that all other Americans have. If I use my right to free speech to declare what I believe the Bible teaches, in some areas it's called "hate speech." In Canada, for example, where they've gone down twenty years beyond us into the abyss, we made a different *Old Time Gospel Hour* television program than the one we air in America.

Thomas: I did not know that.

Rev. Falwell: We cannot mention abortion, we cannot mention homosexuality, nor can we mention any controversial moral issue that might be considered negative to some. Therefore we take the program that I make in America, put about a third of it on the floor—cutting it out, editing it—then we add several songs to make up for the blank spaces that we've cut out so we have a sixty-minute program.

America is heading that way. We're about twenty years behind Canada. Even now, there are many stations in America that will not carry a program like mine, and the courts will give no relief to you for it. You have no recourse. So we have a government today that has abandoned its moorings, its beginnings. We have a Congress that's done the same thing, and we have a White House presently that probably is the most anti-Christian White House in American history. Some say, "What about this Religious Right?" Bob Franken on CNN calls me "the Godfather of the Religious Right." Whether that's an honor or dishonor, I don't know. But what about the Religious Right? What has it accomplished? That is not the right question. The right question is, where would this country be if it were not for the Religious Right of the last twenty years?

Thomas: I want to get into that in a minute, but let me get to some of these other standard questions we're asking.

Rev. Falwell: But in order for the government to get in this convoluted condition—to now have a Department of Education, to violate all states rights that were guaranteed in the Constitution, to run everything from headquarters, and on top of that, Health and Human Services—and when we talk about the cost of the Pentagon, it's minimal in comparison to the dole, to the giveaway, to all the entitlements. Taxes are outrageous because our deviation from who we are is outrageous and we're having to fund all of that, and it's a bottomless pit because once you start giving something to anyone, you can't ever take it back.

Thomas: What are the primary causes of moral decline in America? Is it the quality of the leadership, or is it the followership following after the wrong thing?

Rev. Falwell: I think the ultimate blame for the past generation's radical turn away from our Judeo-Christian ethic must be laid at the doorsteps of the churches. There are about 600,000 pastors in America who lead 600,000 churches—not all evangelical, not all fundamentalists, we have all breeds and brands. But generally, be it a synagogue or a church, if we take our own faith seriously, we agree on the issues that will damn or bless America. It would be an unfair generalization to say that the majority of the churches and synagogues of this country have gone to hell doctrinally. It is fair to say that the deafening silence of the pulpits, the capitulation of the pulpits to the culture, has been the major cause of the sinking and freefall that we are in.

Thomas: So the follow-up question to that suggests itself: Then why are you not more identified in the public mind with trying to fix *that* problem than trying to fix the problem in government, if that's the major problem?

Rev. Falwell: A person is identified in modern times by however the media wish to describe him. He is absolutely helpless to define himself, even if he has 150 television stations, has been on the air for forty-two years, every week, without interruption. The only way that I have maintained my strength and a growing ministry is because of that. Had I not been on national television with all the other national media, and had I not had availability to the secular media—be it the *Larry King Show* or *Crossfire* or whatever—I would be today where Carl McIntire is, where Rex Humbard is, where all the other preachers are who have no way to answer back and defend themselves. But even with the opportunity of nationally speaking for myself, the tremendous weight of the media is so powerful that they define you to most of the public, because most of the public is not informed and studies very little, reads very little, knows very little. That's why surveys can go up and down on any given day on any subject on any person—because you have an uninformed public. If the pollsters call you or me on any subject today, we will be where we were yesterday. And if they call us a year from now, it will be where we are today. That is because we know what we believe and why we believe it. The general public knows neither, and that's why the media can manipulate the nation on any given day. The media have saved Bill Clinton. To this day, had what happened in Bill Clinton's life happened to George Bush, Ronald Reagan, Jesse Helms—you name it—they would have not only been impeached, they would be in prison.

Thomas: Well, I have to follow-up again. If the people don't know and if the churches remain the major source of knowledge and if the pastors like yourself have the greatest opportunity to be an influence, why not focus more on mobilizing—not mobilizing, but informing—and changing pastors to speak the truth rather than working on politicians who are crafty at cutting deals and telling you one thing on one day and something else the next or violating their promises?

Rev. Falwell: A long time ago I decided that was the only alternative.

Thomas: How long ago?

Rev. Falwell: Ten years ago. When I dismantled Moral Majority, it was more than just to get back to my pulpit, but it was to get back to the only way to change the country. For example, this Falwell Fax here goes out every Friday morning; it's sitting on the desk right now of 11,000 pastors. It doesn't cost them anything—it's sitting there. It says that they may use this information without attribution—we rather prefer that they do it that way. One sheet of paper: the information, what's happened this week, and then Action Alerts at the bottom that tell them who to call, who to write, where to write. They take it to the pulpit and mobilize 60–70 million people. We have a newspaper, *The National Liberty Journal,* that goes to 250,000 people, but 162,000 are mostly evangelical pastors—not all evangelical, but 162,000 pastors who want to get it. We've long since heard from the ones who don't want it.

I also do Pastor's Policy Briefings every week somewhere. For example, next week I'm in Oklahoma City with 300 pastors, Congressman J.C. Watts, and Lawrence White, a Lutheran pastor from Houston. We'll buy them lunch—(we pay all the expenses—"we" being businessmen outside our ministries totally, called the National Committee)—and we'll tell those 300 pastors what the issues are. We'll enroll every one of them for the fax or e-mail, whichever they prefer, and the newspaper. We'll also give all of them the "motor voter" things that they carry to their own registrar and get enough for their church—they can get up to 1,000 per church. We inform them, but we don't tell them for whom to vote. We tell them that if you've been preaching correctly, they'll know whom to vote for.

The idea is to get them to vote, and that's legal. You can say that all day long. So we are doing that and more, and next week I'll be in Phoenix doing the same thing. During 1998 I'll be meeting with 50,000 pastors face to face. In those meetings we talk about the things that are going to damn or save America, and stress that you alone have the ability to make the difference. I don't think there's any hope whatever in the Republican party or the Democratic party. (I certainly would prefer just about any Republican over any Democrat right now, because of where the party platforms are—for president or for congressman.

However, I must say that our people voted for a Democrat in this area; Virgil H. Goode Jr. in the 5th District is a pro-life, pro-family, godly man.) I'm very proud of what Newt Gingrich's doing right now, but that's an exception, not the rule. We have the numbers up there in both houses to stop this partial birth abortion, if anybody really wanted to lead the battle, especially in the Senate. Outside of Jesse Helms, there's not a street fighter in the U.S. Senate.

Thomas: You mentioned all these pastors your sending faxes or e-mails to. Gallup found that a third of the evangelical vote went for Clinton last time. How do you explain that?

Rev. Falwell: Well, when you consider the Tony Campolos and the Bill Hybels and the National Association of Evangelicals and many of the "tiptoe through the tulip" guys who want to enjoy the positive connotation of being called an evangelical—a little like Mark Hatfield: Vote and preach wrong about every moral and social issue available. I'm shocked that we got two-thirds of the vote away from them. When you look at the evangelical schools—Wheaton, for example, and Fuller and so forth—I doubt that Ronald Reagan got a majority vote from the faculty at these schools. Of the kids you would, but with the faculty, I doubt it. So there is very little difference in our evangelical schools and anybody else's school.

Thomas: What in your mind—not legally, but spiritually, scripturally—should be the role and limitation of pastors in our society?

Rev. Falwell: Well, my friend Pat Robertson ran for president. I said, when I first heard it, "Wrong is wrong," but I jumped on George Bush's bandwagon from day one, far ahead of his announcement. Pat later rescinded his ordination and did the honorable thing, but at that time he was an ordained preacher. My perception of Pat Robertson for thirty years was that he was a gospel preacher. I didn't know that he wasn't until he told all of us that in 1988.

Thomas: To what degree do you think your political involvement beginning twenty years ago might have alienated anyone from listening to the gospel? In other words, you have your average person out there—maybe a Christmas-and-Easter churchgoer, maybe a little bit more—and they look at preachers on television or in other places commenting heavily on politics, and they may believe some of the

same things, but maybe they get turned off. I know it's a struggle—
your heart is always as a pastor, you started that way, but—

Rev. Falwell: What I did I had to do. For fifty years since Prohibition, the evangelicals of America had been of the strong conviction
that "religion and politics don't mix." They took such a beating back
there that they came to the conclusion that this was not of God, therefore they went to the extreme, saying we should not be involved in
politics. All the surveys taken in the late '70s showed that while 72
percent of the American public were registered to vote, 55 percent of
evangelicals were registered and half of them never voted. So what we
set out to do, I think we did do. We broke down the psychological
barrier that prevented evangelicals—not just preachers, but also laypeople—from being informed, intelligent activists. You would be hard
pressed today to find a Bible-believing preacher who is not an
informed voting person. That was not true twenty years ago. It was
very untrue. Twenty years ago they thought it was a sin to do it,
because somebody in seminary told them that. They now believe that
they should do it.

Now, not all of them will speak from the pulpit. In the Thomas Road
Baptist Church, members are Democrats and Republicans, and a good
way to send them to somebody else's church is to come down on the
side of either party inordinately. Other pastors out there have a far worse
situation than I do. I've been forty-two years in one place, but the pastor who has been with a church three, four, or five years has to be very
careful not to do the stupid thing and tear his church up to prove his
point. So he's got to learn how to teach and preach the issues and honor
those to whom honor is due. A John Ashcroft is due honor. A Jesse
Helms is due honor. And when a guy like Newt Gingrich comes out in
favor of Israel, they ought to do in our pulpits what we did, and say
"God bless the Speaker for standing up for Israel." You don't have to
say, "Vote for this guy for president" or whatever, but as you build values and an appreciation for values in the hearts of your people, they
soon become more principle conscious than they are political party conscious.

Thomas: You mentioned the Republican party a minute ago. A
criticism often heard is that black Americans did themselves in by too

close an association with the Democratic party, where they got taken for granted as a bloc vote. I'm wondering if you think damage was done to your ultimate objectives for the same reason—being taken for granted by your party. It was either *Time* or *U.S. News & World Report* that said of Ralph Reed in a cover story some years ago that the Christian Coalition had finally found "a place at the table." And I remember thinking at the time, "Gee, is this why Christ died, so we can get treated just like the labor unions and civil rights groups and the environmentalists—just one more political group to be thrown a few bones, in our case a few verses quoted (sometimes inaccurately)?" Do you think that our side was "had," at least early on, by the Republicans because they managed to co-opt a lobby?

Rev. Falwell: Moral Majority was born in '79, about the same time I traveled to meet with Ronald Reagan and then down to see John Connally of Texas and a few others who were throwing their hat in the ring, and I became convinced that Ronald Reagan was the man of the hour. So I jumped on the bandwagon with Ronald Reagan up front, and it turned out to be a correct decision. He'd be the one guy in this century that I would still walk out and stand beside today, regardless of the cost of friendships in other places, simply because he was and is a man of such principle that he would never knowingly or intentionally embarrass you. Most evangelicals were not aligned with the Republican party—they were aligned with Ronald Reagan—and that spilled over to the benefit of George Bush in '88. But it wasn't deep enough to spill over in '92 or since then.

It's gone! The evangelicals cannot be counted on by the Republicans the way the blacks can be counted on by the Democrats. The Democrats can just count on it—they own the black population in this country, I think, to the great hurt of African-Americans. The Republicans don't *own* evangelicals. For example, when Virgil Goode stepped up to run for the Democrats in our congressional district, the Republicans were dead in the water. This is a Democratic area, and we vote Republican against the grain here. We went with Eisenhower, and this town went 2 to 1 for Goldwater. We then went for Ronald Reagan, but this town also went for Jimmy Carter in his first run, because of his being born again. They went with George Bush the first time, barely the last time. I think Dole won Virginia, but by the slightest margin. What I'm saying is that right now the Republican party does not have the evangelical vote, and many of them don't want it. They'd rather lose than do what's right.

Thomas: The reason I asked that question is that the first test that we had that I recall was in 1981 when Reagan nominated Sandra Day O'Connor to the Supreme Court. There was tremendous controversy, because even though her legislative and state judicial record was spotty, she had written enough to convince some of us that she was pro-choice. Reagan called you (you told this to Jerry and Deborah Strober for their book) and told you not to worry, it would be okay. Since then she has aligned herself pretty much with the status quo on *Roe vs. Wade.* I remember going on *Nightline* and raising the question as to whether she could be trusted. Someone in Moral Majority chastised me for not being on board with the whole thing. I told him, I thought we were about principle here, not pragmatism. The point I was making, the politicians know so well how to pick somebody's pocket—even good people, even professional people.

Rev. Falwell: Ronald Reagan called me because I'd already commented. (As a result of my comments, Barry Goldwater told me every good American ought to kick my posterior.) Mr. Reagan said to me, "Jerry, I read your comment. I understand your concerns, but I want you to know that I have personally searched this out and I want you to trust me on this one." Well, he had a lot of chips with me, and I said, "All right, I will." I don't regret that I did, because it built a bridge between the two of us that he could talk to me and that I would take his word on things that I didn't fully know the facts on. And she's not the worst person on the court, but neither is she a Clarence Thomas or Antonin Scalia. And there is nobody today who could call me from Washington and change my mind on a candidate for the court if I felt that he or she was not right.

Thomas: Is that because you're more sophisticated now?

Rev. Falwell: That's because I think Mr. Reagan fully thought he was telling me what he knew. I think that the people who brought her to him assured him of her stand on abortion. (I don't think she ever discussed the issue with him.) And she is a lady, a noble lady, and a bright lady and has proved to be a very competent justice. But she is not willing to abrogate *Roe vs. Wade,* and I measure everybody by that.

Thomas: If you had it to do over again—having hindsight with the benefit of everything you know now—and you were starting Moral Majority over again—still 1979, but with the knowledge of everything that has occurred in the past twenty years—what would you do differently, what would you keep the same, what mistakes would you not make?

Rev. Falwell: I would never have had state chapters. That is the only fundamental mistake we made. We had in just about all fifty states a state chairman—and some of them were very good—and state chapters that were funded in their own states, not by us. Therefore we didn't control them. And we had these loose cannons, like the guy up in New York or New Jersey who was looking at a cookie store in a bakery and felt he'd seen an obscene cookie in there and he was going to boycott the bakery. We had these numbskulls out there who put up the shingle "Moral Majority," and every time they did some crazy thing, it got into headlines and it totally (in those areas) changed the subject. Once those chapters were started, we couldn't shut them down. We didn't own them; we didn't control them. So I would say if I were starting all over again, I would have a national headquarters, we would have no state chapters, and we'd run it all from the front office to make sure that the only message going out was ours.

Thomas: That was the only thing you'd do differently—nothing in terms of issues?

Rev. Falwell: I can't think of an issue that we got into in those days that we shouldn't have been in. We were very much with Mr. Reagan on peace restraints and Star Wars; we very much were against the peaceniks, because at that time the Soviet Union was very real and nuclear holocaust was very much looming over us. We had the marchers on the streets, and everybody wanted us to disarm. I remember your comment to Ron Sider or somebody, that we ought to lay our guns down and go to the shores and meet the marchers coming in and they'd shoot us and laugh all the way to Washington. I would say that that and the abortion issue, our upfront support for Israel, a strong national defense—those things were the big issues. I don't think Mr. Reagan could have pulled off what he did in bringing the Berlin Wall down and bringing an end to Soviet Communism without the help of the Religious Right. I don't think he could have done it.

Thomas: If you look at the things we began to address in the public mind in 1979, everything seems to be as bad or worse than it was twenty years ago. We have pornography that's out of—as you used to say—the bad neighborhoods in back of pool halls. Now it's on the Internet. You have drugs—maybe a little different than they were twenty years ago, but still impacting young people and adults as never before. There are slightly fewer abortions—two or three hundred thousand fewer, it appears, per year. What does this say about the effectiveness of Christians trying to change society from the top, through the political system?

Rev. Falwell: As a Christian, I must believe the prophecy in 2 Timothy 3, that in the last days evil men shall wax worse and worse. It is impossible to stop the march of prophecy. It is happening, and it's going to get worse, no matter what we do. The church is nowhere told to control the culture, but we are told to influence it—we're the salt of the earth. The question, I think, should not be "what have we accomplished?" but "what have we prevented?" In view of the fact that there are fewer abortions—one is too many, but a million point two or three as compared with a million five—I have to believe that our message was purely directed to the hearts of men. No laws have changed, except for the worse (partial birth aboritons), so it has been a change of heart. The drug situation is terrible—maybe not quite as bad as twenty years ago, but terrible. But where would it be today? Add to that pornography. We were fighting Hugh Hefner and Larry Flynt twenty years ago—they're Sunday school teachers today in comparison. They still pump out the garbage, but not the hard core. As a result, they are all languishing. Their enterprises are not flourishing as they were twenty years ago because, to their credit, they've at least stopped somewhere—not much credit, but they've stopped somewhere. Of course, there was no Internet to deal with back in those days.

Today the Internet is the most powerful force in the universe. Television was, is no more, and never again will be. We need to use it because it's a way—certainly not *the* way. Radio, likewise. James Dobson and Chuck Swindoll use radio to preach to the choir—the churches. But the unsaved world out there is transfixed to that computer screen right there, so we're spending a lot of time and money here on learning how to use this. You can tune in WRVL radio 24 hours a day as a missionary in Nigeria at no cost to you and listen to everything going on live right here—on the Internet. Web sites: We're going at it like General Motors, because you can get 100,000 hits in two days, and I can't preach to that many in Lynchburg in two days. So let's put the good stuff out there with them.

Everything has changed now, but if we had not been there, I do not know where we would be as a country. Out of Moral Majority was born Christian Coalition, Rutherford Institute, Concerned Women for America—go down the long, long list. None of those were there when we were doing Moral Majority. We closed it, and about that time others hatched right out of it. That is to be expected, because everybody with a vision wants to do it his own way. But we got them out of the church offices and pulpits and out into the streets. They are starting to open up everywhere, and today there's no five-star general needed, just as there's no Martin Luther King Jr. needed. Once you got past the physiological restraints, once you got past the informational absence, from there on out it's purely a matter of doing things your way, doing your own thing.

Thomas: You mentioned Dobson and Robertson. James Dobson's the only one who has refused to do an interview for this book. He thinks we're going to trash everybody, but that's not true. He's trying to assure me that he will be effective because he received these promises from his meeting with this Republican leadership. He mentioned no more NEA funding. They tried that before and a couple of other things. What's he missing? Or to put it another way, can he be more effective than you have been, or than Pat Robertson has been?

Rev. Falwell: Well, James Dobson is a great man, and he is meeting needs everywhere, unlike anybody I know. But he is where I was twenty years ago. You cannot learn anything about that trail without walking down it. So there's no point in my giving any advice. Just walk on down and step off about fourteen miles, and somewhere down there lined up on the side of the hill, with two arms broken and your legs out from under you, you're looking around and nobody else is there—I must have taken the wrong road. What he's doing is great and good—I'm glad somebody is up there beating their heads. I may be a pessimist because of experience, but I don't believe for one moment that any of them will do what they say.

Thomas: The politicians?

Rev. Falwell: That's right.

Thomas: You mentioned prophecy—that's a great line about "it's impossible to stop the march of prophecy"—and said salt is a preservative—it slows down the spoilage, but it doesn't preserve forever. Do you see any signs, any hope, that there might be any kind of spiritual revival, that men and women might turn their hearts toward God again? Maybe all the shootings in the schools, maybe something will cause us, as the Prodigal Son did, to come to our senses before we have to go to the hog pen.

Rev. Falwell: Joel 2 speaks of the outpouring of God's fury in the last days, and James 5 speaks of "the latter rain"—the outpouring, I think, from the march of prophecy. It is inevitable that just before the Rapture—and no one knows when that's going to occur or how—there will be an outpouring of God's Spirit which, I believe, will sweep hundreds of millions into the Kingdom. How long a duration such a thing will have, I don't know. What it will take to initiate that, I don't know. It will take far worse than shootings in the schools or other calamities, natural disasters, hurricanes, tornadoes, and all that to do it. Some speak of a collapse of the stock market, but I don't think that will do it, either.

I think it will perhaps be something beyond human imagination or maybe nothing calamitous—just a still movement of the Spirit of God through the hearts of people. I don't believe it's going to be by Billy Graham, or Jerry Falwell, or whoever. I believe we can constantly be sowing the seed, praying, breaking up the fallow ground, but I believe in a sovereign way God will work worldwide, not just in the USA. God will do something before the sounding of the trumpet, but it's going to be such a radical thing and such a rapid-succession-type thing that nobody is going to have time to sit down and analyze it and write a book on it. God is just going to move in on the scene.

But between now and then, I see things getting worse and worse and worse. All we're doing—all we've ever been able to do—is to have the church put its thumb in the dike, but it's inevitable that it's going to come out. We are supposed to keep it plugged up as long as we can, be a restraining influence. We prevent spoilage—America more than any other country has done that well—the church in America. To the credit of the church today, there is still decency. People are not walking nude in the streets, as in some Scandinavian countries—turn on your TV, and everything is right there.

This is still the most decent place on earth to live, and it's because of the church. But we're kidding ourselves if we think there's any program, any third party, or either of the two main parties, or anything we can do to straighten things out right now, because when you have a society that will support Jerry Springer and give him top TV ratings, when you have a porn industry of 8 billion dollars a year in the U.S.—I'm talking about the hard, dirty stuff and kiddie porn—these things that we have in the country are beyond repair.

NOTES

Introduction

1. Oswald Chambers, *My Utmost for His Highest: Selections for the Year*, New International Version (Uhrichsville, OH: Barbour, 1973), 256.
2. C. S. Lewis, *The Screwtape Letters and Screwtape Proposes a Toast* (New York: Macmillan, 1961), 132.
3. Bakker resigned from PTL on March 19, 1987, amid a sex scandal involving an employee of PTL. He was defrocked by his denomination on May 6, 1987. Later on, charges of financial mismanagement landed him in court, and he was convicted on October 24, 1989. He served more than four years in prison.

Chapter One: What Did We Really Win?

1. Everett Carll and Karlyn H. Bowman, "Public Opinion About Abortion: Twenty-five Years After Roe v. Wade," American Enterprise Institute for Public Policy Research, 1997, 2–3.
2. As reported in "Abortion: Roe vs. Wade Anniversary," CBS News.
3. The figure is 1,195,568, according to the *Corrections Yearbook*, published by the Criminal Justice Institute, South Salem, NY, in 1997.

Chapter Two: The Vast Right-Wing Conspiracy

1. Interview with Matt Lauer, *Today*, 27 January 1998.
2. The historical and theological material is adapted from Ed Dobson, *In Search of Unity* (Nashville: Thomas Nelson, 1985), 31–43; Ed Dobson and Ed Hindson, *The Seduction of Power* (Grand Rapids: Revell, 1988), 43–53; and Jerry Falwell, Ed Dobson, and Ed Hindson, *The Fundamentalist Phenomenon* (Garden City, NY: Doubleday, 1981), 78–89.
3. Jerry Falwell et al., *The Fundamentalist Phenomenon*, 187–88.

4. Ibid., 189–95.
5. Dobson and Hindson, *The Seduction of Power*, 56–59.

Chapter Three: Seduced by Power

1. Mao Zedong, "Problems of War and Strategy," speech on 6 November 1938.
2. Letter to Bishop Mandell Creighton, 3 April 1887.
3. *Merriam-Webster's Collegiate Dictionary*, 10th ed. (Springfield, MA: Merriam-Webster, 1993), 913.
4. Maureen Dowd, "Sinners and Spinners on the Equator," *New York Times*, 25 March 1998.
5. Henri J. M. Nouwen, *In the Name of Jesus: Reflections on Christian Leadership* (New York: Crossroad, 1989), 48–49.
6. Alan K. Simpson, U.S. Senator (R–WY), roast of TV newsman Sam Donaldson, 25 September 1990.
7. Nouwen, *In the Name of Jesus*, 57.
8. Ibid., 59.
9. Fund-raising letter, 1 April 1981.
10. 9 October 1983.
11. Gerald and Deborah Strober, *Reagan: The Man and His Presidency* (Boston: Houghton Mifflin, 1998).
12. *Wall Street Journal*, 16 March 1998, A22.
13. Charley Reese, "The World as It Is Regardless of Whether You Understand That," *Orlando Sentinel*, 11 September 1997, A14.
14. For these biblical images, see Mark 10:31; 1 Corinthians 1:27; Matthew 5:5; Isaiah 40:31; Matthew 13:31–32; Luke 14:7–11; and John 13:1–17.

Chapter Four: Prohibiting Evil

1. R. S. March, ed., *The Temperance Movement* (Lanham, MD: University of Maryland Press, 1998), 1.
2. James H. Timberlake, *Prohibition and the Progressive Movement, 1900–1920* (Cambridge, MA: Harvard Unviersity Press, 1963), 7.
3. Jack S. Blocker Jr., *American Temperance Movements: Cycles of Reform* (Boston: Twayne Publishers, 1989), 79.

4. Ruth Bordin, *Women and Temperance: The Quest for Power and Liberty 1873–1900* (Philadelphia: Temple University Press, 1981), 3.

5. March, *The Temperance Movement*, 1.

6. Blocker, *American Temperance Movements*, 76.

7. Timberlake, *Prohibition and the Progressive Movement*, 125.

8. Blocker, *American Temperance Movements*, 102.

9. Ibid., 106.

10. March, *The Temperance Movement*, 1.

11. Timberlake, *Prohibition and the Progressive Movement*, 178.

12. Blocker, *American Temperance Movements*, 119.

13. Paul E. Isaac, *Prohibition and Politics: Turbulent Decades in Tennessee 1885–1920* (Knoxville: University of Tennessee Press, 1965), 267.

14. Blocker, *American Temperance Movements*, 126.

15. John J. Rumbarger, *Profits, Power and Prohibition: Alcohol Reform and the Industrializing of America 1800–1930* (Albany: State University of New York Press, 1989), 189.

16. Norman H. Clark, *Deliver Us from Evil: An Interpretation of American Prohibition* (New York: W. W. Norton, 1976), 168.

17. Blocker, *American Temperance Movements*, 125.

Chapter Five: Crossing the Line

1. Phil Evans and Eileen Pollock, *Ireland for Beginners* (New York: Writers and Readers Publishing, 1994), 113.

Chapter Six: The Use and Abuse of God

1. Tucker Carlson, *The Weekly Standard* (28 December 1998), 25.

Chapter Seven: Better Weapons

1. Personal recollection of the author.

2. *Time*, 15 May 1995, 28.

3. C. S. Lewis, *The Screwtape Letters and Screwtape Proposes a Toast* (New York: Macmillan, 1963), 35, letter 7.

4. Quoted by Charles Stanley in an address to the Southern Baptist Pastors' Convention, 1994.

5. The Clinton Chronicles, by Citizens for Honest Government, Jeremiah Films, 1994.

6. Marvin Olasky, *Abortion Rites: A Social History of Abortion in America* (Washington, DC: Regnery, 1992).

Chapter Nine: Focus on the Family, Not on Politics

1. *New York Times*, 12 February 1998, A22.

2. Poll conducted Election Day, 5 November 1996.

3. *Washington Post*, 29 March 1998, A6.

4. *Wall Street Journal*, 20 February 1998.

5. See www.fedworld.gov.

6. *Wall Street Journal*, 20 February 1998.

7. Personal slogan and the title of his book, *Why Not the Best?* (Nashville: Broadman Press, 1975).

Chapter Ten: Losing Where We Ought to Win

1. Josh McDowell, *Right from Wrong: What You Need to Know to Help Make Right Choices* (Dallas: Word Books, 1994), 19.

2. Neil Howe and Bill Strauss, *13th Generation: Abort, Retry, Ignore, Fail?* (New York: Vintage Books, 1993).

3. Centers for Disease Control and Prevention, Atlanta.

4. McDowell, *Right from Wrong*, 19.

5. Wesley G. Pippert, *The Spiritual Journey of Jimmy Carter* (New York: Macmillan, 1978), 18–19.

6. Ibid.

7. Ray Bradbury, *Fahrenheit 451* (1953; reprint, New York: Ballantine, 1979), 60.

8. The Web site http://www.plannedparenthood.org/ includes this information: "Most teenagers consult their parents before an abortion. But telling a parent is not required in all states. Many states do require a woman under 18 to tell a parent or get a parent's permission. If she cannot talk with her parents, or chooses not to, she can speak with a judge. The judge will decide whether she is mature enough to make her own decision about abortion. If she is not mature enough, the judge will decide if abortion is in her best interest. Find out about the law in your

state. Your local Planned Parenthood can help you with this process." What Planned Parenthood and such groups say and what they do are two different things. I have talked to many women around the country who have gotten abortions at Planned Parenthood clinics, and they say they were misled by Planned Parenthood counselors who told them that their "product of conception" was not fully human, and say that counselors are not forthcoming about other opinions.

9. *Washington Post*, 14 January 1998, A1.
10. Commencement address, 1 June 1990.

Chapter Eleven: Learning From Our Mistakes

1. *New York Times*, 23 March 1998, A1.
2. Ibid.
3. Ibid.
4. *New York Times Magazine*, 19 April 1998, 17.
5. Dick Morris, *The Weekly Standard*, 30 March 1998.
6. *Wag the Dog* (New Line Productions), 1997.
7. *Primary Colors* (Universal Pictures), 1998.
8. Psalm 11:3.
9. William Murchison, *Dallas Morning News*, 8 October 1997.
10. Ibid.
11. Ibid.
12. Harry Blamires, *The Christian Mind* (London: SPCK, 1963), 3–4.
13. C. S. Lewis, "Answers to Questions on Christianity," in *God in the Dock: Essays on Theology and Ethics*, ed. Walter Hooper (Grand Rapids: Eerdmans, 1970), 58–59.

Chapter Twelve: Let the Church Be the Church

1. Eugene Peterson, *Working the Angles: A Trigonometry for Pastoral Work* (Grand Rapids: Eerdmans, 1987), 17–18.
2. H. M Kuitert, *Everything Is Politics But Politics Is Not Everything* (Grand Rapids: Eerdmans, 1986), 146.
3. Ibid., 149.
4. Ibid., 151.
5. Ibid., 171.

6. Francis John McConnell, *Evangelicals, Revolutionists and Idealists* (New York: Abingdon-Cokesbury Press, 1942), 164.
7. William Wilberforce, *A Practical View of Christianity*, ed. Kevin Belmonte (Peabody, MA: Hendrickson, 1996), 251–52.

Epilogue: Let's Do It His Way

1. Nicholas Lemann, "The New American Consensus: Government of, by and for the Comfortable," *New York Times Sunday Magazine* (1 November 1998), 38.
2. William Safire, *New York Times* (5 November 1998), A25.
3. *Washington Post* (4 October 1998), A23.
4. Ibid.